For Review in:

Contemporary Sociology
University of Connecticut
Storrs, CT 06268
_____500_____ words
Date 11/30/82

Issues in Macroanalysis

The Analysis of Educational Productivity

Volume II: Issues in Macroanalysis

Edited by:

Charles E. Bidwell
Douglas M. Windham

Ballinger Publishing Company • Cambridge, Massachusetts
A Subsidiary of Harper & Row, Publishers, Inc.

This project has been funded at least in part with Federal funds from the Department of Health, Education, and Welfare under contract number 400-77-0094. The contents of this publication do not necessarily reflect the views or policies of the Department of Health, Education, and Welfare, nor does mention of trade names, commercial products, or organizations imply endorsement by the U.S. Government. The Department of Health, Education, and Welfare holds a royalty-free, non-exclusive and irrevocable right to reproduce, publish, or otherwise use and to authorize others to use this work for government purposes.

International Standard Book Number: 0-88410-192-4

Library of Congress Catalog Card Number: 79-28508

Printed in the United States of America

Library of Congress Cataloging in Publication Data

Main entry under title:

Issues in macroanalysis.

    (The analysis of educational productivity; v. 2)
    Bibliography: p.
    Includes index.
    1. Educational planning — Longitudinal studies — Addresses, essays, lectures. 2. School management and organization — Addresses, essays, lectures. 3. Educational sociology — Addresses, essays, lectures.
I. Bidwell, Charles Everett, 1923- II. Windham, Douglas M. III. Series: Analysis of educational productivity; v. 2.
LA132.A53 vol. 2   370.19s [370.19]   79-28508
ISBN 0-88410-192-4

Contents

List of Tables   vii

List of Figures   ix

Acknowledgments   xi

Introduction—*Charles E. Bidwell and Douglas M. Windham*   1

Chapter 1
Levels of the Educational System and
Schooling Effects—*John W. Meyer*   15

Chapter 2
Linking Education to the Larger Society with Social
Indicator Models—*Marcus Felson and Kenneth C. Land*   65

Chapter 3
The Efficient Use of Educational Data: A Proposal
for the National Longitudinal Study of the High
School Class of 2002—*Bruce K. Eckland*   93

Chapter 4
Time and Time Again: Some Analysis Problems in
Longitudinal Research—*David Rogosa*   153

Chapter 5
Educational Production Theory and Teacher
Inputs—*Henry M. Levin*   203

Chapter 6
Choice in Education—*James S. Coleman*   233

Index   257

About the Editors   265

List of Tables

4-1   Correlation Matrixes at Time 1 and Time 5   165
4-2   Estimation of Models for the Berkeley Growth Data   184

List of Figures

1-1   Some levels of education and their potential effects   20

2-1   Heuristic diagram depicting initial model found in
Felson and Land   76

2-2   Thirteen types of descriptive and analytical indicators
in a social indicator model of education in the context of
a larger society   84

4-1   Causal relations built into each variation of the model   164

4-2   Representation of the structural model for data from
a 2W2V longitudinal panel   180

4-3   A structural regression model used in the analysis of the
Berkeley growth data   183

4-4   The array of population correlations in a 2W2V panel
relevant to the method of cross-lagged correlation   190

Acknowledgments

The papers published in this volume and in its companion volume were written under the auspices of the Educational Finance and Productivity Center, Department of Education, University of Chicago. The Center was generously supported by the National Institute of Education (Contract No. 400-77-0094) and benefited particularly from the efforts of Michael Cohen and Virginia Koehler.

The papers were originally presented at a two day conference held at the Department of Education in June 1978. We are most grateful to the authors themselves as discussants of each others' papers; to Professor Jacob Michaelsen, University of California, Santa Cruz; and to members of the Advisory Board of the Center: Professor John E. Coons, University of California, Berkeley; Professor Robert M. Hauser, University of Wisconsin-Madison; Professor Luvern L. Cunningham, Ohio State University; and Professor W. Lee Hansen, University of Wisconsin-Madison.

We are especially indebted to Ruth Melville for editing the manuscripts for both volumes and to Linda Budd and Sharon Rosen for taking administrative responsibility for the entire enterprise.

We wish to thank the following members of the staff in the Department of Education for their valuable assistance: Robyn Beatty, Aimee B. Collier, Yvette Courtade, Martha Harris, Karol Noble, and Nancy Ward.

Introduction

Charles E. Bidwell
The University of Chicago

Douglas M. Windham
The State University of New York at Albany

In two senses national systems of education may be thought of as hierarchical. In a more general sense, the form of these systems appears as subordinate to the institutional form of their surrounding societies. In a more specific sense, these systems appear as nested hierarchies in which public policy for education is transmitted and specified to the classroom through such intervening levels of educational organization as the school district or the state department of education.

Two of the chapters in this volume address in theoretical terms issues of hierarchy in modern national systems of education. A third describes in substantive terms varieties of public policy that may affect the kinds of schooling to which students are exposed. Three more consider suitable research designs and procedures for studying schooling in its institutional and organizational contexts. In this introduction, we will comment selectively on certain of the theoretical and methodological issues posed by viewing these essays in juxtaposition.

THEORETICAL ISSUES

Schooling denotes what teachers and students do, together or separately, when they are in classrooms or elsewhere engaged in tasks set by their classroom activities. To the extent that schooling affects what or how much students learn, it affects the academic productivity of schools—either the nature of the product (what students learn) or the rate of production (how much they learn). In this connection, the notion of the subordination of education to the

1

institutional form of societies implies a broad historical covariation of institutional forms and forms of schooling, through which societies in effect select what is learned in school and how quickly various students move along the selected paths of learning.

To postulate a covariation of forms of social institutions and forms of schooling leads us at once to ask how this covariation may arise. It also leads us to ask how institutional forms in societies may shape or otherwise affect the structure through which the conduct of schooling is controlled—for example, the institutional conditions that have fostered that nested hierarchy of governance that appears to be so characteristic of present-day societies.

The idea of the covariation of forms of social institutions and forms of schooling and the consequent idea of the social selection of what and how much students learn have an honorable place in the social science literature on education. Max Weber (1946), for example, postulated three types of authority, three concomitant forms of social organization in the history of societies, and three resultant types of education. Societies in which domination is based on the magical gifts of a leader, on the traditional political prerogatives of elite status groups, or on the rational-legal authority of experts and bureaucratic officials give rise to charismatic, aristocratic, or specialist-vocational education, respectively.

In the charismatic situation, education is sporadic and rudimentary, dependent upon the appearance of a recruit with gifts that are to be awakened by an older hero or magician. In traditional societies, educational systems may be quite extensive and may enroll large proportions of birth cohorts. However, their chief function is differentiating: to "cultivate the pupil for the conduct of a life . . . the conduct of a status group" (Weber, 1946:426). The purpose of education is to inculcate the moral norms, tastes, and manners of a status group: "its internal and external deportment in life" (Weber, 1946:427). What the student is taught and how rigorous and extensive is the demand for attainment are dictated directly by the student's social rank; popular, superficial versions of the aristocratic curriculum are likely to be extended to children of lower rank in the interest of social order. Historical variations of aristocratic education arise from differences in the openness of the stratification of traditional societies and in the lifestyles of the dominant status groups that set the schools' curricula.

In contrast, in bureaucratic, rational societies, although universal school attendance appears, the content of schooling becomes less universal: it represents a departure from education for life conduct toward training for the conduct of specialized occupations. With the dissolution of traditional authority, control of the content of education and of access to it moves away from dominant status groups toward the play of special interests within the polity of the national state. Partisan politics becomes the mechanism for the selection of what students learn, and how much they learn (at least how far they go in school) becomes a matter of state policy. Weber argued that education itself becomes bureaucratized, a process that promotes the power and autonomy of educational organizations and occupations in the political arena. Thus, the selection of what is learned, control of students' access to curricula, and their rates of progress through these curricula become in good part consequences of the ideologies and interests of educational organizations and occupations.

Émile Durkheim, like Weber, stressed the historical institutional sources of what and how much students learn, but with a different substantive focus. For Durkheim (1956:65), education is above all "the means by which society perpetually recreates the conditions of its very existence." How education performs this function occurs through an adaptation of its organizational form and instructional means to the beliefs and institutional structure characteristic of its environing society.

Modern societies, he said, are marked by the decay of kinship and tradition, the fragmentation of social formations, and the individualization of human consciousness. Hence, the specific function of education in these societies is nothing less than to construct the normative basis of the national state: widespread respect for national political and moral authority and disciplined cooperation balanced against trained, skeptical intellect and specialized scientific and technical preparation.

The inexorable development of science and rational modes of thought in modern societies, according to Durkheim, can be relied on to provide the curricula for training intellect and specialist skills. Fortunately, too, the extreme differentiation of such societies not only creates the conditions that specify the function of education as moral as well as intellectual training, but also provides the means for this moral education. The organizational separateness of the school and classroom, set apart from family and other parochial social units, and the emergence of teaching as a specialist vocation provide a school setting in which the classroom, dominated by a disinterested and cosmopolitan teacher, provides in its daily life regular practice in the group loyalties and cooperative predispositions that its students will later require to act appropriately as citizens of a national society.

Presiding over the modern educational system is the state. Its ministry officials and educational experts, themselves rational analysts of the social functions and means of education, construct the curricula, guide the teachers, and frame the policies that determine what and how much students learn. The state emerges as the dominant educational agency, the source of social guidance that shapes and directs the conduct of schooling.

Thus, explicit though undeveloped in Durkheim's writings is the idea of a nested hierarchy of educational governance—a chain of authority that runs from the national ministry to the classroom teacher. For Weber, the governance of modern educational systems is less clearly ordered. Educational bureaucracies do attain a substantial degree of power and autonomy in a national state, but the play of political forces, in which educational interests (including those of school organizations and educational occupations) may become variously dominant, is problematic and shifts with the flow of short-run circumstance.

In the present volume, the essays by John Meyer and Henry Levin both argue for the historical covariation of institutional forms of societies and forms and processes of schooling. Meyer's, in essence, is a Weberian argument. Meyer views the onward march of bureaucratization as a pervasive and inexorable trend in all contemporary societies. Bureaucratization is a powerful force toward the definition of life roles primarily as work roles and of work roles as specialized occupations. These occupations require for entry some formal certification of competence. Economic and state bureaucracies lie athwart access to almost all kinds of work, and certification of educational attainment becomes a central component of rationally, bureaucratically ordered job entry.

At the same time, the interests of an increasingly dominant and bureaucratic state, in the course of generally successful efforts to control the prevalence and rates of political and economic participation by its citizens, create a political theory of socialization in which the statuses and accomplishments of children and youth and their readiness for one or another kind of adult social participation are defined in the formal, authoritative terms of membership in and progress through the levels and branches of the national educational system. Consequently, the statuses of childhood, youth, and adulthood are rigidly separated and defined by location in the formal categories of this system or by certified graduation from one of these categories.

Under these conditions, teachers and school officials, themselves semiautonomous actors on the bureaucratic stage, find that they can extend their own organizational and occupational power by subsuming the workings of classroom and school under the formal societal rules of educational classification and certification. By making students' passage through the educational system conform to these rules, the political and economic significance of formal education is maintained or enhanced. Ritual replaces substance. As Meyer observes, the actual activities of schooling "can be adapted to the vagaries of students' (and others') preferences and capabilities, while the binding and authoritative general categories are maintained." The practice of education in schools and classrooms is "decoupled" from ritual observance of the societal rules that define the categories of student and curriculum and establish the meaning of certification and diplomas. In an ironic revision of Weber, the process of bureaucratization produces not the "demystification of the world," but the transformation of myth from a traditional to a pseudorational base.

Hence, bureaucratic societies select what and how much students learn by virtue of the subordination of the process of schooling to the institutional definition of the categories of student, curriculum, and certificate. In this selection, the various school organizations and occupational groups, however bureaucratized themselves, have no effective power. The formal structure of educational governance may take on a nested form, but whatever this structure does, it does not influence the consequences of schooling for the students who are schooled. Instead, the school and classroom directly embody the institutional structure itself. Teachers, principals, and superintendents may design the work of schooling to suit local tastes, but any resulting variation in the substance of the work of schooling is epiphenomenal to its outcomes for students.

This is not to say that what students experience in school is of no consequence. For Meyer, students are rational, purposive actors. Responding to the institutionally defined value of categories of schooling and of the educational certificates that they can earn, students govern their lives in school to maximize the utilities that they set on these ritualized components of education. What counts are the student's immediate experience with the institutional form that the school or classroom embodies and his or her calculating use of the opportunities that this form provides. Because schools and classrooms are institutionalized so uniformly within contemporary societies, the usual production function approaches to the study of school effects (discussed in some detail in the companion to this volume) must yield negative results. To see the consequences of the organization of schooling for what and how much students learn, historical or cross-societal comparisons are essential. To discover the mechanisms by which institutional forms affect what students learn and at what rates, one must move below the collective levels of school or classroom to observe the actions of individual students as they encounter the institutional forms embodied in their school and classroom surroundings.

Levin presents a contrasting account of the context of educational production. Like Durkheim, he stresses the autonomy of the school as an effective agent shaping what teachers do and what students therefore learn. He accepts Weber's notion of the autonomy of educational bureaucracies but gives little attention to Weber's additional analysis of the governance of education as a problematic outcome of politics.

Like Meyer, Levin accepts the premise of historical variation in the processes and outcomes of schooling. Unlike Meyer, Levin gives no attention to the student's goals or actions. For him, the teacher is the central actor in schooling. Variation in what and how much students learn, Levin's argument suggests, is a function of variation in teachers' command of the subject matter and instructional skills (which he combines to call "capacity"), how much effort they put into the use of capacity, and how much time they give to instruction in each portion of the curriculum. The student, in effect, is treated as a passive recipient of whatever kind and amount of instruction the teacher is able and willing to give.

In this formulation, local educational organizations emerge as key sources of variation in the outcomes of schooling, and local decision-makers appear as key actors. Within the broad institutional limits of national labor markets, variation in teachers' capacities rests on the incentives that schools or districts can provide to attract and retain teachers and on the degree to which these incentives are deliberately used to this end. Within broad limits set by markets for texts and other instructional materials, national or regional tradition, and state laws, the time that teachers spend on curricular elements can be influenced by local district and school policies. Similarly, the effort that teachers put into the use of capacity is subject to local organizational influence through teacher recruitment and re-training, performance incentives, and "organizational climate."

Levin recognizes that such variables as teachers' effort, the directions to which they turn their capacities, and the time that they spend teaching one thing or another are subject to the specific influences of their own preferences and the different capacities and interests of their students. Nevertheless, he argues that the thorough bureaucratization of modern societies carries over into the schools, reducing teachers from professionals to employees and thus opening their work to control by their employing bureaucracies. Here, as in Meyer's chapter, the key institutional variable is bureaucratization, but for Levin it enhances rather than reduces the potency of local organizational influence. Presumably, then, a large portion of observed historical and cross-societal variation in what and how much students learn is to be explained by variation in the institutional conditions that shape educational organizations and the cumulative consequences for students' learning of organizational constraint on what teachers are able and willing to do.

Levin does not assume that organizational controls can be so powerful as to reduce the within class experiences of students to one common pattern. Quite the reverse: he sees that an important problem in the study of educational production is accounting for variation in teachers' preferences and in their responses to the particularities of the student membership of their classrooms. However, present-day educational systems contain potent local organizations that can limit in significant ways how teachers respond to the vagaries of their own tastes and of the tastes and capabilities of their students.

Juxtaposition of the Meyer and Levin chapters raises a number of interesting issues for the student of educational productivity. Among these, clearly, is the degree of internal autonomy of educational organizations and its consequences for what and how much students learn. This issue in fact has two facets, not clearly separated in either essay.

First, what are the consequences of historical or cross-societal variation in institutional forms for the internal autonomy of the various kinds and levels of educational organizations? The Meyer and Levin arguments can be read to suggest that one consequence of institutional change is to alter this autonomy. Meyer's formulation implies that the bureaucratization of societies weakens the effective autonomy of schools and school districts by subordinating their structures and activities and the interests of their members to the myth of the rationality and universalism of the labor market. Levin's perspective implies the opposite—that bureaucratization, by favoring organizational over professional control of schooling, strengthens the effective autonomy of local school organizations.

The relationship between institutional forms and the autonomy of educational organizations is an interesting research problem that requires the cross-national or historical comparisons advocated by Meyer. Such research, however, will not speak to the second facet of the issue of autonomy: whether the incentives and policies of local educational organizations have any consequence for events in classrooms and thus for what and how much students learn.

On this problem, negative findings of between school or between classroom school effects (such as those that have accumulated at the school level for the contemporary United States), while consistent with Meyer's argument, need not be inconsistent with Levin's. If Western societies are indeed as thoroughly bureaucratized as Meyer and Levin contend, the local organizational means available to affect what teachers or students do (curricular policies, normative or monetary incentives, "climates," or whatever) may be too uniform to covary with outcomes. Perhaps bureaucratization has crossed a threshold above which variation produces decreasing increments of change in those organizational means that affect what and how much students learn. In principle, similar arguments could be made about any societal variable likely to affect local educational organizations, such as public investment in education.

Thus, we come to two interesting possibilities. On the one hand, institutional forces and organizational policies and procedures may be related in a contingent way, as Meyer suggests and as Weber's writings imply. In its strongest form, this proposition states that such institutional differences between societies as the prevalence or intensity of bureaucracy suffice as conditions for the effectiveness of policies or procedures for schooling. In Meyer's essay, the proposition is put less strongly—that under certain institutional conditions (e.g., pervasive bureaucratization), no organizational policy or procedure will be effective. Under other institutional conditions, presumably, the effectiveness or ineffectiveness of policies and procedures may be explained by appeal to other causes.

On the other hand, institutional differences between societies may generate corresponding differences in the availability to schools of potent organizational means to influence schooling. This proposition is Levin's, and it was Durkheim's as well. When in a given society or historical period (e.g., bureaucratic or capitalist) there is sufficient agreement on the goals of schooling and sufficient similarity in the organized work of schooling, the uniformity of potent means masks their potency. When institutional constraint is less strict, there may be more variation in the availability of potent means and, thus, more evidence of their potency.

Either possibility leads to comparative research, allowing variation in institutional parameters to be observed over societal or historical settings. Such research must be designed so that for each society or period, the distribution of organizational policies, structures, and activities of schools can be described, the between and within school or classroom variance in pertinent schooling outcomes calculated, and the partitioned variance related to the measured organizational attributes of schools.

This is a design for comparative social research of a scope and complexity not often undertaken. To conduct it would require much more thorough theoretical elaboration than either Meyer or Levin could provide in their brief essays, specifying the institutional constructs, the pertinent organizational policies, structures, and activities, and the pertinent schooling outcomes. The specification required would be sufficiently detailed and unambiguous to guide the selection of measures that would provide epistemic comparability across the societies or periods to be studied.

Investigators engaged in such research would do well to remember that close observation of classrooms reveals remarkably diverse instructional practices, even within the same school or locality. Meyer regards this diversity as inconsequential for the outcomes of schooling. For Levin, it is of consequence, but limited by the controls of the bureaucratic school.

Perhaps neither Meyer nor Levin is right. Instruction may affect what or how much students learn, but the diverse realities of instruction may be little influenced by organizational controls. Organizational influence may be present, but less direct than Levin suggests: for example, school policies that govern the size or the ability or motivational composition of classrooms rather than incentives that govern teachers' effort. If so, the variation within societies in schooling as it is conducted by teachers and experienced by students may be very much greater than the variation between them.

METHODOLOGICAL ISSUES

Whatever the merits of Meyer's or Levin's theoretical arguments, they surely are correct that efforts to relate the institutional or organizational contexts of schooling to productivity criteria require investigation into the beliefs and activities of the individual actors in the schooling process. A principal purpose of comparative studies of schooling is to determine how such beliefs and activities (e.g., the calculations of rational student actors, the effort expended by teachers, or the interplay of the two) vary from one organizational or societal context to another and how these variations are related to what or how much students learn.

These studies, then, require adequate specification of an educational production function: an attempt to go beyond present production function approaches to capture the realities of schooling and their consequences for the content and rates of students' learning. To specify the function adequately is a major task and the subject of the companion to this volume. Levin also suggests directions toward this specification. Comparative macrolevel studies that are based on information about the beliefs and activities of the individual actors in schooling are of a piece with this specification effort. Such studies will be necessary if we are to understand how the means of schooling operate and the conditions under which they operate well, badly, or not at all.

It will be essential to base such research on longitudinal panels of students. We cannot rely on the cross-sectional designs that characterize the current production function methodology. Schooling is cumulative. To measure schooling requires measurement of the sequences and amounts of student exposure to instruction. Moreover, schooling outcomes must be measured as difference scores: gains or losses in pertinent cognitive or affective states of individual students. Efforts to use data from the recent multinational educational assessment conducted by the International Association for the Evaluation of Educational Achievement (IEA), which provides only cross-sectional measures of students' attainment, show how risky it is to draw inferences from such data about institutional or organizational sources of cross-national differences in scholastic outcomes. The difficulties arise especially because student cohorts entering various national systems of education differ markedly in capacity for school work.

Earlier efforts at longitudinal analysis have been flawed. David Rogosa provides a trenchant account of the shortcomings of earlier designs for the analysis of effects over time. Fortunately, he suggests the great potential for studies of such social processes as schooling that is provided by recent developments in the analysis of longitudinal panel data.

Once we see that studies of the productivity of systems of education require measures of institutional and organizational context, measures of individual student and teacher activity, and longitudinal panel data on these activities and on learning, it becomes evident that the data bases for such work must follow successive cohorts of students through the school years and through the various branches of differentiated educational systems. Moreover, as Marcus Felson and Kenneth Land and as Bruce Eckland rightly stress, students must be followed through experiences in their family and in other out-of-school learning environments as well. To provide strong support for inferences about institutional or organizational effects on the outcomes of schooling, it would help to follow the out-of-school experiences of members of birth cohorts who do not enter formal education (in societies where such persons exist in some number) and of persons who leave formal education at successive exit points. Meyer is cogent on this point.

Such data have never been gathered for one society, let alone for enough societies to make adequate comparisons. Historical studies, however useful for information about the covariation of institutional and organizational variables or of these variables with such information on school attendance or achievement as is likely to be a matter of public record, cannot link institutional or organizational variables to the activities of teachers or students or to the learning of individual students. Advances toward methods for building macro-level social indicator models from the requisite individual level longitudinal panel data, described and interestingly applied by Felson and Land to questions about the institutional context of educational systems, promise the feasibility of research of the kind that theoretical arguments like those of Meyer and Levin require.

Clearly, too, such research must incorporate multiple levels of analysis: levels that correspond to whatever hierarchy of societal and organizational contexts of schooling one's theory postulates. Rogosa shows that, at least in principle, it is possible to incorporate a hierarchical design into the treatment of longitudinal panel data.

Constraints on our ability to conduct comparative analyses of the productivity of educational systems will be less those of the design and techniques of analysis than of the logistics and costs of providing the necessary sets of longitudinal panel data on successive cohorts of students and on their proximate schooling and other learning environments. Were such data collection limited to the United States, the expense of conducting the surveys and in situ observations and of coding and maintaining the resulting data in accessible form would probably not be prohibitive by comparison with that portion of the U.S. educational research and development budget now given over to disparate studies that, however valuable in themselves, yield fragmented, noncumulative information about the contexts, processes, and outcomes of schooling.

Nevertheless, Eckland's chapter provides an arresting and sobering account of the substantial political and management difficulties surrounding the collection of data in the National Longitudinal Study of the High School Class of 1972 (NLS), many of which arose from the multiple and conflicting interests of the researchers, policy-makers and analysts, and subject groups legitimately involved in the collection and use of the NLS data. Eckland's sensible proposal for a longitudinal study of the class of 2002 would surmount many of these difficulties, especially if serious attention were given to his arguments for large relative investment in special studies and samples and a carefully limited national sample of students to be surveyed. This proposed study, however, would require a reallocation of federal research moneys and a subordination of particular interests not likely if recent experiences of social scientists with the federal educational research establishment are a reliable guide.

Eckland's proposal, viewed in the light of the new modeling and data analysis procedures described by Felson and Land and by Rogosa, would yield data of such richness and importance for the study of institutional and organizational contexts of schooling that the social science and policy analysis communities would be well advised to consider mechanisms for developing it and ultimately supporting it vigorously as a logical progression from the initial class of 1972 NLS and the class of 1982 NLS now underway.

Such a research program, however, even if fully implemented, would produce data on but a single case—U.S. society of the present and the near future. Of necessity, analysis of this case cannot provide insight into the consequences for schooling of variation in such institutional parameters as bureaucratization. The prospects for developing comparable individual level data sets in societies that afford adequate variation of institutional parameters, even if such parameters could be specified in precise theoretical terms, are discouraging. The agency for selecting the societies to be studied, developing and coordinating the research design, negotiating with governments and educational organizations for the conduct of the research, and overseeing its conduct is nowhere at hand. The heroic efforts behind even the relatively limited IEA study are instructive. The difficulties described by Eckland that surrounded the first NLS would be multiplied manyfold in an international effort. Nevertheless, as we have said, retrospective historical comparisons or other uses of the public record, however helpful for certain purposes, lack the essential individual student data that inquiry into educational productivity demands.

Before one accepts this counsel of despair, a closer look at the Meyer and Levin chapters is in order. Each is notable for its failure to consider structures of educational governance or regional or other within society differences in the incidence of public policy for education. Weber, let us recall, asserted that the very forces that lie behind bureaucratization, and the force of bureaucratization, make partisanship and the play of political interests powerful agents of social control. Public policies in education are, he said, a not inconsiderable object of partisan and interest group politics. One need

Book undersigns customs which the ... earlier others ... any sees possibilities.

not espouse Durkheim's ready assumption of the state as paramount to engage the notion that the structures and processes of educational governance, at least in contemporary societies, should interest the student of educational systems.

Here James Coleman's account of various schemes for family or student choice in education is suggestive. Meyer contends that by its sway in schools and classrooms, the bureaucratic myth weakens students' appreciation of the intrinsic value of what is to be learned and of membership in a classroom or school. Schooling becomes an instrument of status attainment, its value derived from the status rewards of years and types of schooling and the certificates that they yield. Durkheim argues that the intrinsic value of school membership is a principal source of the power of schools to form students' moral commitments. One might go further to argue that to experience schooling as intrinsically or extrinsically valuable is to form the very modes of valuing.

From these few remarks, it follows that one might look within a society—in American society, for example, at alternative mechanisms of choice among kinds of schooling or schools—for approximations to natural experiments to reveal the differential consequences of public policy for the nature and the meaning of students' experiences of schooling and for some of the things that students may learn from these experiences.

The policy variations that Coleman describes are not widespread and may never be. The brief argument just presented may be vacuous, while the normative outcomes of schooling that it addresses may be of little current theoretical or practical interest. Nevertheless, the more general point may hold: contemporary societies vary markedly in the differentiation of school organization and curricula, at least above the common school level. The United States remains at the extreme of organizational and curricular homogeneity in education. Thus, there should be numerous opportunities for interesting within society comparisons.

True?

Even in the United States, state governments make rather different provisions for the fiscal support of education, with certain states taking notably variant approaches to the provision of equity in tax burdens and school revenues. State-by-state and within state comparisons provide potentially important variation in the length of the school year, in responsiveness to federal initiatives in fiscal and substantive educational policy, in judicial intervention into the conduct of education, and in curricular content—to mention only a few obvious examples.

The general point is that theoretically sensitive use of state, regional, or even local variation in educational policy and in legislative, judicial, and administrative governance of education might be combined with a national educational survey of the kind Eckland proposes and with the modeling and analytical procedures that Felson and Land and Rogosa describe to tell us a good deal about the consequences of variation in public policy and policy implementation for the conduct of schooling and its effects on what and how much students learn.

Such studies would say little in a direct evidential way about the correlates of such broad institutional variations as the intensity or pervasiveness of bureaucratization, although informed speculations might be justified. Nevertheless, comparisons within societies of the kind that we have suggested would have considerable uses. Positive findings would speak to the value of a formulation like Meyer's that reads governance and organization out of the productivity equation. They would elaborate and specify a formulation like Levin's that fails to say precisely how bureaucratization provides potent organizational means of schooling.

Negative findings would have less clear theoretical implications, but they would help us assess the value of the heroic effort required to conduct prospective cross-national investigations. They might also force us to reconsider the usefulness of current modes of policy-making and implementation in the governance of American education.

A systematic program of social accounting in education, even within one national society, holds out the unique promise of capturing the realities of schooling in relation to societal contexts and student's learning. This promise justifies the undeniably large costs in money and effort that such a program would entail.

REFERENCES

Durkheim, Émile. 1956. *Education and Sociology.* Translated by Sherwood Fox. Glencoe, Ill.: Free Press.

Weber, Max. 1946. *From Max Weber: Essays in Sociology.* Edited and translated by Hans Gerth and C. Wright Mills. New York: Oxford University Press.

Chapter 1

Levels of the Educational System and Schooling Effects

John W. Meyer
Stanford University

Educational systems are organized at many structural levels. There is the microorganization of the experience, interaction, and learning of the individual student. There is the classroom, which may be coterminous with, nested within, or overlapping with the grade or "class" in school. Sometimes there are programmatic levels in which the grade or classroom may be located (e.g., vocational program, college preparatory program, English major). There is the school itself and the larger district of which it is a part. The school is an element in a general type or category of schools (e.g., comprehensive high school, vocational high school, elementary school, junior college) that cuts across the boundaries of particular districts. Then there are state and national levels of organization and to some extent a world level (defining in small ways, and sometimes even funding, education in particular national societies).

These are all levels at which some structuring of education is maintained. But paralleling and cutting across them are a whole series of levels of social structure that contain important definitions and controls over the system—informal levels of family and peer organization, the community and its various constituents, national society, a welter of relevant occupational and interest groups, and so on. These are important too: in some cases they are known to substantially affect the schooling process and its outcomes.

The problem of this chapter is to discuss how we are to think about, and study empirically, the effects of these various levels on schooling and its outcomes. Clearly, educational outcomes cannot be assumed simply to reflect the classroom experiences of individual students—in some way, properties of the other levels must be brought in too. The problem is how—with what kinds of arguments and methods?

The general argument advanced here is that the schooling levels of importance are institutional, not organizational, in character. "Institutional" refers to roles and rules and definitions shared (with more or less consensus) in society at large (Berger and Luckmann, 1967). Societal institutional categories generally control definitions of the present nature and social futures of students and thus are critical in determining and defining outcomes. Examples of important societal educational institutions include educational levels, such as the fourth grade, high school, or the first year of college. Others include types of schools: college, vocational training school, elementary school. Others include standardized educational topics: arithmetic, sociology, business administration, reading, chemistry. Still others include standardized roles: elementary school teacher, fourth grade student (or student in general), professor of physics. These are all societal institutions. First, their meaning is importantly derived from societal definitions, rather than from particular organizational circumstances, as is their power to affect and dominate student life and outcomes—the power of the fourth grade teacher to control student instruction derives centrally from a secure and accredited location as a proper societally defined fourth grade teacher, rather than from the particular personal relationships and organizational roles characteristic of a specific school and its fourth grade. Second, there is no way to know through any direct inspection of organization and interaction that a given classroom is "really" a fourth grade classroom—such classrooms vary enormously on all sorts of dimensions organizationally, none of which define them as fourth grades. The real defining characteristic is the institutional definition and accreditation process: a classroom is a fourth grade if and only if it is defined as a fourth grade—the definition inheres in the institutional label.

A student's position vis-à-vis the institutional structure of education is a crucial determinant of future success and opportunity: it may be good to know something, but for a wide variety of purposes, it is crucial to be a graduate (high school, college, professional school, etc.). Students perceive this and presumably adapt to the dominating importance of the institutional structure. Organizational factors are important in this view mainly insofar as they are linked with the general institutional ones. I confront a literature showing weak organizational effects on schooling outcomes by calling attention to the institutional factors usually held constant in such research and by proposing research on them (e.g., studies of the decision to attend college usually start with samples of high school seniors and leave out those who do not occupy this institutionalized category). Education is thus conceived to be more importantly an institutionalized system than an organizational structure. And the student is seen as an occupant of a highly socially defined role more than an organizational member and object.

I further argue that participants in educational organizations understand the overriding significance of proper conformity to, and accreditation in terms of, institutional considerations and for this reason tend to deemphasize strictly organizational patterns of conformity and control. In this view, the often-discussed "loosely coupled" (Weick, 1976; Meyer and Rowan, 1978; March and Olsen, 1976) properties of educational organizations—the tendency for structures to be disconnected from each other and from outcomes— is seen as resulting from the relative unimportance of organizational coordination and the critical importance of maintaining categorical conformity with the legitimating rules of the institutional environment.

To simplify the discussion, I restrict the dependent or outcome variables under consideration to the two broad classes most commonly discussed in the literature: what (and how much) students learn and the extent to which they choose to participate in the educational system—in the present, in the future, and on into the preferred (high status) occupational and social roles to which education gives entry. This simplified student learns more or less and invests more or less participation in the system. Many other variables of interest are left out—values, personality characteristics, social relations, family-forming behavior, misconduct, and so on.

The task is further simplified because the two dependent variable clusters are known to be reciprocally related. Students who learn more tend to participate more in the system. And those who participate more and longer learn much more. I proceed in four steps:

1. First, the nature of the problem is discussed. It has often been given a methodological cast, with attempted methodological or metamethodological solutions. This effort has failed. The problem turns out to be substantive (and theoretical), and the remainder of the chapter focuses on such issues.

It further turns out that the problem lies not only in defining the nature of the independent variables involved (i.e., the levels of educational structure), but also in explicating their impact on students. We need not only to discuss education as an institutionalized system, but also to conceive of students as participants in a societal institution whose effects on them then become plausible and comprehensible. The remainder of the chapter thus focuses on theoretical conceptions of students and of education.

2. Ideas are then developed about the institutional nature of the educational system and thus about the nature of the social position of students—ideas that are more realistic than those conventionally discussed and that make it easier to understand how it is that properties of higher levels of the educational system have their impact. The line of attack is to think of the student not as a primitive individual and object of education, but as the fairly rational agent of a highly socially organized career line. The social future is therefore very real to the young person and student.

Thus, some theory is formulated about the action of students as well as some theory about young persons that explains how various levels of educational organization might affect their involvement in the student role and the learning and participation appropriate to it.

3. Given these theories about the people who are the targets of the educational system, ideas are developed about the effects properties of different educational levels may have. Attention is given to both organizational and institutional aspects of the system.

4. Given the ideas developed in earlier sections, I proceed to discuss how it comes about that educational organizations are structured as they are. Relationships among the various levels of educational organization are known to be oddly decoupled (Weick, 1976). This becomes comprehensible when we understand more about the nature of educational institutionalization, the social organization of young persons, and the student role.

Throughout the chapter, certain facts must be borne in mind. First, the need for this study arises because the field of schooling effects has reached an interesting disaster point. Our present research models have led to the conclusion that characteristics of the student and the student's immediate situation and experiences are of overwhelming importance and that higher organizational levels may have little effect. This violates our common sense in so many ways as to generate intellectual discomfort, but it follows from the way that we have thought about the problem. We therefore need to think about the problem in different ways. In view of this situation, perhaps the peculiar language and research models suggested here can be tolerated in the interests of intellectual innovation.

Second, our task is to think in terms of needed lines of future research. Throughout, I suggest concrete research designs, both to illustrate general ideas and to further real research possibilities. My aim is not to construct an integrated theory, but to open up new lines of research.

THE NATURE OF THE PROBLEM

The Methodological Nonproblem

In principle, the research issue is clear: What are the independent effects on student outcomes of characteristics of various levels of the educational system? Figure 1-1 illustrates the possibilities in a simplified form. Student outcomes can be affected by properties of the student, families and peers, classrooms, grades, schools, districts, and states and countries. These effects may be direct (a–g) or indirect (u–z, combined with one or more from a–f).

Though adequate for the present, Figure 1-1 is too simple. First, a number of levels noted earlier (e.g., type of school) are omitted for simplicity. Second, many arguments are currently made that effects of the various levels are interactive (e.g., that classroom size is more important for lower-class than for middle-class students). Such effects are omitted but could easily be added. Third, Figure 1-1 shows the various levels as nested. This is imprecise: they are not always nested organizationally (e.g., grades transcend the boundaries of particular organizational units and are nationwide in meaning, as I discuss at length later), and even when they are nested, effects may skip levels (e.g., national changes may affect classrooms without first affecting school or district organizations). This is an important point: the later discussion emphasizes institutional levels in which many organizational elements are (quite independently) nested. Fourth, aggregative effects, by which lower levels modify higher ones, are left out (e.g., the cumulation of higher status students in a school modifies curricular arrangements, which themselves have direct effects). Such effects are omitted from this chapter, although it can be argued that some of the most important effects of education occur on higher level elements of the system—for instance, on members of the community who are not even attending the schools (see Meyer, 1977, for a discussion). Even with such omission, Figure 1-1 is complex. Many attempts at simplication have been made, and I briefly review them here.

Methodological Simplifications. Many social science models attempt to reduce the multilevel complexity of social explanation by concentrating on only one level of analysis at a time. In its extreme form, this has followed Durkheim's dream that one could analyze the group properties (social facts) that create rates of a given social

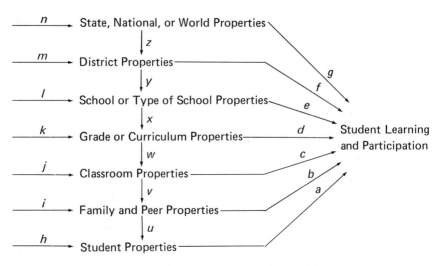

Figure 1-1. Some Levels of Education and Their Potential Effects.

behavior (other social facts) entirely separately without considering the individual properties affecting the individual behavior making up the rates. The converse fantasy—that one could study the effects of individual properties on each other without considering the collective processes of which these relations might be artifacts—is still common in the social sciences (e.g., to an unknown extent, findings that students with college-going peers are more likely to attend college may simply reflect joint membership in a college-going curriculum or school that possesses its own direct allocative power).

Methodological inquiry since World War II has made these positions untenable (see Hannan [1971] for a review). It is now clear that evidence on relationships at any one level of analysis can be contaminated in any direction by uncontrolled processes at other levels.

A later methodological attempt at simplification in the same direction also failed. Sewell and others (e.g., Sewell and Armer, 1966; see also the responses in ASR, 1966) argued by fiat that the contextual effects depicted in Figure 1-1 c–g (effects of type b were arbitrarily given a separate status) were somehow inferior in methodological status to the individual level effects a and should not be estimated directly. They chose to interpret not direct estimates of such contextual effects, but only estimates of the increment in explanatory power produced by adding contextual variables to models in which individual variables were already entered. Because the relevant contextual properties (e.g., school status) were highly correlated with individual ones (e.g., individual status), contextual effects were practically eliminated. A long, involuted methodological discussion followed in the field, leading to the conclusion that this position was unjustified and that more straightforward procedures for estimating contextual effects were appropriate (see the covert concession by one of Sewell's followers in Alwin, 1976).

All these efforts ended back at the starting point: the complex model in Figure 1-1 cannot be simplified by methodological sleights of hand. A student's learning may be affected by properties of many different structural levels. Remaining efforts at simplification have taken a substantive turn.

Substantive Simplifications. Methodological issues aside, many researchers are uncomfortable with higher level, direct contextual effects on student outcomes (i.e., c-g in Figure 1-1). They suppose that if higher level effects occur, they should be rendered indirect by discovering what lower level and individual variables mediate them. The effort is to move toward a model in which only a effects operate directly: b-g are eliminated, and the effects of properties of these levels are mediated through u-z and then through a. Preferences for such models are in principle very reasonable, since most educational processes affecting learning, participation, and other variables can be understood to be mediated by some sort of individual level variables, broadly defined. Only occasionally is the individual entirely left out in practice (as when parents enroll a biochemically disabled and unaware child in college, or a registrar reclassifies a subsequently informed student as a sophomore rather than a freshman, or a student is terminated or graduated without his or her prior knowledge). Even highly institutional effects (e.g., the greater likelihood of university attendance among given students in countries that have universities) are usually mediated by proximate individual variables (e.g., knowledge of, and intentions to attend, universities).

Research in this area is often slipshod—frequently the individual variables thought to mediate contextual ones (commonly, individual intentions) can be seen as incidental by-products of aggregate phenomena that directly cause individual consequences as much as they are causes of this behavior. (Subjectively, for instance, many college students report never having decided to attend college—the assumption that they would do so was a part of their status throughout their lives.) But this objection is not fundamental: better specified models would still find individual level processes involved. Some of the styles of substantive reasoning that have developed following this general intellectual line of attack can be described briefly.

Narrow Economism. The problem could be greatly simplified if the whole educational system could be conceived to be built around a simple, more or less additive, production function, absorbed in a unified economy. Education would then result from monetary resource flows through the organization and down to the teaching of the student. Where more money flowed, more learning and probably more participation would result. Higher levels of the system would have indirect effects by passing funds down to lower ones.

This simplification is no longer taken very seriously. A generation of studies has shown few important direct effects on educational outcomes of the monetary resources of schools, districts, or states when a reasonable set of individual student characteristics (with which organizational resources are correlated) are held constant.

Simple Sociologism. Much sociology arises as a counterpoise to economic models—adding the additional utility of social prestige to economic resources. Sociologists have looked for the educational effects of high school status, ordinarily measured by the aggregated social status of students or of people in the community. They have typically found disappointingly small positive effects on the performance and college intentions or attendance of students.

This line of thought opens up the possibility that the various levels of education create, through social interaction, their own systems of value or prestige not integrated with the national status system. This would make possible all sorts of contextual effects beyond those arising from a simple economic model (i.e., operating from the ability of each subsystem to add to or eliminate the value created by the wider system, as indicated by effects i–n in Figure 1–1). But the absence of findings showing large amounts of between school or between district variance in outcomes (individual controls held constant) has been very discouraging. This line of thought has been mainly used to encourage research on peer groups and student cultures—levels at which distinctive systems of value seem most clearly to be created. But occasionally it is also used to justify research on the effects of the classroom as a little social system of its own. Clearly, the isolation of the individual classroom in the educational system and the high rates of internal interaction it contains make possible the creation of rather distinctive social values and resources. These processes are sometimes thought of as operating interactively.

Interactive Models. General attempts have been made to suppose that the simpler models discussed above fail because they are built mainly around additive effects and that contextual effects often take an interactive form. Psychologists looking for ways to incorporate social structure (e.g., Cronbach and Snow, 1977), economists interested in paralleling traditional production functions, and some recent sociological arguments (e.g., Sørensen and Hallinan, 1977) propose such effects.

These ideas take on more meaning when infused with substantive imagery. The most useful ones have been organizational in character: the educational system as a complex organizational structure channels resources with more or less effectiveness toward different classrooms, which in turn organize these resources in ways that interactively affect different kinds and groups of students differently (Thomas, 1977). The effects of the resources depend on the way they are organized, and the types of students who are affected also depend on the organization of the classroom work.

By and large, these kinds of ideas have not been tested enough to make an evaluation possible. But at least they do not run against what evidence is available. This is particularly true when they are applied to within school levels of organizational structure. The available evidence suggests that between school and between district variation (independent of individual student characteristics) is small and does not lend itself to optimism about either additive or interactive effects at these levels. There is much less evidence about how much outcome variation there is between classrooms. And indeed, the belief that this is the level of analysis that will finally show large contextual effects is currently widespread in the sociology of education (see, for instance, the papers in NIE, 1978). The classroom is the organizational level that most clearly shapes many educational decisions, and school or district decisions apparently have little effect on classroom practice (Meyer et al., 1978). Thus, it is at least plausible that variation in classroom organization will prove to be important. If schools are almost random collections of classroom organizations and if classrooms are the level at which educational outputs are affected, we have a plausible account of why school effects are ordinarily found to be small.

In any event, classroom effects (whether additive or interactive in nature) are at least not at odds with the available evidence and deserve more investigation. They are now much discussed in the literature, and I develop other lines of attack here.

The Problem

The social scientific imagination on the ways in which higher levels of education affect students has been very limited:

1. In the absence of substantive clarity, there has been a tendency to see the problem as methodological. It is not, and a good deal of energy has been wasted. My reconceptualization below discusses effects of educational levels that can be studied either with individual data or with data on higher levels of the system.

2. Available research on contextual effects has looked mainly at organizational levels of the educational system—schools and sometimes districts—and has found little. Conceiving of the system as integrated organizationally runs against the grain of the literature on educational organization itself (Bidwell, 1965; Lortie, 1973; Meyer and Rowan, 1978). The institutional levels of the system have usually been held constant in empirical reserach and ignored in theories. The discussion below emphasizes the system as institutionally integrated and controlled (see also Meyer, 1977). Do similar students learn differently if they are in different grades, in different types of schools, in different courses? Do similar young persons learn different things if they are in what is defined as a school than if they are not? The obvious answer to these questions is affirmative. I argue below that these are the fundamental levels in terms of which the education system is structured: if so, they are also the levels at which we should obtain variance to study.

3. Not only is the system usually seen organizationally, but levels within it are usually seen as nested—the student within the class, the class within the school, and so on. This conception eliminates some of the most interesting possibilities. The third grade in any school, for instance, is directly linked to a nationwide set of social definitions and opportunities. I argue below that such institutions as the third grade have considerable power to generate educational effects, independent of the school and district in which, in particular instances, they appear.

4. The prevailing research tradition, by conceiving of the educational system as organizational in character, creates a very peculiar and limited conception of the student. This student is not really a member of society in any direct sense but is primarily the object of organizational activity (constrained by other immediate organizational networks in the family and peer group). The student is complex, but in a peculiar and passive way; he is endowed with a great many cognitive and affective dispositional properties that make difficult material for organizational processing. But the student is not seen as organizing his own work around his own purposes

and future enterprises: the family may have instilled some virtuous or defiant values, as may the peer group, but these are not linked to a project of the student's own.

In order to develop a more coherent picture of educational effects, it will be necessary to redefine the student and the young person who chooses student roles. In the arguments below, then, I modify the perspectives noted above. I underplay methodological issues by emphasizing individual level data (often experiments). The educational system is seen as an institution, not primarily as an organization. Each part of the system is seen as directly infused with institutional meaning, not as a nested organizational component.

And most important, I redefine the student. In the prevailing tradition, the sociological perspective is that of an organizational psychologist, and the student is seen as a mildly intelligent monkey (or occupant of a monkeylike role), constrained by the immediate distribution of rewards. I take a more sociological perspective and see the student very differently. Because the larger institution of education is rationalistically organized and linked up with future rewards, the student as a member of society is similarly rationalized. I see the student as a fairly well-informed economist—alive to the system and on the lookout for main long-run chances within it.

THE STUDENT AND THE INSTITUTIONAL STRUCTURE OF EDUCATION

Theory of the Student

Let us begin with the most narrow posture, formulated in polemic contrast to the literature (I broaden it in the subsequent section). Imagine that a student is only a student—not a broader social person at all. The student's world, that is, is only that of the educational system. In this system, continued success and participation are necessary for survival, and the main desideratum is entry into the later social positions in "adult" life to which educational success gives access. The student is thus a kind of firm (or more precisely, an agent of a career as a corporate actor) acting to insure success and survival in the educational marketplace. This student has no attachments, only a variety of consultants (peers, teachers, counselors, parents, etc.) who aid by providing information of varying accuracy.

How this student will act, of course, depends very heavily on the structure of the educational world in which action is to occur. (This is deceptive, as noted in the next section: in some respects the student identity or role is in the first place a construction of the educational system.)

The Institutional Structure of the Educational Market. The student confronts the modern educational system, which has some distinctive properties:

1. The system is organized around the goal of learning, but success in this respect is only very probabilistically related to success in the system.

2. It is tightly organized around a rather rigid sequence of steps—a ladder over time. Each step must be completed before the next can be taken. No matter what the student knows, ordinarily, the fourth grade must be completed properly before the fifth grade is entered.

3. Further, completion of a step gives enormous advantages for entry into the next step. No matter what the student knows, proper completion of the fourth grade gives almost certain entry into the fifth grade. At later steps this is less certain, but great advantages still accrue to those who have properly completed the previous step.

4. The knowledge gained in the system is useful in obtaining entry into valued social positions. But independent of this, proper completion of more steps in the system confers great advantages for obtaining entry into valued positions. Often this is legally or socially required.

5. At its higher levels, the system is laterally differentiated into many programs. But this differentiation has the same structural form as the vertical one discussed above. It is built around the goal of acquiring differentiated knowledge, but programmatic membership is more certainly vital than knowledge. Membership in the college curriculum in high school helps in obtaining college entry. Having properly completed a premedical program helps in obtaining entry into medical school. And having the proper certificate—entirely over and above knowledge—is commonly vital to entry into desired positions in society.

6. Practically all the vertical and lateral differentiations noted above are uniform across the country—the whole system is institutionalized at the national level. Knowledge levels may vary a good deal across individuals and organizations, but a student's fundamental social position is defined in terms of the nationwide categories discussed above and transcends any given organizational structure. Properly completing the fifth grade is crucial to obtaining entry into the sixth grade; it does not matter very much, formally, where one has completed it. Similarly all through the system: a student who has completed the proper program at an inferior school of education may have slightly lower prospects of becoming a teacher, but prospects that are vastly superior to those of a very able student

who has not completed the proper program at all. Understanding this central property of the educational system is vital to understanding why resources and organizational variations among schools often have such small effects: the fundamental resource any high school has is its legitimate authority to define its students as nationally valid graduates (Meyer, 1970b).

Even special forms of organizational success—being in a "good" college or being a very successful student within a program—are attenuated in their social significance. It is necessary to complete high school to go to college: it is nice, but not necessary, to have done so in an admired school, or to have received good grades, or to have learned a lot. The success that matters most is that achieved with respect to the educational categories of national significance.

7. The general educational categories of nationwide meaning are linked to concrete topics of education: topics, therefore, vary in their institutional centrality. Some (e.g., reading and arithmetic in elementary school) are everywhere understood to be defining ingredients of schools. Others are more peripheral. Still others have only local organizational meaning—defined in a particular classroom or school.

Further, time-defined centrality varies. Some topics are understood to be more vital to future programs than others: mathematics, for instance, is broadly necessary and is also organized in long chains of requisite steps.

The institutionalized national education system importantly consists of sequencing rules and topical definitions. Some variation exists among various legal and public organizational definitions, but there is a broad base of widely shared definitions. Educational organizations are astonishingly homogeneous in that they all fall into a few general categories and have common topical and general sequencing rules within categories. Even so evanescent a topic, in terms of actual knowledge, as sociology can be found in almost every American college.

I have described the institutional structure of modern education: consider briefly what it is not. It is not primarily a system of discrete classroom, school, and district organizations, each producing measured learning of each child. Some assessments of this kind are made and are built into the grades received by the student; but these assessments, and the controls they represent, are of uncertain meaning and secondary significance both to the market and to the students who receive them. The organizations that make up the educational system derive their significance, their external status, and their power over students from the institutional classification system with which they link up. The student confronts particular organizational units; these units have power not in their idiosyncratic organizational details, but inasmuch as they carry the authority of the wider institutional system.

The Rational Student. How then will a reasonable student, approaching the social system in good faith and interested in the main chance, learn and participate? The necessary core propositions of any sociology of education are often ignored.

Proposition A: Students, in contrast to nonstudents, will learn and will participate in learning knowledge appropriate to success in the educational and occupational systems.

1. They will learn and will participate in learning central topics more than peripheral topics.
2. They will learn and will participate in learning topics linked to valued futures more than those linked to less-valued futures.

Proposition B: Students will learn, and participate more in learning, knowledge relevant to immediate success in their programs and categories.

1. They will learn and will participate more in learning required material more than less-required material.
2. They will learn more and will participate more in programs or categories that are linked to valued futures than in those linked to less-valued futures.
3. They will learn more and participate more in programs that are more certainly linked to valued futures than in less certainly linked programs.

Students generally understand that the system is built around a knowledge gradient and that the knowledge is important for future educational and occupational success (Proposition A). But the system offers much more certainty than this—knowledge is useful, but completion of the immediate program or category is vital and more or less ensures successful access to the next step. A probabilistic relation is institutionalized and made certain, and the rational student will do what is required. Even very young students understand the importance of school and of schooled subjects, as well as the great importance of properly completing given grades and proceeding to subsequent grades.

Thus, from the perspective of the private interests or tastes of individual students, the educational system is a huge knowledge-creating and knowledge-distorting structure in two ways. First, it is infused with knowledge relevant not to the present life of the student, but to various social futures. Second, through its programmatic structure, it makes certain types of knowledge (which may be of little future use) crucial to present (and thus future) success and makes other types of knowledge (which may be of actual future utility) unimportant or irrelevant. Like any institution, education is a structure of pluralistic knowledge and pluralistic ignorance. It distorts the learning and participation of young people from the issues relevant to the present to those relevant to the future; and it further distorts learning and participation from issues that may be of actual future relevance to those that are, through collective political and organizational processes, built into the educational programmatic structure. (And as with any institution, one can make different moral assessments of the distortion as virtuous or fraudulent. In this instance, they depend on one's assessment of [a] the importance of the childish state of nature—as with the current children's rights movement; [b] the adult world—as with manpower planners; and [c] the autonomous authority of the educational system—as with cultural emphases on the independent virtues of knowledge.)

In any event, once in the student role, a whole rather standardized program of learning and participation is laid out and made useful and necessary to valued futures. This has extraordinary effects, as can be seen most easily in those few studies that compare students with otherwise similar nonstudents (e.g., Holsinger, 1974). Assessments of educational effects should look to such research designs rather than to those that compare schools and programs that may be essentially identical from the point of view developed here. If schooling inheres in institutional definitions, its effects may be ascertained by comparing those acting within the institution to those acting outside its penumbra.

Simple experiments can show these effects. How much more will young experimental subjects choose to participate in any given instructional situation if it has a properly schooled label or definition? Given participation, will they learn more under this label? How much more will they participate and learn if the instruction is for credit? If it is required for proper completion of their program?

Further, experiments can show the effects of institutionalized educational topics. Students should learn and participate more if the knowledge involved is understood to be very central to adult status. For instance, attaching the label "mathematics" to given instructional play should make it more efficacious than calling it a game (or game theory). And college freshmen should learn more from a taped lecture called "political philosophy" than from the same lecture called "personal political opinion": perhaps they would learn still more if it is called "economics" and less if it is called "sociology."

Beyond topical labels, other programmatic elements of education should make a difference too and can be studied experimentally or in other ways. Students located in programs of lower value or of less certain success should participate less in and learn less from given instructional situations. Given students should learn less from a course called "third grade" than from one called "fourth grade" material. And students in a vocational program should learn less from a given course than similar students in a college preparatory program. Students in formally inferior types of schools should acquire less commitment to learning and participation (some evidence that this is true in the case of British schools is shown by Himmelweit and Swift, 1969; Kerckhoff, 1975; and Treiman and Terrell, 1975; American studies comparing curricula include Rosenbaum, 1975; and Alexander, Cook, and McDill, 1978). American research has unfortunately rarely compared vocational with general high schools and college preparatory high schools, but the effects should be substantial.

Beyond the overall future status conferred by a given categorical program, topical relevance is also established. Medical and law students should learn rather different things from a course in forensic medicine. And while we generally expect vocational students to learn less from their work, this should be especially the case with courses removed from the main definition of their programs, such as English or mathematics courses.

It follows from this discussion, of course, that learning and participation in stigmatized courses or programs (remedial courses, for instance) or by stigmatized students should be lower. This should especially be the case if the stigmatization confers genuine disabilities for future success (we are not discussing here subtle reactions of students to the attitudes of those about them, but rational responses to sharp differences in future value).

In addition, it follows that idiosyncratic instruction—peculiar to a particular teacher, program, school, or whatever—is less likely to be efficacious. The instructional power of a given element is greatly enhanced by its presumed structural necessity and universality. As students understand that an element is not "really" central either to future knowledge or to widely shared definitions of their programs, doubts about its utility arise. It may be necessary to learn the material here and now, for practical purposes. But if it is easy to imagine that other students occupying the same educational category and going through the same institutionalized program do not learn the material at hand, this material begins to seem arbitrary—a gratuitous exercise of authority—and resistance arises. I return to this point later in this chapter.

More subtle studies than those proposed above can show exactly what contextual cues operate to establish the properly schooled (and hence valuable) character of knowledge and educational work. Will students participate and learn more if the instructional leader is defined as a teacher? If the instructional materials appear to be "educational"? If other participants appear to be students? If the physical setting is that of a school? Such experiments explore the phenomenology of education. They show some of the processes that locate value in given work and knowledge. But they are mainly of analytical interest; in the real world it is usually very clearly defined whether a given learning situation is schooled or not. As discussed later, it is greatly in the interest of educational managers and teachers to gain power and control over the situation by maintaining these definitions in real life.

Societal Effects. Let us, for the moment, assume the argument that the educational system tends toward homogeneity across the country and further tends toward isomorphism with nationally defined educational categories and topics. The arguments above then make it clear that this system tends to generate nationwide bodies of knowledge and to instill them into the citizenry. Clearly, for instance, a national agreement that astrology (or economics) was vital to elementary education would produce vast increases in participation in and knowledge of this subject. Or as another example, American students often learn the names and locations of the American states but know almost nothing about the Canadian provinces (and we would expect the gradient on this dimension as one neared the Canadian border to be very small). One inch across the border, however, and the situation would undoubtedly change dramatically, despite relatively little national structuring of the curriculum in any direct way in either country. Unfortunately, much of the important cross-national research emphasizes commonly valued topics (e.g., mathematics, science) rather than areas where differentiation seems "obvious."

These examples suggest useful comparative research, but they are introduced here for another reason. The general argument of this section is written, for polemic emphasis, as if students do all the educational work—operating through their anticipations of future requirements and future value. This is clearly not the case. Hosts of consultants help them with parents, peers, and counselors all playing some role. But the organizational structure of education plays a very direct role in this capacity. I have argued that it is a mistake to see this organizational structure as the main show, but it is also a mistake to ignore it completely. Throughout the educational system, administrators and teachers work to link up concrete educational materials and topics to the general national classificatory system and to give this system local and specific meaning. The important point is that they do this not as a coherent organizational structure, but as loosely coupled elements of a binding national institutional system.

Summary. Working from a naively sociological conception of the student, we are able to consider the "obvious" effects of education. The organization of value and life chances in a nationwide system with restricted structural properties produces an enormous amount of learning and participation along highly directed lines. Symbolically, though not in organizational details, the system is homogeneous. By thinking of the student not mainly as a person or network role occupant, but as a member of a nationwide institutional category, we are able to think about some fundamental aspects and effects of the system—effects that might not vary much among organizational settings.

I could easily go on to elaborate this model. Students are better or worse informed about the structure of the system; those poorly advised by parent and peer consultants may participate and learn less. And programs differ in the detailed ways in which they manage transitions and confer certainty of success upon completion. Differing discount rates can be applied to success in the nearer or further future. Detailed arguments can be worked out, and some suggestions are made in the following section.

But I must now deal with the major embarrassments of this simple theory. The theory has it that, barring mistakes, all students will learn everything they are supposed to, will participate in the system to the highest professional levels, and will attain the nirvanas that the stratification system has to offer. The theory further has it that students have no other interests—nothing else to do—but to pursue long-run status goals.

To a surprising extent, modern postindustrial educational systems and societies are like this. But qualifications need to be introduced.

Theory of Commitment to the Student Role

Imagine now that our young person is a broader and more variable kind of firm, not simply an automaton embedded in the student role. We have now a young social careerist, with multiple interests and capacities, multiple roles, and many desirable futures, not all of which are linked to the educational system. Further, our young firm has problems of internal organization, of structuring life and action so as to make effective success possible. Again, I assume that there are no real attachments, although diverse consultants offer more or less accurate information (I avoid the case of the present-oriented, attached personality, since this case is too highly developed in the literature already). Our problem is to consider the conditions under which this young firm will make a greater investment in (commitment to) the educational system and the learning and participation that are involved.

My description of the institutional structure of the educational system must also be modified. Not all possibilities are open to everyone. There is selection and success and failure: some of the desired educational and occupational outcomes are difficult to obtain. The selection and success and failure, however, are defined primarily in the educational system itself—in the transitions from categorical step to categorical step.

The starting point is obvious—we need only a primitive social psychology here. I add to the earlier propositions one central idea:

Proposition C: Commitment to the student role (and the learning and participation involved according to Propositions A and B) is a positive function of the perceived and actual rewards and a negative function of the costs involved. Among other things:

1. Commitment is a positive function of the relative gains in occupational and educational success to be obtained.
2. Commitment is a negative function of the attractiveness of the alternatives to education.
3. Commitment is a positive function of the rewards and meaningfulness available in the present student role.
4. Commitment is a negative function of the effort required to obtain success.

Clearly, educational systems maximize commitment if they gain monopolies over the conferral of status, expand the total amount of success available, maximize the present rewards and meanings available to students, and lower the effort required. The social psychology involved here requires little discussion, partly because the available literature deals with it fairly well, and much research has been done.

The sociological implications, however, are little studied. But they are of great interest, because the dimensions maximizing commitment cannot themselves be simultaneously maximized. Substantial trade-offs are involved. School work that is meaningful and rewarding in the present is often poorly linked with future success. In a fixed occupational system, maximizing the total amount of educational success created minimizes the occupational success available per educational step. Minimizing the effort involved lowers the likelihood of future success. A jungle of structural constraints exists.

The fundamental problem is simple: both present and future rewards and meanings increase commitment to the system. But the maximization of the present rewards and meanings available to the student results in sacrifices in future rewards and meanings. And conversely, the maximization of educational control through close linkages with future success constrains the present rewards and meanings available to the young person (for an empirical example, see Arnove, 1971). Compromises must be made—different compromises depending on the goals of the system and on the properties of young persons. These compromises are typically (1) between the expansion of educational success and the occupational success provided per unit of education and (2) between shorter run and longer run educational success.

A second feature of the system offers further complexities. Proposition C operates partly through the realities of the system. But these are never entirely clear, and the process operates substantially through the perceptions of the young persons and their consultants. Systematic distortions in these perceptions can be created through organized action. At every point in the educational system, inflation occurs; to maximize commitment, more success is offered than is objectively available. This works, but at some cost to the meaningfulness of the future and of the educational work that leads to future success. Educational systems reach different compromises, depending on educational goals and on the properties of young persons, between inflation and realism in the definition of meaning and opportunity.

In some areas, however, system properties can expand commitment without trade-offs. They can increase the extent to which young persons are generally attuned to the educational system through socialization, can increase the autonomous value of education, can sometimes increase accurate understanding of the linkages and rewards involved, and can expand overall occupational success in postindustrial society.

I discuss these issues in the following two sections. The discussion is organized around particular variables and levels of analysis, rather than theoretically. Given the purpose of encouraging research, some clarity may be sacrificed, but perhaps potential research designs will be clearer.

LEVELS OF EDUCATION AND THEIR EFFECTS

In laying out a "theory of the student," I have addressed some of the most central issues of educational effects. The system operates by organizing learning and participation in a sequenced set of institutionalized categories and by making success in each of these categories vital to future prospects. Schooled learning and participation become much more valuable than nonschooled learning and participation. In acquiring or linking up to the larger (partial) institutional monopoly, each level of the educational system gains power over the young. Many of the effects here are obvious, although they have not often been studied. Research designs mainly involve contrasts between students and nonstudents, members and nonmembers.

I turn now to the more complex effects arising from the broader issues brought in by the "theory of commitment" and the related discussion above. What follows is organized in terms of the effects of various levels of educational structure in order to suggest specific research issues.

Individual Factors
Two individual variables are almost universally found to affect learning and participation—family social status or resources and ability. Status operates to affect ability and, mostly through this, learning. But it directly affects crucial decisions to participate (e.g., in America, the decision to attend college). Ability directly affects both learning and participation. Many efforts have been made to account for these effects with various intervening variables. (The effect of ability on learning is, however, ordinarily treated as very direct, since the ability assessed is practically defined as the capacity to undertake schooling tasks.) Without attempting to structure the field generally, a few comments may be useful.

Family Social Status. Family social status (mainly parents' education and educational expectations for the child, rather than economic resources) increases the perceived value of educational success. It may also lower the value of the alternatives (this has not been studied adequately). Higher status families provide a much clearer depiction, to the young person, of the linkages of the whole educational and occupational system—linkages that make the student role much more valuable. Young people are often very poorly informed about these linkages, and better information may, by making the institutional connections clearer, make current activities seem more certainly tied to more valued futures. The experientially irrelevant knowledge comprising the educational system may become more relevant if a young person understands its substantive and organizational links with valued futures. Future status attainment studies should incorporate variables measuring young persons' comprehension of the structure of the system that confronts them. Researchers should also measure rejection of the lower status careers to be obtained without participating in the system, as well as the commonly measured desire for the high status options (see Rodman and Voydanoff, 1978).

Ability. Family status, and especially ability, measure the degree to which the young person is in tune with the requirements and meanings of educational work. Both may increase not only the perceived value of this work, but also the ease with which it can be understood as meaningful and with which it can be done.

Relatively little is known about the way intelligence is generated in children, considering that this has been a main research problem for perhaps eight decades. This is partly because intelligence has been conceived to be a kind of personality property—integrated in the motivational and perceptual structure of the person as a bounded subsystem. Intelligence might be better seen as a reflection in the person of a peculiar phenomenal world outside (one related conceptually and empirically to what is now called modernity; see Inkeles and Smith, 1974). This is a world, and a way of acting, that would have seemed alien to most people in human history. Its properties include:

1. Order—the world is a dense network of causal flows; events have origins and explanations, and problems have answers.
2. Rationality—calculation can decipher the order and solve problems.

3. Objectification and impersonality—the real world is external to social life and human meaning, and answers to problems are both objectively correct and the same for everyone.
4. Authoritative individualism—individual persons have the collectively defined right and obligation to approach the world and its problems. They do not act as agents of larger corporate entities, whose rules and traditions define correct approaches to the world, and do not need to consult such authorities. Each individual is directly linked to the rational, orderly, objectified cosmos.

This world is so real in our society that most individuals are deeply imbued with its perspective. (We do not have many terms to describe someone who acts intelligently in a negative way.) As a result, IQs in modern societies are much higher than those in others. As a further result, research on the nature of intelligence might better proceed by finding experimental devices that can temporarily lower IQs rather than those that may raise them. Some suggestions can be made: Will experimental groups do less well on ability tests if they are informed that there may not be correct answers to all the items? Will they do less well if they are informed that the correctness of answers may depend on the perceptions of individuals or on these individuals' backgrounds? Will they do less well if authoritative corporate groups are invoked? (Katz, Epps, and Axelson [1964] suggest that blacks do less well in these situations.) For example, if individuals spend a prior day or two working on tasks where they do not, and group leaders do, have access to data on the correctness of task activity, will IQs be lowered? Or will children do less well on an oral test if their parents are present? Research of this kind (see Sarason [1978], among others) can isolate properties of the context that support a world in which individual ability is a relevant dimension for action.

The lines of research advocated here may be especially useful in interpreting the large racial differences in America on ability tests (social status held constant). Clearly, blacks have occupied a status one step removed from the "real" world on which ability is constructed—a status linked to that world through corporate political relationships. The technical structure of the world around them has been less relevant for their action than the social linkages that locate their identities. One would expect to find large racial differences in the ability of individuals to focus clearly on the kinds of tasks found in ability tests—to take these tasks seriously as a main order of business.

Aggregated Individual Factors

To some extent, classroom, school, or district social class and ability factors operate the same way individual ones do. A student surrounded by able and high status peers has better consultants, higher standards of work, and so on: such a student may value education more, understand its logic better, and find its immediate activities more meaningful.

However, additional complexity is introduced here. In high status schools and classrooms, the effort required is greater, but the success offered is not increased proportionately (in America, at least: other systems sometimes publicly define such schools as better and offer better futures to their students). These factors lower commitment in some measure. This is the often-discussed "frog-pond effect" (Davis, 1966; Meyer, 1970a; and many others) by which the aspirations and participation of given students are slightly reduced by the presence around them of more able competitors. This effect is smaller than might be supposed; no convincing data show it at the college level, and few studies show it as a consequence of tracking in elementary schools (e.g., Goldberg, Passow, and Justman, 1966). And the studies that report this finding in high schools are methodologically suspect: the aggregated ability measures they use are obtained from tests administered under conditions common to a given school but perhaps variable between schools. Thus, aggregate ability measures may simply reflect a source of error in the measurement of individual ability (which is held constant in such analyses). If the effect really exists, it is very small.

The reason for this is clear. The informal world around each school and classroom makes corrections for the competitive level involved. Counselors, college admissions officers, and teachers in their grading practices increase the rewards available to students in high status schools enough to make up for the lowered competitive situation within those schools. In some contexts this is formalized, and schools are publicly stigmatized with formal categorical labels in such a way as to eliminate frog-pond effects—on the main consequences of education, at least—entirely. It is still possible that more subtle negative effects on commitment occur, but so far they have not been discovered. Some of them may show up in investigations of the formation of student subcultures and other modifications of the student role: high status schools sometimes generate (in America, at least) student cultures with lower competitive pressures that are at considerable odds with the private interests and goals of the students (Coleman, 1961). The process

I discuss here may be involved: if so, comparative research would be useful in showing it. High status schools whose competitive structure is adequately corrected for by positive public stigmatization should show fewer tendencies toward such student cultures.

Student Role Properties

I have emphasized the extent to which the student role derives meaning from its links to the future. Access to valued positions in adult life depends on successful action in this role. But this feature of the student role generates a peculiar problem—the student role is heavily defined by the presumed incompetence of its incumbents and by their lack of present direct linkage with the centers of meaning and value in adult life. Success in the student role requires effective choice and action, but it also requires acceptance of the role and of the ineffectiveness that is its defining characteristic. This paradox explains the relative educational ineffectiveness of the most brutal kinds of educational systems, which our "theory of the student" implies might be the most effective. A system of instruction clearly linked with the requirements of adult life—which organizes tasks in terms of these requirements, emphasizes selection and failure, and so on—tends to generate and reinforce a sense of meaninglessness and lack of commitment in students.

In most educational systems, a solution is the expansion of the student role to incorporate more matters of student interest and taste and more expanded legitimations of students' present identities. The student role expands into a legitimate social space of its own, far beyond the point implied in our "theory of the student." The curriculum is organized to fit the present interests and perspectives of the students as persons, and a huge extracurriculum is created. Students are given a status of their own in society, with areas of jurisdiction over their own lives and some areas of autonomy. The effect of this expansion of the student role on learning and participation is complex. Learning and participation are in some measure enhanced. But at the same time this expansion slowly undercuts the highly meaningful linkages between the student and the future.

So also with the expansion of the student role created by young persons themselves. They are caught by the problem of giving present meaning to activity valued mainly for its future outcomes. And they are caught by the need to give meaning to the dense social relations with each other into which they are thrown by the ecology of the educational system. Faced with this, like dependent populations everywhere, students create a culture of their own, albeit a fragile one (Coleman, 1961; Berger, 1971). To some extent, this culture and its associated social organization enhance the meaning of student life enough to reinforce learning and participation. But greatly elaborated, they undercut links with the future, and the meaninglessness and uncertainty so created begin to lower commitment. The relation between the expansion of the student role and commitment to it is probably curvilinear.

However, another effect is created here that lies outside the boundaries of our initial formulations. In some respects, learning is enhanced by expansion of the student role, but the character of the learning itself changes. Learning and education become decreasingly related to the types of knowledge relevant to adult life and become tied to the student subworld.

Aggregated Student Roles

These modifications of the student role are only in part local to each classroom, school, and so on; in large part they are nationwide and worldwide phenomena. The creation in modern societies of hugh classes of young persons institutionally segregated from adult life and located in the educational system has substantial effects. Perhaps one-fifth of the people in the world have as their primary social status the position of "student." This aggregate fact increases the separation of individual young persons from adult life. It surrounds them with meanings and social relationships organized on their own terms, thus continuing a historical process discussed by Ariès (1962). This reinforces the processes described in the section above; it expands the student role, decouples this role from adult life, and increasingly organizes educational work and learning in terms that are independent of the knowledge desired or required by the adult world. Its relations to student commitment are quite possibly curvilinear—the elaboration of the student role in a society probably first increases and then decreases student commitment to education, at least in adult terms. And it also changes the character of the commitment and learning involved, as noted above.

Vertical and Lateral
Institutional Differentiation

The vertical differentiation of the student role into the twenty-odd "grades" of the modern educational system (from nursery school to postdoctoral study) is the institutional parallel to the phenomena discussed above. It increases commitment by organizing work in ways that are directly related to the student's present capacities, perspectives, and interests. And it clearly lowers commitment by separating students more and more sharply, with more and more intervening steps, from their futures. Clearly, there are trade-offs between the *shtetl* school organized around adult knowledge and authoritarian in its imposition (Zborowski and Herzog, 1962) and the modern school, with its carefully graded program, tuned to prevailing social conceptions of the child.

Most important, what is learned changes. The modern educational system, in order to fit the child, creates and organizes types of knowledge that have few counterparts in adult life, but that nevertheless made necessary to the successful attainment of adult life. Long curricular chains are created, which in their earlier stages alter to unrecognizability the types of knowledge ultimately desired. Paralleling the informal student subculture, a whole official subculture of childhood arises, with separate books and libraries; separate music and games; peculiar versions of language, history, science, and mathematics; and so on. The more highly graded the school system, the more elaborate this official subculture, and the more differentiated from adult knowledge is the knowledge actually learned in school. (Schooled knowledge, of course, also feeds back into the adult world, altering the knowledge base of society; but this is beyond our scope.)

Lateral differentiation of majors, curricula, types of students, and even, in a small way, courses and topics operates mainly in the opposite direction from vertical differentiation. It increases the meaningfulness of student roles in relation to occupational and educational futures and decreases their present meaningfulness; and again, it undoubtedly has a curvilinear effect on commitment and learning. Further, it probably lowers the extent to which the official bodies of student culture and knowledge are completely separated from those of adult life.

These two features of modern educational systems seem to fall into a shifting balance. In the earlier years of life, vertical differentiation predominates, and the little subworld appropriate to each age and grade is elaborated (along with justificatory ideologies from educational and developmental psychologies). Later, vertical differentiation is accompanied by more and more lateral differentiation, linked more closely to the adult world. As noted later, the shifting points depend on the extent to which educational systems are built around participation or, alternatively, around social selection. But however this may be, these shifting points drift upward in age with social modernization and with emphases on egalitarian nation building.

Some forms of lateral differentiation, however, have more complex effects. The construction of stratified programs or curricula, built around subsequent social selection, increases realism, but for subordinated groups of students it creates a paradox. Subordinated programs may be linked to adult life, but to adult roles that involve relative failure. They may through their "relevance" increase commitment, but this is overshadowed by the fact that this commitment is to a social gangplank. The actual commitment generated by such programs may be fairly low. Even the fact that they are frequently tailored to the "needs," tastes, and interests of the students in the immediate present is unlikely to make up for the highly meaningful failure they imply.

Research Designs on the Student Role

The ideas developed above can be studied in a variety of ways: comparative research is not inevitably necessary. For instance, one could compare student learning and participation over time in social studies courses that follow authoritative traditional models of curriculum and instruction with others that incorporate more and more student choice and interests, even allowing central topics to be chosen by the peer culture. Curricula built along the latter lines, even though organized to maximize interest, would eventually come to seem meaningless in terms of "real" educational requirements. This might occur less if the autonomous world and life of children and students were more legitimated in society. American students, for instance, would be expected to find student-directed curricula more appropriate than would, say, French students. And both groups would find them more appropriate than would students in less modern societies.

One could also compare, with survey techniques, extant schools and curricula. One of the adaptations of the American educational system to students who are very low in status and ability is to tailor curricula to their interests and qualities. For instance, in extreme cases teachers employ curricular materials unrelated to official topics and use a great deal of positive affect to encourage students (Dornbusch et al., 1974). They sometimes also employ grades to reward participation of any kind, independent of learning. These short-run strategies obviously have some negative consequences: the work that students do decreasingly has long-run educational and occupational meaning, and students lose clarity on the links between what they are doing and the future. It would be easy to study empirically students' reactions to programmatic stigmatization and to the weakening of educational content.

Vertical differentiation could be studied in the same ways. Experiments could show the reactions of students to curricula that move further and further from their own experience and toward the realities of adult life—or, on the other hand, to curricula that are increasingly adapted to their situations and interests. The trade-offs in learning and participation so created would almost certainly show up if experimenters were willing to try unrealistic extremes in these respects. Survey data could show many of the same kinds of effects.

In all these studies, of course, the degree to which students are a status group highly legitimated in society would be an important variable, supporting more disconnection from adult life and more relevance to present situations and interests. One could also compare societies directly: Do those that broaden the social definition of the student role enhance learning and participation? Can one find a point on this scale after which negative consequences appear? And in any case, is the knowledge instilled in students decreasingly related to the adult world?

Organizational Factors

In some measure, school organizations manipulate the student role in the ways discussed immediately above: they construct the curriculum and the extracurriculum to expand the possibilities for commitment. Here I note some additional aspects of these effects.

Our simple "theory of the student" suggests that a school organization attempting to enhance learning and participation would do well to build in real threats of failure. But beyond a certain point prospects of failure lower commitment, and the effects of this variable are probably curvilinear. On the other hand, the external world clearly earmarks many students for failure. How can the school adapt?

A solution for the school organization would be to provide some kind of success for almost all students and to let the future world figure out how to "cool them out" (Clark, 1961). This can be done by creating special curricula aimed at futures that in fact are not available (e.g., vocational curricula, for the most part, in America), by expanding the curriculum to include topics of marginal relevance, by processing more students through to diplomas than there are positions available for, and so on.

Most of these strategies work to some extent, particularly as students are poorly informed or misinformed. And students are likely to be misinformed; the longer they retain high aspirations, the higher and more meaningful their present status is. To a certain extent, the organizational expansion of the student role increases commitment. Eventually, however, these strategies again reach a point of negative gain: the losses and gains, however, will undoubtedly be different for different groups of students. Strategies of incorporation produce maximum benefits (at least in the short term) for marginal and low status students. Their costs are more apparent for able and high status students, whose positions and virtues are undercut by the overall meaninglessness generated.

These issues can clearly be studied with experimental data or with data from school organizations. Are students more likely to learn and participate if success rates are higher and if programs are broadened to incorporate more kinds of students and knowledge? And does the perceived meaningfulness of school work decline under these circumstances? One might compare, for instance, the effectiveness of various mathematics programs that successively broaden the range of topics, the categories of students, and the possibilities of organizationally defined success. The programs should be compared overall and also in terms of their effectiveness with various types of students.

In all these studies, degree of program stigmatization is an important variable. Programs stigmatized as disabling with various public definitions (e.g., remedial, "slow" track, "noncollege") should have fewer positive consequences for the participants and fewer negative consequences for the nonparticipants than programs that are given formal public equality.

Societal and Educational System Factors

The individual, role, and organizational properties discussed above are greatly affected by larger attributes of societies and societal educational systems:

1. Modern societies increase the proportion of individuals who are attuned to the educational system—namely, those who have educationally appropriate world views and who come from social strata closely linked to the educational system.

2. Modern societies increase the extent to which access to desirable social positions is dependent on educational success. Given social positions come increasingly under the jurisdiction of educational credentials. This increases the value of education, the learning and participation of students, and the commitment of young persons to the student role. Other factors constant, the more modern the society, the more students should learn and participate in school.

3. Modern societies expand the set of desirable positions that depend on educational success. They not only gound given elite positions in education but also expand their elites (primarily in the tertiary or service sector) to take control over a wider range of social activities. Access to these new service elite positions (e.g., civil service, educational system, and professional positions) almost universally depends on education. These social changes give education more and more authoritative control over young persons and their life chances and thus enhance educational effects.

4. The social changes discussed above (especially point 3) also broaden the legitimate content of the educational system. I noted earlier that schools may expand their curricula to incorporate a wider range of topics in an effort to coopt student commitment, but that unauthorized expansions may lower the meaningfulness of education. The expansion of rational collective authority (nowadays, mainly in the state) to cover more domains, and the rooting of this authority in education, legitimizes such changes. Thus the educational system is broadened and is able to legitimately absorb student interests in its broader domains. A student can, for credit, study the culture of his or her ethnic group, the mechanics of the female orgasm, a variety of games, favorite types of popular music or literature, and so on. These subjects come to be not merely devices to absorb student interest, but legitimately schooled topics, each broadly understood to link up to desirable adult and occupational roles in the enormously expanded service sector. Such changes increase learning, although they also expand the set of dimensions on which learning occurs. They also increase participation. They produce these effects both by increasing the importance of educational success and by linking the educational system to a wider range of students and student interests.

5. Modern societies can increase the authority and value of education directly, not only through enhanced educational opportunity. Education itself takes on value beyond its instrumental significance. This increases educational effectiveness. Apart from its immediate allocative powers, the larger assumption is created that schooled knowledge is authoritative and will (and should) dominate in the long run. This widespread assumption that social progress of a rational kind is possible and likely and that education is closely linked to it puts the burden of proof on the doubter. Even the most alienated students tend to affirm the value of education (Dornbusch et al., 1974). The effectiveness of education is increased, and the student role is expanded to an even more enveloping degree. Faith in the possibility of obtaining

success in life through noneducational channels is similarly lowered.

6. Modern societies expand and alter commitments by creating more and more elaborate and independently justified social identities for students and children, separate from those of adult life. They bound childhood from adult society with credentialing systems, restrictive labor laws, ecological segregation, and the elaboration of separate youth cultures and differentiated bodies of curricular knowledge and extracurricular activity. By and large these changes increase educational commitment (although to some extent they also lower it, as discussed above) by organizing both young people and the schooling system to be in tune with each other. But they also alter the substantive character of the kinds of learning and participation involved, directing them along lines not necessarily relevant to adult society in any direct way.

Research on all these societal effects can most obviously take a comparative form. In what kinds of societies is commitment (and learning and participation) enhanced? The properties above are suggested factors. Experimental studies—in which students are asked to make educational choices in hypothetical societies varying on the dimensions suggested above—are also relevant. Would a given student not be more likely to consider a wide range of curricular topics if society is described as containing many positions for which these would be appropriate training on if society is described as containing distinctive youth cultural preferences toward such topics?

Summary

I have reviewed a number of properties of higher level contexts that might transform the meaning of the student's role and choices, often tacitly assuming that the immediate interactional and organizational context is held constant. Properties of the student role in society, of broad organizational rules, and of society itself enter in.

Of course, many of these effects would be partly mediated by the local social structure around the student—the messages conveyed by parents, peers, teachers, and patterns of instruction. I have deemphasized such issues in calling attention to more macrosociological effects, but there is no real conflict here. In some measure, students figure out the educational score on their own. To some extent, advisors help them. This issue should be no more central to the macrosociology of education than it is to the theory of the firm.

All of the arguments have been built on the assumption that young persons are fairly sensible about the whole thing. They make heavier educational investments than might arise from personal interests and tastes, since education confers valued futures. These commitments become heavier still as education acquires a monopoly over future status. They also become heavier if the work is easier, in terms of individual abilities and tastes, and if students become more certain of the dependence of success on education.

Educational work will be distorted (both by students and by the system) in the direction of the students' personal interests and preferences, but eventually present meaningfulness is gained at the cost of future meaningfulness, so a kind of equilibrium results. The deflection of educational work is partly created by school and society in an effort to absorb the interests of the young, but it is also a result of young persons' efforts to create enough meaning to make their present positions and social relations plausible.

Through all this, the wider system definitions play a dominant role. Students choose to study and learn mathematics not only because they are taught it, but also because (1) mathematics is central to the social requirements for future educational careers, (2) it is central to many occupational entry requirements, (3) it is central to educational content as defined by all sorts of social parties (teachers, parents, and the wider culture), (4) it is built into the students' own conception of important knowledge, and so on. Most of these variables are little manipulable by a local classroom, school, or district. They are highly linked to education as a wider institution. We should not be surprised to discover few effects or organizational variations, unless these are linked to, and given meaning by, the wider institutional system.

RATIONAL EDUCATORS AND THE EFFECTIVE SCHOOLING SYSTEM

Given the educational institutions and students discussed above, how do participants in the organizational structure of education behave? How do they organize, and how do they take action within the organizations they create? For simplicity, assume that we educators are not much less sensible than young persons. Assume further that educators play roles as agents of a system whose goals are to enhance young persons' learning and participation (though in varying proportions). We can usefully ignore their attention to private or subgroup interests or any distortions that might conceivably result from any "professionalization"—a term of very uncertain

meaning. I consider first the activities of organizational functionaries (principals, superintendents, and other administrators), second
those of teachers, and third those of societal and educational states-
men. Throughout, I assume that all parties respond to young persons
as described above—that they understand that these young persons
are deeply embedded in a context of meanings densely linked to
the present and the future.

Administrators (see Meyer and Rowan 1977, 1978)

The power of any given school or educational organization arises
principally from its linkages to the bottom nine-tenths of the educational iceberg—the institutional structure of education. The main
problem for the administrator, if learning and participation are to
be sustained, is to clearly link a particular educational organization
or program to this wider institutional system. The school must
be wholly accredited in everyone's eyes, or commitment and resources will rapidly decline. Ideally, it should be accredited as
properly within a nationwide category of schools of general meaning
and substantial allocation power—for example, it is better to be a
college than a junior college, better to be a general high school
than a vocational school, and so on. Much organizational activity
must be devoted to maintaining institutional legitimacy. A stock
of properly credentialed teachers is necessary, along with approved
facilities and students who are themselves appropriately defined
and credentialed.

Clearly, the topics or categories of instruction should parallel
those of the broadest meaning: they should reflect the standardized
categories of instruction required by the state and understood to
be appropriate by all constituents. Even at the level of higher education, it is important to incorporate as many of the standardized
national "fields" as one can. Otherwise questions may be raised,
and the college considered limited or partial or incomplete.

Further, the types of students internally distinguished should
conform to categories with the broadest institutional meaning and
authority. In America, one distinguishes students in grades running
through twenty-odd vertical categories (and many laterally differentiated ones). Omitting categories increases uncertainty and raises
doubts in the minds of students and others about the legitimacy
of the program.

By linking the school structure to the wider institutional system,
the administrator maximizes its effective authority and incentives.
The student is no longer moving from freshman to sophomore

status in a particular school; the transition is meaningful throughout American education, and the authority and incentives are nationwide in meaning. The student will know the transitions that must be made to be a high school sophomore, a graduate, a chemistry major or graduate, and so on. No incentives that the weak organization of the school, standing alone, could generate would approach this institutionally derived baptismal power.

As a result, schools and curricula and courses tend toward isomorphism with national systems of categories. This tendency is strongest where education is most highly institutionalized. Formal educational homogeneity is generated even in a national society (like the United States) in which educational control is decentralized.

Within any general category, administrators struggle to increase the status or prestige of their programs, but this is a minor and relatively unimportant process at the level of a given program (though it may be an important source of innovations for the system as a whole). They try to find innovations that are, or will be, fashionable—that is, that have some chance of attaining institutional status in education generally. On occasion, some may even innovate on their own—sometimes in a desperate attempt to maintain survival prospects and to find their niche within the general categorical system.

We have, thus, a system in which institutional conformity is much more important for effectiveness than is technical instructional efficacy or technical innovation: the real technology of the system lies in its institutional exoskeleton, not in organizational machinery. But what if, as is often the case, the students are uninterested or disabled or the prospects of real educational success are slight? One solution is the incorporation in the school of different programmatic categories—vocational curricula, and so on. Sometimes these may be linked to real occupational opportunities; on other occasions they will be justified by standardized categories of instruction. In either case, this solution, if carried too far, can result in the loss of status and meaning and can lower learning and participation by engendering doubts about the validity of the program. Students in such programs probably learn less than comparable students in regular programs—but much more than if they did not participate at all.

A second, and common, solution is to allow and encourage inflated levels of participation in regular school programs. This involves the partial disconnection of educational programs and the social futures that they are ordinarily supposed to lead to: students are allowed and encouraged to participate in programs leading to futures that are not in fact open to them. This has the advantage of maximizing participation and can easily be justified with democratic ideology (e.g., equality of opportunity). It is a central characteristic of American education and permits and encourages student aspirations far in excess of the available opportunities. It is one of the mechanisms by which American education has always sustained extraordinarily high levels of participation throughout the life cycle.

A disadvantage of this strategy is the loss of reality involved, the potential doubts about the real meaningfulness for real future outcomes of the educational system. But it is safe to say that rational administrators desiring to maximize learning and participation in school do well to expand valued programs in excess of the available opportunities. What exact levels of such institutional deception best maximize learning and participation—bearing in mind the costs in meaningfulness—are uncertain. The optimal level differs for each school and for the system as a whole: a rational minister of education would probably permit less inflation than results from the activity of a group of rational school principals. Each principal will hope that someone else will be forced to bear the costs of maintaining social realism.

A third solution arises from the second, but also from other considerations. Maintaining clear organizational isomorphism with valued educational categories is best accomplished through a studied organizational inattention (loose coupling, it is now called; see Weick, 1976) to actual educational work and learning. The moral fact that a course or program belongs to a given valid institutional category is crucial. The social reality of this category, and of a given unit's attachment to it, is undercut by the introduction of variance—of public definitions that this teacher or these students are really doing arithmetic, not algebra, or are doing it better or worse than average. Several forces are involved here.

First, the institutional validity of the curricular unit is maximized by defining the situation as a moral dichotomy—by creating the dramatic opposition between algebra and not algebra. Technical systems usually work better with the introduction of more variance in measures of activity and output—more feedback is obtained, and more precision is possible. But institutional systems work by a logic of categories—an educational program is most binding and effective if its attachment to a valued general category is absolute, definitive, and unquestioned. Structured invisibility helps here, justified by the ideology of educational professionalism (which is mostly invented and maintained by institutionalized educational bureaucracy and is not really in conflict with this kind of bureaucracy).

Second, the advantages of the buffering, or loose coupling, of educational categories and instructional reality are increased by the fact that the two are inevitably inconsistent. Teacher preferences and capacities, parent tastes, student interests and competencies, and the inflationary processes noted above all operate to create useful gaps between what is going on and the general categories that give meaning to what is going on. This is made more extreme by the lack of coherence and plausibility of the general category systems, which are general cultural ideologies as well as specific educational dicta. Inevitably, requirements and customs exist in the institutional structure that make little sense when built into actual practice (e.g., requirements for instruction in "values" or state history, instruction in calculus when many students have forgotten algebra, fashionable definitions of proper mathematics, or college level English composition courses for students who cannot write). Acknowledging practical realities in public may sabotage the legitimacy of the program. It may be more rational to retain institutional supports by programmatic conformity to general rules, combined with concealed practical adaptation to local realities.

Obviously, there are limits to the degree of decoupling that is possible: at some point the educational meaningfulness of the program to students, parents, and teachers is threatened. The rational administrator can, for the most part, rely on teachers to maintain the necessary boundaries and to avoid scandal. Further protection is offered the administrator (especially in the presence of scandal) by a permanent posture of reform. A certain amount of moralism is also a useful device in institutional organizations, as is a good deal of gossip (which maintains the larger moral fabric while partially acknowledging practical realities).

A Qualification. The theory of administration laid out here emphasizes the American context. Local control is strong, and institutionalized educational categories are defined very abstractly. Equilibrium solutions to the problem of maximizing learning and participation involve balancing the gains created through program incorporation, program inflation, and decoupling against the loss of reality to local constituents and students (although many of these have the same interests as administrators). In this context, resulting equilibria involve high levels of incorporation, inflation, and decoupling.

In countries with more central controls, equilibria involve lower levels on these dimensions. Nationwide tests required for completion of each educational level, for example, greatly alter the point at which adaptations undercut the meaningfulness of programs. It is hard to convince parents and students that the local algebra is really algebra if none of the students can pass the nationwide tests. Consequently, centralized systems tend to have tighter controls over instruction and learning and probably obtain less participation and thus less total learning.

But centralization is not really the crucial variable. The real issue is the nature and purposes of the collective action that manages schooling and the balance between the learning desired of those who participate and desired participation. Centralized systems often (but not always—some socialist systems and others oriented heavily toward nation building are exceptions) act in terms of narrowly rational societal goals. Education is a device for securing personnel for roles in a fixed or planned society, and the educational problem is one of proper selection and the training of those selected (Turner [1960] called this "sponsored mobility"). Maximizing participation, or the learning of the unselected, is less important.

The American system (along with many contemporary state-centered systems focused on nation building) is organized to maximize participation and the supposedly attendent extensions of democracy, opportunity, self-conceptions, and membership in society. Decentralization is simply part of the general American political strategy of maximizing involvement by putting responsibility in the hands of individuals and subunits. Since education, unlike some commodities, does not have many "zero-sum" properties, this results in a good deal of optimism, local boosterism, and educational inflation. It also results in very high levels of participation and in a society permeated with faith in education—even in the lower strata.

Research Designs. The ideas discussed here lead rather directly toward research (see Meyer and Rowan, 1978). One can compare administrative action in different countries or experiment with administrators located in different hypothetical systems. One can thus study strategies for expanding participation as pressure for this increases. Most important, one can study the value, from the point of view of administrators, of effective isomorphism with institutional categories compared with technical instructional effectiveness. What sacrifices in wider institutional conformity would administrators make in order to increase technical effectiveness?

What sacrifices in the other direction? What kinds of data would administrators choose to look at, given a variety of choices (between, say, output data and program data)? And how would all these choices vary depending on the actual or described wider context? Our arguments fit well with American data: administrators shed information on instruction and its technical effectiveness and retain information on the programmatic aspects of their schools. Presumably, this would be altered with contextual changes.

Teachers

Too much research looks at the technology of teaching as if it were the mechanical action of a person on an object. Even discipline is seen as separate from instruction or as reflecting a distinct set of goals, although teachers clearly do not see it that way (Dornbusch and Scott, 1975). Attention is focused on the mechanics of organizing ideas, materials, and time: some of this may be justified, although much of the research is discouraging. Our discussion leads in a different direction.

The fundamental technology of teaching is exoskeletal to the classroom or the school: it lies in the effective activation of the larger institutional realities that give the local setting "educational" meaning. Our (rationalist, individualist, materialist) language tries to move this offstage by calling it moral or normative or, in the case of teaching, discipline. But teachers sensibly spend a great deal of time maintaining the "third gradeness" of the third grade—defining and maintaining appropriate behaviors and orientations, locating work in general topical categories, and so on. The object is to activate in the students their own membership in the categorical structure of the educational system and with this to mobilize their commitment. This structure is the central control the educational system has: it can be used by any teacher, but is not located in the classroom or school. If the child does not learn the appropriate things in the third grade, the entire social system—not just the teacher—may classify the child as a failure—inadequate in the fourth grade or a repeating third grader.

A variety of strategies is available to teachers to adapt the child or to bend the curriculum to the available children (as discussed above in the case of administrators). A good deal of inflation and decoupling can occur; playing in the sand becomes science, and games become mathematics. Faced with difficulty, teachers resort to diffuse and affective controls to maintain student membership and commitment. They physically touch little children (Henry, 1971) and display great positive affect toward potentially dissident bigger ones (Dornbusch et al., 1974). Throughout, the object is to enmesh the student in the educational apparatus—to attune him to the educational facts of life and to hope that these facts will make learning and participation a main order of business.

Herein lies the problem with much instructional innovation. In the interests of "technical" effectiveness, the compelling power of the institutional structure is lost. Mechanistic reward systems lower the student's own commitment and attachment to the institutional system. Innovations sacrifice the categorical meaning of topics and rely on the intrinsic interests that they may be able to arouse. Technical changes can easily weaken the institutional status of the student and the institutional meaning of educational activity. We do not need, here, to impugn all technical innovation— it is enough to point out that its effects depend on the real structure of the system, to which it is marginal commentary.

From a technical point of view rather than an institutional one, teachers are almost unrelievedly authoritarian: they talk all the time, completely dominate interaction and agenda, and so on. Yet students rarely experience education in this way; they experience the larger, invisible reality of education, in terms of which teachers are "helping" them "learn the material."

Because they are attending to the larger reality of "teacher" as an institutional category, students are often surprisingly inattentive to the particular characteristics of their individual teachers. These do not loom large in students' subjective accounts of their experiences (Thielens, 1977). Perhaps effective teaching requires less the creating of a distinctive local world in the classroom than the activation of the larger institutional one, and perhaps this requires the partial concealment of the individual identity of the teacher behind the general role. Ritual leaders—priests, for instance— submerge their individuality in the conduct of ceremony. Inasmuch as teachers play a ritualized role in activating the institutional reality of education, similar patterns may be found. It seems possible, even, that a teacher who blandly plays the conventional role—and is considered deadwood by younger innovators—has found the most effective educational strategy.

Research Designs. Empirical studies should find teachers, like administrators, reaching various kinds of equilibria and succeeding as they do so—conforming to the larger transcendent educational realities, but also adapting to local circumstances. Different solutions occur for different students: with older and more able students, the classroom becomes more an enactment of the standardized categories; with younger and less able ones, decoupled compromises are made. Similarly, different emphases on participation versus the learning of those who participate produce different equilibria. As participation becomes more important, teachers make more compromises; and as selection becomes more important, they conform more closely to standardized categories.

A useful way to study the hidden instructional properties of the teacher role is to compare instruction in school with similar behavior outside the institutional arena. How do adults act differently teaching math in school and teaching the same material (under a different name) to a group of children assembled in the summer? How does a professor address and treat differently a group of interested adults and a class of students? Understanding these differences can tell us something about the larger context of modern education. One could even try to modify experimentally the institutional features of the system (hypothetically) to see how teachers would propose the act.

Classroom decoupling can easily be studied: How do teachers differently describe their courses to their different constituencies— to students, to colleagues, to administrators, and so on? How do these general legitimating descriptions relate to the actual educational work going on in these courses? How do descriptions change as contexts (actual or hypothetical) change?

An Example. Some partially hidden recent changes in American secondary schools bear on the process described here. The events of the late 1960s created changes in the institutional roles governing secondary school participation (Meyer, Chase-Dunn, and Inverarity, 1971). The legitimacy of what had previously been called truancy increased, student interests and choices became more important, and the wider system's support for compulsory attendance rules (e.g., the support of the legal system) declined sharply. Attendance rates dropped, and student customs legitimating very partial attendance (skipping many days or skipping some hours each day) developed, especially in low status and minority group schools.

These changes produced few formal or programmatic changes in school organization or curricula, and the traditional institutionalized definitions were retained. Thus, teachers were left to deal with the problem. This apparently produced many classroom adaptations of the kinds discussed above. Student commitment could no longer be taken for granted and had to be negotiated by teachers. Teachers made many curricular adaptations to try to "interest" students, deviating from standard topics though retaining their labels. As a result, of course, student learning along the traditional dimensions declined (especially at the high school and junior high school levels). The past few years may have produced something of a return to the previous situation.

Changes of these kinds should be studied much more carefully. Many educational changes of considerable importance—affected by widespread contextual changes—that are not really reflected in formal categorical data seem to occur. Most studies of educational innovation and practice rely on the reports of administrators and occasionally of teachers—the very data that the system itself is organized to distort.

Societal and Educational Statesmen

For reasons beyond our scope, modern societies and states are deeply committed to the expansion of citizenship and to the use of educational expansion toward this end (Coombs, 1968; Meyer et al., 1977; Boli-Bennett and Meyer, 1978). They construct a social table of organization in which every person's most central starting status is educationally defined and thus defined by society itself. The push is for maximal participation; and participation rates, in both rich and poor countries, have risen astonishingly. We are now in a situation in which something over 90 percent of the world's elementary school population received at least some formal schooling—a figure perhaps twice what it was twenty-five or thirty years ago. Secondary and higher educational enrollments have risen at even more rapid rates, since they are less hindered by ceiling effects.

Given these general goals, certain rational administrative strategies have become worldwide:

1. Homogeneous nationwide systems of educational definition—levels, types, and topics—are created. To maximize participation, all schools at a given level are integrated under a single type that is given the most favorable definition. Lateral differentiations are eliminated or delayed until later in the life cycle. Thus, formally stratified types of schools within a given level (e.g., teachers colleges, gymnasia, vocational and technical schools) are eliminated, and all schools fall into a relatively prestigious type (comprehensive schools; colleges or universities). This presumably maximizes commitment.

2. Rigid systems of selection by internal national tests decline, and again the American solution—allowing each school to define its own standards of performance in order to maximize participation—has become more common. Educational credentials come to be defined more by levels (or types) of schooling and less by externally imposed tests.

3. Educational credentialism—the linking of more and more social positions to education—increases, increasing commitment.

4. The tertiary occupational sector is expanded—expanding just those sets of positions that depend most heavily on education. This again enhances the value of educational participation. Governments expand very rapidly, sometimes directly expanding civil services in order to incorporate unemployed educated personnel, whose existence is thought to be directly threatening and indirectly delegitimating. These changes, of course, lower educational inflation by the partly perverse strategy of inflating the occupational status structure. Prestige is inflated vis-à-vis income when the latter is measured in terms of the prices of "hard" commodities. This is made possible by the almost complete control that the world system gives each nation state over its internal labor force and labor market. Even with that, the system is maintained by tax and tariff structures directing "consumption" expenditures away from world commodities and toward the services that the expanded state (and educational system) is defined as providing—in good part by social fiat rather than by market choices. These organizational changes (1) increase the extent to which success depends on education and (2) increase the amount of success that education can provide in total. Participation, and presumably learning, increases.

5. In two ways, states directly expand the domain of education. First, they expand the knowledge domains organized around rational collective authority—the legitimate content of rational national action and, thus, the knowledge required of proper citizens and elites. Second, they expand their direct controls over the differentiated social statuses of children (Boli-Bennett and Meyer, 1978). Expanding these controls, they lower the legitimacy of traditional mechanisms of socialization and control, expand the independent role of childhood, define this role in terms of societal socialization requirements, and so on.

Broadly speaking, then, postindustrial society separates the worlds of children and adults. It tends to link both worlds directly to the state (in the adult world by means of the service structure and in the world of children by education). The connections between these worlds become—both in ideology and in organizational reality—the institutionalized theories of socialization built into the rules of the educational system and managed by state authority. The life cycle decreasingly becomes individual or familial biography and increasingly becomes an enactment of rationalized rules controlled at the collective level. The educational system is the implementation of these rules and so gains great power.

CONCLUSIONS

I take as given that (1) modern educational systems are constructed around societal rules of educational and occupational certification—sequential rules defining progress to valued positions in the educational system and in external society; (2) young persons try to obtain positions of general value; and (3) the systems are designed to maximize participation (in varying degrees) and learning (emphasizing, in varying degrees, total learning and the learning of those selected to participate).

My conclusions are as follows: Young persons try to acquire the knowledge and certifications appropriate to short- and long-term success. They do so better if they understand the structure of the system, if the work is easier for them, if the system expands to legitimate their status and incorporate their interests (to the point where substantive and certificational meaning is lost), and if more success can be provided.

Schooling personnel gain power to produce learning and participation by linking their activities with the general categories of the broader certification system. As they succeed in doing this, the meaning and authority of these activities for students are increased. Within limits, the categorical status of an activity, course, program, or school is likely to be more important in producing effects than are particular details of content and organization. For this reason, research within the boundaries of important educational categories such as "high school" or "third grade" shows weak effects. And studies contrasting categories such as levels of education show extraordinary educational effects on almost every variable of relevance in modern society.

In the course of maintaining categorical conformity with the wider rules of educational certification, the schooling system becomes internally decoupled in substantive matters. Ritualized conformity to the rules of the wider system is crucial: variations in activity can often be ignored to advantage. Actual activities can be adapted to the vagaries of students' (and others') preferences and capabilities, while the binding and authoritative general categories are maintained by the educational drama. This solves many problems, but may always run the risk of costing more in resulting meaninglessness than is gained.

What levels of the educational system, then, make the most difference in student outcomes? Those levels that define and control the meaning and larger status of the student and of educational activity—namely, the system as a whole and the authoritatively defined categories within it. Organizational features of classrooms, schools, districts, and so on that are not clearly linked to these institutional variables are likely to be less relevant. In the view taken here, what is often seen as rhetoric is in fact educational rationality; what is often seen as rational organizational action is likely to be irrelevant decoration. If the rhetorical exoskeleton of education is its central ingredient, effective manipulation should focus there. Note how often researchers discuss education as if it were static and ineffective and difficult to change or improve, despite much evidence that many very large-scale changes occur rather rapidly. The changes in the American secondary school created after Sputnik and the contemporary parallel changes being made in reaction to the events of the 1960s occur through large-scale changes in institutional rhetoric that diffuse to parents, teachers, and students throughout society. They do not occur primarily through formal organizational mechanisms.

A Note on Institutional Structure

In an effort to simplify the counterposition of institutional effects to organizational ones, I have defined the former only evocatively, by example. This allows some mistakes to creep in, correction of which would add further complexity to already complex arguments, but which might also add some more ideas.

1. I have described the institutional classification systems as if they were very highly codified in nationwide law and custom and as if consensus were very high. For many important rules, this is true, but there is substantial room for disagreement and interpretation. Students, teachers, parents, community personnel—as well as the national educational elites—engage in such processes, defining and redefining, for instance, what a high school graduate is. An extension of my argument would have it that these are important institutional processes too—that the rhetoric involved is more effective than particular organizational implementations, that the rhetoric is likely to be decoupled from organizational practice, and that the presence of this rhetorical work (which is really collective action) further increases internal organizational decoupling (schools have to conform simultaneously to diverse and inconsistent institutional environments; see Meyer and Rowan, 1978).

2. Even the consensual institutional structure works through local interaction and communication. Educational institutions not only affect students directly (Meyer, 1977), but also affect them through reconstruction of the surrounding social world. The

student is not so much influenced by others, though, as informed by them of prevailing social realities (e.g., one affects an undergraduate more by informing him that statistics is important in graduate school than by advocating an interest in the subject). To convey this point, I have described the social relations around the student as containing consultants, rather than using the standard term "significant others" (which has been perverted from its original Meadian meaning to refer nowadays to something like the collection of zookeepers who surround an animal, offering affection, esteem, and food pellets). The networks of social relations are less likely to be primarily organizational in character than they are to reflect complex social processes of diffusion. Like the student, the student's consultants are directly linked to the larger meaning system: only the most naive and irrational will take as authoritative the reports of organizational superiors on such matters.

3. Institutional rules include both normative social fictions and cognitive assessments of social organizational reality. I have described the two as if they were the same and as if they could both be comprehended by the single term institutional. They are distinct, and both have effects along the lines of our discussion. The occupational choices of female students are undoubtedly affected by both (a) the known low proportions of women in the high professions and (b) the normative description of these positions as available (and increasingly so) to women. Effects may be more or less additive, so no great distinction must be made on this account.

But the relation between the two types of institutional structures is more complex. "Unrealistic" institutional descriptions—elementary school texts filled with pictures of female doctors and political leaders or television shows depicting black executives—are important devices for concealing, controlling, changing, and maintaining parallel conditions in social organization life. To maintain our democracy, we describe it to children as much more democratic than it is—publicly acknowledging the truth would change it. To change our racial inequalities, we sometimes institutionally conceal them and almost always describe them and their origins in very misleading ways. The "right answers" that we as social scientists would give on scales measuring authoritarianism or prejudice or equality are very different from the "right answers" we would give as citizens to the same questions (e.g., about the intelligence of blacks).

In some aspects, the collective action represented in our normative institutions closely parallels that represented in our cognitive descriptions of social organizational life, but often the two must be systematically different if the system is to be maintained (let alone changed). In modern societies, given their ideological dependence on education, this system is a main locus of our "hypocrisy." To maintain and improve our society, we lie to little children about it (Ariès, 1962).

More to the research point, highly normative institutional rules often develop in reaction to differing social organizational realities— that is, one type of collective action is balanced against another. The normative system is unrealistic and is known to be so by participants: it therefore has fewer pure effects than a simple reading of my arguments might suggest. Subworlds and subcultures arise to informally correct them. Even if students (and the educational systems) are organized as I have described, action and effects are really composites of sets of structurally inconsistent larger realities. The student must learn to act not only in terms of important truths, but also in terms of truths that are not true.

REFERENCES

Alexander, K.; M. Cook; and E. McDill. 1978. "Curriculum Tracking and Educational Stratification." *American Sociological Review* 43:47-66.

Alwin, D. 1976. "Assessing School Effects: Some Identities." *Sociology of Education* 49:294-303.

American Sociological Review (ASR). 1966. "Communications on 'On Neighborhood Context and College Plans' (I), (II), (III)." *American Sociological Review* 31: 698-707.

Ariès, P. 1962. *Centuries of Childhood: A Social History of Family Life.* New York: Alfred A. Knopf.

Arnove, R. 1971. *The Impact of University Social Structures on Student Alienation.* New York: Praeger.

Berger, B. 1971. *Looking for America.* Englewood Cliffs, N.J.: Prentice-Hall.

Berger, P., and T. Luckmann. 1967. *The Social Construction of Reality.* New York: Doubleday.

Bidwell, C. 1965. "The School as a Formal Organization." In *Handbook of Organizations,* edited by J. March, pp. 972-1022. Chicago: Rand McNally.

Boli-Bennett, J., and J. Meyer. 1978. "The Ideology of Childhood and the State." *American Sociological Review* 43:797-812.

Clark, B. 1961. "The 'Cooling-Out' Function in Higher Education." In *Education, Economy, and Society,* edited by A. Halsey et al., pp. 513-23. Glencoe, Ill.: Free Press.

Coleman, J. 1961. *The Adolescent Society.* New York: Free Press.

Coombs, P. 1968. *The World Educational Crisis.* New York: Oxford University Press.

Cronbach, L., and R. Snow. 1977. *Aptitude and Instructional Method.* New York: Irvington.

Davis, J. 1966. "The Campus as a Frog Pond." *American Journal of Sociology* 72:17-31.

Dornbusch, S., and W.R. Scott. 1975. *Evaluation and the Exercise of Authority.* San Francisco: Jossey-Bass.

Dornbusch, S.; R. Espinosa; C. Fernandez; K. Wood; D. Hinders; M. Harris; G.C. Massey. 1974. *Student Perception of the Link Between School and Work.* Report to the Vocational Educational Research Section of the California State Department of Education. Palo Alto, Calif.: Stanford Center for Research and Development in Teaching, November.

Goldberg, M.; A.H. Passow; and J. Justman. 1966. *The Effects of Ability Grouping.* New York: Teachers College Press.

Hannan, M. 1971. "Problems of Aggregation." In *Causal Models in the Social Sciences,* edited by H. Blalock, Jr., pp. 473-508. Chicago: Aldine-Atherton.

Henry, J. 1971. *On Education.* New York: Random House.

Himmelweit, H., and B. Swift. 1969. "A Model for the Understanding of School as a Socializing Agent." In *Trends and Issues in Developmental Psychology,* edited by P. Mussen, J. Langer, and M. Covington, pp. 154-81. New York: Holt, Rinehart & Winston.

Holsinger, D. 1974. "The Elementary School as Modernizer: A Brazilian Study." In *Education and Individual Modernity in Developing Countries,* edited by A. Inkeles and D. Holsinger, pp. 24-46. (Leiden): Brill.

Inkeles, A., and D. Smith. 1974. *Becoming Modern: Individual Change in Six Developing Countries.* Cambridge, Mass.: Harvard University Press.

Katz, I.; E. Epps; and L. Axelson. 1964. "Effect upon Negro Digit-Symbol Performance of Anticipated Comparison with Whites and Other Negroes." *Journal of Abnormal Psychology* 69:77-83.

Kerckhoff, A. 1975. "Patterns of Educational Attainment in Great Britain." *American Journal of Sociology* 80:1428-37.

Lortie, D. 1973. "Observations of Teaching as Work." In *Second Handbook of Research on Teaching,* edited by R. Travers, pp. 475-97. Chicago: Rand McNally.

March, J., and J. Olsen. 1976. *Ambiguity and Choice in Organizations.* Oslo: Universitetsforlaget.

Meyer, J. 1970a. "High School Effects on College Intentions." *American Journal of Sociology* 76:59-70.

——. 1970b. "The Charter: Conditions of Diffuse Socialization in Schools." In *Social Processes and Social Structures,* edited by W. Scott, pp. 564-78. New York: Holt, Rinehart & Winston.

——. 1977. "The Effects of Education as an Institution." *American Journal of Sociology* 83:55-77.

Meyer, J., and B. Rowan. 1977. "Institutionalized Organizations: Formal Structure as Myth and Ceremony." *American Journal of Sociology* 83:340-63.

——. 1978. "The Structure of Educational Organizations." In *Environment and Organizations,* edited by M. Meyer et al., pp. 78-109. San Francisco: Jossey-Bass.

Meyer, J.; C. Chase-Dunn; and J. Inverarity. 1971. *The Expansion of the Autonomy of Youth: Responses of the Secondary School to Problems of Order in the 1960's.* Palo Alto, Calif.: Laboratory for Social Research, Stanford University.

Meyer, J.; R. Rubinson; F. Ramirez; and J. Boli-Bennett. 1977. "The World Educational Revolution, 1950-1970." *Sociology of Education* 50:242-58.

Meyer, J.; W. Scott; S. Cole; J. Intilli. 1978. "Instructional Dissensus and Institutional Consensus in Schools." In *Environments and Organizations*, edited by M. Meyer et al., pp. 233-63. San Francisco: Jossey-Bass.

National Institute of Education (NIE). 1978. *Papers of the National Invitational Conference on School Organization and Effects, San Diego, California, January 27-29.* Washington, D.C.

Rodman, H., and P. Voydanoff. 1978. "Social Class and Parents' Range of Aspirations for Their Children." *Social Problems* 25:333-44.

Rosenbaum, J. 1975. "The Stratification of Socialization Processes." *American Sociological Review* 40:48-54.

Sarason, I. 1978. "The Text Anxiety Scale: Concept and Research." In *Stress and Anxiety*, edited by C. Spielberger and I. Sarason, vol. 5, pp. 193-216. Washington, D.C.: Hemisphere.

Sewell, W., and M. Armer. 1966. "Neighborhood Context and College Plans." *American Sociological Review* 31:159-68.

Sørensen, A., and M. Hallinan. 1977. "A Reconceptualization of School Effects." *Sociology of Education* 50:273-89.

Thielens, W. 1977. "Undergraduate Definitions of Learning from Teachers." *Sociology of Education* 50: 159-81.

Thomas, J. 1977. *Resource Allocation in Classrooms.* Chicago: Educational Finance and Productivity Center, University of Chicago.

Treiman, D., and K. Terrell. 1975. "The Process of Status Attainment in the United States and Great Britain." *American Journal of Sociology* 81:563-83.

Turner, R. 1960. "Sponsored and Contest Mobility and the School System." *American Sociological Review* 25:855-67.

Weick, K. 1976. "Educational Organizations as Loosely Coupled Systems." *Administrative Science Quarterly* 21:1-19.

Zborowski, M., and E. Herzog. 1962. *Life Is With People.* New York: International Universities Press.

Chapter 2

Linking Education
to the Larger Society
with Social Indicator Models

Marcus Felson and Kenneth C. Land
The University of Illinois at Urbana-Champaign

A GENERAL OVERVIEW OF SOCIAL
INDICATORS RESEARCH

Introduction

The extreme complexity of education's role in society suggests a need to organize investigation of education quite carefully. The complexity of this and other aspects of the social system has generated a movement to collect social indicators and to organize these indicators into a system of social accounts. Recent efforts to build social indicator models linking social indicators to one another have forced researchers to face the unpleasant fact that social theories (especially at the macro-level of analysis) are not always well suited to such model building. Since social indicators, social accounts, and social indicator models parallel to some extent economic indicators, economic accounts, and econometric models, social indicator researchers have been faced with decisions about whether and when to mimic, adapt, or reject the theoretical and statistical strategies that economists propose for investigating social conditions. Hence, researchers must deal with important theoretical and practical questions, often relying on substantial improvisation.

This chapter reviews some of the experience that we have had in building social indicator models and provides suggestions about

Funded in part by grants from the U.S. Army (RI/DAHC 19-76-G-0016) and the National Science Foundation (SOC-77-13261).

how such models can be developed for education. We begin with an overview of social indicator research in general, including reports on both other efforts and our own experience. Then we discuss applications of this approach to education and include a report on our thirty-four equation macrosocial indicator model of educational enrollments, attainments, and organizations in the United States from 1947 to 1974 (Felson and Land, 1978).

While the ideas for studying social change are often old ones, the expense and complexity of putting those ideas into action require more than the discrete efforts of individual researchers. Social indicator research may be interpreted as an organizational effort, made possible in part by discussions among researchers and government officials designed to produce some common terminology, research goals, and means for carrying out these goals. One important element in this organizational effort is the development of social accounts, which we consider in the next section.

The Design of Social Accounts

During the past four decades, econometricians have developed quantitative, empirically-based models capable of simulating and forecasting trends and fluctuations in economic (and some noneconomic, social) indicates. Such model-building efforts have depended upon three interrelated theoretical and empirical building blocks. First, many time series of economic indicators have been collected and made available for analysis, some on a monthly or quarterly as well as a yearly basis. Second, economists have the advantage of an accounting system that—despite its flaws and limitations—is suitable for collecting and communicating information in terms of a single monetary unit of measurement. This accounting system facilitates quantitative analysis. Third, economics as a discipline has a set of macroeconomic theories that, even if oversimplified, incomplete, and imprecisely specified, nonetheless can be made operational without great difficulty. For instance, Keynesian theory can be expressed in the form of a number of stochastic equations and indentities. We shall return to the question of how theory can be applied in social indicator research in the next section, and how this applies to educational research in subsequent sections. But first we consider how social accounts can be designed.

As some social scientists have noted (e.g., Gross, 1966), the "national income and product accounts" (see description by Ruggles and Ruggles, 1970) provide a systematic framework for economic data that facilitates their use for macroeconomic model building. The obvious suggestion is to construct a similar system for social indicators. Social accounts could provide social indicator models with a framework for building an internally consistent system of equations determining many indicators simultaneously, a function that the national economic accounts perform in the case of econometric models. Of course, macromodels can be built without an accounting framework, and this is just what happened in economics in the pre-Keynesian era. Thus, to explain variations in particular social indicators, one could proceed to employ various middle-range sociological theories. However, piecing these parts together into a consistent system would be difficult without some underlying social accounting framework.

Recently, several proposals for systems of social accounts have been advanced. Part of the reason for the existence of various proposals is that an accounting system usually requires some common unit in which components can be expressed. Possible units for social accounting include money (dollars), time, and people. For example, Ruggles and Ruggles (1973) propose extending the national income accounts to include a system of social and economic accounts in which the basic accounting unit would be the dollar, whereas Fox (1974) gives an approach to social accounting based on dollar equivalents of time allocations.

Other possible units of measurement that might be employed for social accounting are sometimes found in the literature on social change or in compilations of social statistics. For example, travel researchers often tally trips and classify them by purpose, length, number of persons involved, travel mode, and so forth (see, e.g., Keefer, 1966). One might learn a great deal about American society if there were a set of social accounts in which trips were classified by, for example, the activities they involved or the population they brought together. While no social indicator researchers have, to our knowledge, considered this alternative, it is at least a reasonable idea that might produce good results for some purposes. However, one cannot classify the changes in activities that occur at a single site with indicators measured in trips.

Trips are a subset of a much larger set of events that involve or affect more than one person. Other examples from this category are divorces, natural disasters, marriages, births, and crimes. Yet we think it would be difficult to decide precisely when some events begin and end and hence to build a set of social accounts on events alone. Nevertheless, events sometimes capture useful data about social conditions.

Another type of data sometimes used to measure social change consists of summary statistics for larger distributions of data. While it has long been common to report such indicators as median income or mean per capita income, one also finds such indicators as "standard deviation of occupational prestige" (see Pampel, Land, and Felson, 1977) or Gini ratios employed as social indicators. In addition, Felson (1976) uses correlations among lifestyle items as social indicators of lifestyle coherence. The construction of social accounts from such statistical indicators would probably be very difficult, but it poses the possibility of disaggregating changes in means, standard deviations, and correlations, using standard statistical techniques as a method of social accounting.

Some types of social change have also been captured by tallying and classifying words. Content analysis of text, newspaper headlines, or speech employs this technique. Some use has also been made of bibliographical citations as indicators of the transmission of information (see Hubert, 1977). Since printed text is stored in libraries and is increasingly amenable to computer analysis, social accounts based on counts of words or citations might prove useful for describing and analyzing certain social phenomena, especially the growth and dissemination of ideas, attitudes, and knowledge. Yet such indicators often oversample the words of intellectuals, newspaper writers, and editors, providing limited evidence of general social conditions.

A variety of other units have been used to measure particular social phenomena. For example, Evers and McIntosh (1977) discuss social indicators of human nutrition in terms of such indicators as percentage consumed of recommended requirements of nutrients, weight, height, skinfold of persons, and mean age of menarche. Another example is found in Kinsey's research (Kinsey, Pomeroy, and Martin, 1947) on sexual behavior, which includes a rather elaborate accounting of sexual behavior taking sexual orgasms as the unit of measurement. While Kinsey's study was not a study of social change, he compared males of different age cohorts in order to estimate how sexual experiences change over the life cycle, using number or percentage of sexual orgasms classified in various ways to draw his inferences. The use of trips and Kinsey's use of sexual orgasms are two examples of how substantive researchers interested in particular topics utilized what seemed to be the closest unit of measurement to the phenomena they were studying and built up a variety of interrelated evidence from these units of measurement. To be sure, none of the examples actually represents a fully developed system of social accounts, and each is limited in its breadth of applicability.

Such successes in enhancing knowledge on specific topics suggest to us an important dilemma involved in setting up social accounts.

On the one hand, a national system of social accounts needs to be uniform enough in its organization to allow relating one type of social condition to another. On the other hand, one can only purchase this generality at the price of specificity.

A number of social indicator researchers have emphasized the goal of generality, seeking to build a single set of social accounts based on a single measurement unit. Often researchers have chosen monetary units, since the already established economic accounts are based on them. It would be simple if every social phenomenon involved a market transaction in which money were exchanged: one need only tally and classify money allocations to keep track of social conditions. Since this is obviously not the case, several researchers have found ways to compute "dollar equivalents" for other units of measure. For example, economists sometimes take a woman's potential market earnings as a measure of how much her time is worth. If a woman who earns $8 an hour allocates one hour a week to visiting her father, spending $1 in driving costs, that indicates that visiting him is worth $468 a year to her. If fifty million Americans in the same situation make the same allocation, paternal visiting of this type would then take on a value of $23.4 billion that year. One could tally all such dollar equivalents, add them to the gross national product calculated from economic accounts, and thereby arrive at a gross national social product (see Ruggles and Ruggles, 1973).

Such calculations require a variety of assumptions about the value of goods and services for which individuals do not necessarily spend money directly. Since alternative ways can often be found to compute these values, a good deal of disagreement is possible. For example, the cost-benefit ratios computed by the Army Corps of Engineers might indicate that it is beneficial to build more locks and dams, while the ratios calculated by environmental groups may show quite the opposite. Frequently, nonmarket processes and even market processes involve implicit or explicit third- and fourth-party payments that distort the value of goods and services to those consuming them. For example, because many of the health care expenditures of Americans are covered by insurance programs, patients have an added incentive to obtain what benefits they can from the program, since they do not have to pay the full costs themselves. Hence, the $40 billion spent on health care in the United States in 1976 includes individual consumer demand and the national political "value" of health care for the aged, as well as the aspirations of health care providers for new equipment, career advancement, and so on. One cannot assume that the whole figure represents national preferences.

Perhaps the dangers inherent in constructing a single set of social accounts using a single unit of value is best illustrated by returning to Kinsey. While translation of sexual behavior into dollar values seems intrinsically unromantic, the importance of sexuality in social life suggest that no gross national domestic product would be complete without its inclusion. Should we figure out a mean dollar equivalent of orgasm? How should this be done? If done, it would imply not only that orgasms can be expressed in dollars but also the reverse, hence allowing translation of the gross national product into units of orgasm. These absurdities illustrate the problems inherent in constructing a system of national accounts based on a single resource unit. Moreover, this particular example requires that a number of debatable assumptions be made to arrive at a dollar value for an activity and tends to ignore norms, institutions, physical abilities, and the requisite coordination of activities with others. We do not deny that such calculations are possible or that they may be carried out with great care and sophistication. We merely wish to warn that there is a risk that reduction to a single unit of measurement may lead to distortions.

We also wonder whether each individual has a single equation for maximizing satisfaction given available resources. Perhaps everyday life is segmented into different sets of activities involving different choices and constraints, not all of which compete in the same terms. For example, allocations of unpaid time may well be made independently of allocations of money, physical needs somewhat independently of social needs, and so on. While these different subsets of activities and resources may indeed compete at certain times and places, they may not do so universally. Hence, a system of social accounts may require greater flexibility than a system of economic accounts and may employ different resources as appropriate.

In our own research we have so far opted for number of persons in various classifications as the most flexible and useful unit of measurement. One can classify people according to a variety of activities, roles, and statuses, including their income category and the value of their expenditures. Most social indicators are already or can be defined in people units. For example, one can classify numbers of persons experiencing various events (including taking trips), citing or being cited in bibliographies, writing various ideas or being written about, earning certain incomes or spending them in various ways, participating in various activities, and so forth. Since social conditions usually concern what is happening to people in their daily life, accounts based on people avoid some of the risks inherent in translating one type of resource unit into another. Thus for our purposes it is more convenient to build an accounting system on the basis of "people" or "demographic" units and thus a system of "demographic accounts." This type of framework for social accounting has been explored primarily by the British economist Richard Stone (1971, 1975). Appendix A of Land and Felson (1976) illustrates how demographic accounts can be constructed for the United States from available sources.

The virtue of demographic accounts is that they provide a means of organizing the entire population of a society in terms of inflows and outflows on a year-to-year basis. Moreover, these flows can be classified into various states or activities, such as schooling, employment status, and health status.

Despite practical limitations on the construction of unified social accounts, the current availability of a variety of social data, much of it appearing in the statistical abstract of the United States, has allowed us to begin using social accounting ideas for building macro social indicator models, as the next section discusses.

Building Macrosocial Indicator Models

We have shown elsewhere (Land and Felson, 1976, 1977) how models of social change can be derived by defining parameteric indexes based on demographic accounts, yet one does not need a full set of demographic accounts to accomplish such a task. Demographic accounts are to some extent a way of thinking about a problem, even if the data are absent or only partly available. By specifying a variety of alternatives that compete with one another (e.g., military service, college enrollment, full-time labor force participation), one can evaluate how changing the opportunities for one alternative serves to influence individuals' choices of another. To the extent that many social activities parallel a market in competing for people's time, this information helps to specify macrosocial indicator models. This is an example of how economic reasoning might be applied to social indicator modeling. However, social indicator models are often constructed for social activities that, instead of competing with one another, are mutually dependent. For example, completion of high school is a requirement, in most cases, for college enrollment; marriage a requirement for divorce; arrest a requirement for imprisonment. Hence, social indicator models must consider those social statuses, roles, and activities that subject people to risk of or opportunity for other experiences. This notion of being "subject to risk," while often considered in demographic analyses, is less likely to emerge from an economic perspective. In any case, the terms "opportunity" and "risk" are vague unless they are based on a clearly defined and well-articulated substantive theory.

Although efforts at social indicator modeling initially emphasized competitive processes of the sort found in the labor market (see Pampel, Land, and Felson, 1977), other efforts have concentrated on the "subject to risk" approach (e.g., Land and Felson, 1976; Felson and Land, 1978). Perhaps the most extensive substantive development of this sort of reasoning outside of demographic theory is found in recent work by Cohen and Felson developing the "routine activity approach" to analyzing trends and cycles in crime rates (Cohen and Felson, 1979). This approach treats direct contact predatory crimes (specifically, those crimes in which at least one person directly takes or damages the person or property of at least one other) as routine activities that feed on other routine activities. These offenses generally require the convergence of three minimal elements—a likely offender, a suitable target, and the absence of a guardian capable of preventing a violation. Any social processes affecting the location of people in space and time may therefore influence the probability that a direct contact predatory violation will occur by arranging or preventing the convergence of these minimal elements. In addition, social changes that affect the structure of routine activities that occur as a part of everyday community life may have a major indirect impact on crime rates by affecting this convergence. For example, Cohen and Felson (1979) argue that households with only one adult and those in which there is a female labor force participant will experience higher rates of personal and property victimization, since these social phenomena expose people and their property to greater risk of attack. The general hypothesis stated is that crime rates vary inversely with the tempo of routine activities within families and households. Both micro- and macrodata consistently support these propositions (see Cohen and Felson, 1979).

Two unique features of this approach are, first, that it seeks to isolate the minimal conditions necessary for certain social events to occur and, second, that the physical convergence of people in time and space is considered the key to providing such conditions, with social phenomena such as roles, statuses, and norms having an indirect effect on crime rates through their impact on the spatiotemporal structure of activities. Finding its antecedents in human ecological theory, especially as presented by Amos Hawley (1950), the routine activity approach suggests that illegal activities depend on legal activities, so that analysis of the latter is often necessary for understanding the former. It even appears that government policies influencing household structure and activities may be more important for their effects on crime rates than are the policies of the criminal justice system itself. This inference is controversial and, indeed, subject to continued research, but the lesson is unmistakable: *building social indicator models profits greatly from looking beyond the conventional boundaries of each substantive topic to consider as well those seemingly unrelated activities that—perhaps inadvertently—influence social change.*

In addition, the routine activity approach offers a reminder to researchers not to commit what Samuelson (1974) calls the "fallacy of composition." Behavior patterns of individuals may not provide sufficient information for inferring behaviors of aggregates. Finally, the routine activity approach represents a general effort to focus on the most "obvious," tangible, and clear-cut relationships, carrying them as far as possible in modeling social trends and cycles. For this reason, we have attempted to use age, household structure, and labor force participation as most likely antecedents of certain social changes.

Most important, our efforts have tended to concentrate on specific activities of people as they depend on one another. This is not to say that cultural and legal changes have no importance, but such changes are difficult to monitor. They often take very long to become manifest, while changing activity patterns are often visible within a year or two, or even in some cases month by month or hour by hour. We allow, nonetheless, for normative and institutional effects by employing difference equations that assume noninstantaneous adjustments of dependent to independent variables. In general, the demographic accounting perspective has helped us to think in terms of stocks and flows of population engaging in various activities or passing through various roles and statuses and about how these transitions relate to individuals' competition and cooperation with others as well as their exposures to risks and opportunities. For example, such a perspective helps one to think about how occupational, household, education, and criminal justice indicators relate to one another. More generally, such an approach facilitates learning about structural interdependencies by helping to organize such investigations.

APPLICATIONS OF SOCIAL INDICATORS RESEARCH TO EDUCATION

An Initial Model of Education Enrollments, Attainments, and Organizations

We review here our baseline thirty-four equation model linking several changes in educational enrollments, attainments, and organizations to one another and to certain social, demographic, and economic trends for the United States during the years 1947–1974 (see Felson and Land, 1978). Within the social indicators literature, some studies explicitly consider changes in education (e.g., Rivlin, 1973; Car-Hill and Magnussen, 1973; Ferriss, 1970; Duncan, 1968). We also consider trends in educational enrollments and attainments to be important social indicators, and we begin our model with them. Research on the flows among educational statuses and between educational and noneducational statuses is a well-established endeavor, especially with respect to school drop-out rates, completion rates, and transition rates (see, e.g., Koshal, Gallaway, and Akkihal, 1976; Stone, 1971, 1975; Legare, 1972; Ferris, 1970; Galper and Dunn, 1969; Thonstad, 1969).

In our specifications of equations describing school enrollments and attainments, we have defined schooling rates in terms of a ratio to the overall population and have allowed school enrollment and attainment rates to be affected indirectly by age composition. Our specifications consider that preceding educational attainments affect subsequent ones, that reentrance into the educational system by persons who at some point left it may be important, and that noneducational opportunities compete with educational enrollments and attainments. (The timing of education in the life cycle is itself a complex topic, treated in sophisticated fashion by Beverly Duncan [1965a, 1965b, 1967, 1968]);

Our initial thirty-four equation model is calculated from various annual social indicators aggregated for the United States as a whole for the years 1947–1974. The equations themselves are calculated from as many years as possible through 1972, then employed to forecast 1973 and 1974 rates, and the forecasts are in turn compared with observed values.

A summary of the model can be gleaned from Figure 2–1, which shows how the exogenous population and economic structure feed into the educational system. The model shows how educational enrollments and attainments respond to these exogenous changes, how educational organizations respond to the changes in enrollments, and how labor force changes both influence and are influenced by educational changes.

Although we lack the space to present the model in further detail (see the list of variables accompanying Figure 2–1), we can illustrate the technique with two equations.

First, our kindergarten enrollment rate equation is presented as follows:

$$ENKR_t = 196.67 + 251.85 \ \%POP_t^5 \ -44.20 \ \%FPOP_t \quad (2\text{-}1)$$
$$(2.04) (5.25) (21.39)$$

$$+ \ 25.57 \ FLFPR_t + error.$$
$$(21.28)$$

where the variables in order of appearance are:

$ENKR_t$ = total enrollment in kindergarten in the academic year beginning in the fall of year t per 100,000 mid-year population;

$\%POP_t^5$ = total number of persons aged five as a percentage of the total midyear population in year t;

$\%FPOP$ = total farm population as a percentage of the total midyear population in year t;

$FLFPR_t$ = the female labor force participation rate—the total number of females aged sixteen and over in the labor force (annual average) as a percentage of the total noninstitutional female midyear population.

In this equation, the R^2 adjusted is 0.975, with twenty-three degrees of freedom, while the Durbin-Watson value of 2.29 allows us to accept the null hypothesis that autocorrelation is absent. The t ratios in parentheses indicate that the kindergarten enrollment rate responds greatly to increases in the female labor force participation rate and to declines in farm population, with some effect found for age structure as well. What is perhaps most interesting about this equation is that it shows the vulnerability of enrollment to social trends besides age structure alone.

Of course, enrollments and attainments do not necessarily determine the level of intellectual growth. Perhaps the best available social indicators of intellectual change are the achievement and aptitude tests administered to students. One of the most consistent findings in these tests is a trend toward declining scores during the 1960s and early 1970s in the United States. For example, recent compilations of the evidence (Harnischfeger and Wiley, 1975; Munday, 1976) reveal declines in median or mean scores since the early 1960s in such tests as the SAT, PSAT, ACT, MSAT, ITED, and ITBs. Moreover, these reports have demonstrated that the observed declines appear to be robust when controlling for various aspects of the composition of test takers, such as their year in school, race and sex. Although a larger number of women have taken the American College Test (ACT) in recent years and received lower scores, tests administered in several earlier grades manifest no such change in composition of the test takers but also indicate

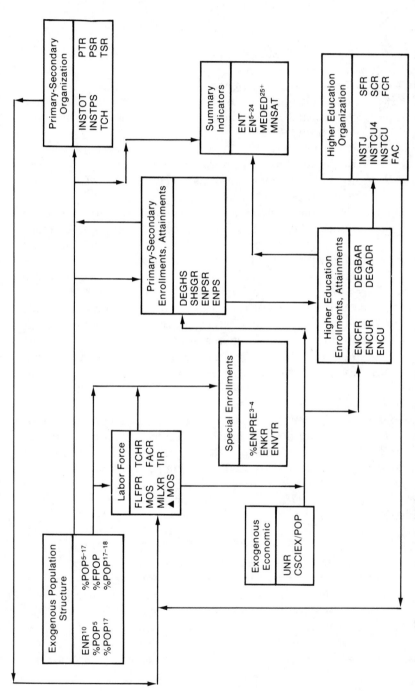

Figure 2-1. Heuristic diagram depicting initial model found in Felson and Land (1978). Reprinted by permission from the publisher.

Short Descriptions of Variables Depicted in Figure 2–1 (see Felson and Land [1978] for full definitions).

CSCIEX/POP	Science Expenditure Rate*	INSTPS	Number of Primary and Secondary Schools
DEGADR	Advanced Degree Rate*	INSTU4	Number of Four Year Institutions
DEGBAR	Bachelors Degree Rate*	$MEDED^{25+}$	Median Education, population 25 and over
DEGHS	High School Degree Rate*	MILXR	Military Expansion Rate
EN^{5-24}	School Enrollment Rate, ages 5–24	MNSAT	Mean Scholastic Aptitude Test Score
ENCFR	First Enrollment in College Rate*	MOS	Mean Occupational Status
ENCU	College-University Enrollment	ΔMOS	Change in Mean Occupational Status
ENCUR	College-University Enrollment Rate*	$\%POP^x$	Percentage of Populations, ages x (ages vary)*
ENKR	Kindergarten Enrollment Rate*	PSR	Pupil-School Ratio
$\%ENPRE^{3-4}$	Preschool Enrollment Rate, ages 3–4	PTR	Pupil-Teacher Ratio
ENPS	Primary-Secondary Enrollment	SCR	Student-Institution Ratio for Colleges and Universities
ENPSR	Primary-Secondary Enrollment Rate*		
ENR^{10}	Grade 10 Enrollment Rate*	SFR	Student-Faculty Ratio for Colleges and Universities
ENT	Total School Enrollment, all levels		
ENVTR	Vocational-Technical Enrollment Rate*	SHSGR	Standard High School Graduation Rate
FAC	Number of Faculty	TCH	Number of Primary and Secondary Teachers
FACR	Faculty Rate*		
FCR	Faculty-College Ratio	TCHR	Teacher Rate*
%FPOP	Percentage Farm Population*	TIR	Total Instructor Rate*
FLFPR	Female Labor Force Participation Rate	TSR	Teacher-School Ratio
		UNR	Unemployment Rate
INSTCU	Number of Colleges and Universities		
INSTJ	Number of Junior Colleges		
INSTOT	Total Number of Educational Institutions		

*Resident population of United States in denominator.

declining scores. Some changes in content and scaling of tests has occurred, but neither report finds evidence that these changes were responsible for the declines. For instance, the mean scores of the Scholastic Aptitude Test (SAT), administered to high school juniors and seniors by the College Entrance Examination Board, declined from 478 in 1963 to 445 in 1973 in verbal scores and from 478 to 430 during the same period in mathematical scores. Harnischfeger and Wiley (1975: Table 1) calculated scores corrected for changes in scaling procedures that indicate even stronger declines of 48 and 40 points for verbal and mathematical mean scores respecitvely, representing 41.7 percent and 24.8 percent of their standard deviations. It is highly unlikely that the declines reflect random sampling error, since millions of students were tested over a nineteen year period on at least fifty different dates in thousands of locations.

The increased rates at which young persons complete high school and go on to college probably produce an increased number of poor students taking college entry tests. However, test score declines are observed at lower grade levels for which enrollment rates have been almost constant since the 1950s, and declines in ACT and SAT scores have continued despite a leveling off of the proportion of the relevant birth cohort taking these tests and of the high school graduation and college entrance rates. Nonetheless, it is worth exploring whether rising high school graduation rates correspond to declines in SAT mean scores.

Harnischfeger and Wiley (1975) have considered the possibility that declines in the exposure of students to academic courses may be responsible for declines in test scores. Indeed, they document a decline in such enrollments between the 1970–1971 and 1972–1973 school years, during which time SAT scores also declined. For example, English and language arts courses per pupil declined 14 percent during this period. However, academic course enrollments increased between 1960–1961 and 1970–1971, also a period of test score decline. The data are not consistent, nor are enough time points available for assessing the impact of changing exposure to academic courses. While lack of exposure to schooling could be a factor in test score declines during other periods, it could not have been very important for the decline during the 1960s.

Several social and educational attributes might affect test score decline, including school and classroom organization, pupil motivation, curriculum, teaching staff characteristics, discipline, drugs, alcohol, and television viewing. These various potential "causes" of test score decline (some of which were discussed by Harnischfeger and Wiley [1975]) are difficult to subject to rigorous testing. All are associated with an underlying demographic change—namely, the so-called "baby boom" first noticeable in 1942, starting in earnest in 1946, and peaking in 1957–1958. The 1946 birth cohort was aged seventeen in 1963, the year in which SAT scores peaked, while the 1958 birth cohort was aged seventeen in 1975. Although it is too early to determine whether this is coincidental, it is almost exclusively the baby boom birth cohorts that experienced the declines in SAT scores. It is also noteworthy that many of the educational and societal problems associated with test score decline—crowding, hiring of inexperienced teachers, and discipline problems, for example—can be associated with large birth cohort size. Even changes in curricular content, including premature innovations and weakening of intellectual requirements, may be in response to the burden of teaching larger cohorts. We therefore consider birth cohort size a possible driving factor in the test score decline.

Zajonc (1976) has used a somewhat different set of arguments that infer a similar empirical linkage between demographic trends and trends in SAT scores. He argues that family size and birth order vary inversely with the ability of families to provide an intellectual environment for a particular child. Additional theoretical support for his assertion can be found in Spaeth (1976), where it is argued that the teaching of children by parents is more effective when the number of children is fewer and that such parental teaching plays a central role in the development of intellect. Spaeth's arguments are consistent in several respects with those of Zajonc and suggest that trends toward larger family size or higher mean birth order will correspond with trends in lower test scores, a linkage specifically supported by Zajonc's data analyses. In our current equation, we have not sought to test this perspective directly but have made the more general prediction that demographic pressures (especially the pressure of larger birth cohorts) will put strains on institutions, including both school and family. This reduces their capacity to impart knowledge, leading to a decline in test scores. Since cohort size reflects both family size and mean birth order, the following equation incorporates Zajonc's approach into a more general specification of the consequences of demographic change (based on data updated since the earlier paper):

$$MNSAT_t = -39.27 + 1.06 \ MNSAT_{t-1} - 21.31 \ \%POP^{17}_t \quad (2.2)$$
$$(0.32) \quad (9.20) \quad (2.38)$$

$$+0.19 \ SHSGR_t + error$$
$$(0.44)$$

where the variables in order of appearance are:

$MNSAT_t$ = the sum of verbal and mathematical mean SAT scores in year t;

$\%POP_t^{17}$ = population aged seventeen as a percentage of the total midyear population in year t;

$SHSGR_t$ = standard high school graduation rate—the total number of high school degrees awarded in the academic year ending in the spring of year t divided by one-half the number of persons aged seventeen and eighteen at midyear of year t.

This equation has an R^2 adjusted of 0.925 with eleven degrees of freedom and allows acceptance of the null hypothesis that autocorrelation is absent (Durbin-Watson = 2.45). The impact of the standard high school graduation rate turns out to be negligible and statistically insignificant, while the impact of the size of the age cohort is statistically significant in the direction predicted.

In addtion to the foregoing topics, we have considered several changes in the organizational characteristics of American schooling, especially changes in the number of educational attainments and of teaching personnel. Heretofore, most research relevant to this section of our model has taken an economic approach, considering educational costs, expenditures, and other financial attributes (see, e.g., Grubb and Michelson, 1974; McMahon, 1970; some consideration of supply and demand for teaching personnel is also found, e.g., Folger, Aston, and Bayer, 1970:61–65, 103–14). Most of the models in the educational literature are based on cross-sectional data, comparing either states or school districts in terms of their financial attributes. Although some time-series analysis exists (e.g., McMahon, 1970), such research usually studies school districts or states as semiautonomous economic decisionmaking units and does not examine the aggregate school organizational trends over time.

In Felson and Land (1978) we treat the formation, growth, and dissolution of educational institutions as characterized by substantial inertia. Many institutions survive in some form for hundreds of years, while external pressures on survival can often be met by merger or consolidation. Perhaps of more importance for the present modeling efforts is the fact that organizations can handle increased aggregate work loads without increasing in number if they expand their size or change their organizational characteristics in some respect. Thus, we prefer to treat organizational variables in terms of numbers rather than rates per 100,000 persons.

Primary and secondary schooling in the United States is a very old industry indeed, yet an industry that has faced the double onslaught of higher age-specific enrollment rates and the rapid infusion of younger age cohorts into the system. At the same time, much education at these levels has been the responsibility of very small institutions that are costly to maintain. During the years under consideration here, a major trend toward consolidation of small schools into larger schools was occurring. At least two factors are probably important in motivating schools to consolidate—namely, the increased urbanization and suburbanization of the population and the pressure of higher enrollments. This consolidation is reflected mainly in the reduction in the number of one teacher schools and the total number of primary and secondary schools. Enrollment pressures are also likely to increase the number of teachers, although the declining number of one teacher schoolhouses conserves labor, which means some reduction in the number of teachers employed.

Since many communities had no institutions of higher education at all in 1950 (and many do not even today), the spread of higher education required in many cases the development of new institutions rather than the consolidation of old ones. Indeed, the number of colleges and universities in the United States was only 1,859 in 1950, allowing plenty of room for new institutions to be created from scratch. On the other hand, these organizations had another option available to them. Since higher education students are capable of changing residence to attend school, and since the notion of separate college campuses was widely accepted, higher education could expand the size of existing campuses to accomodate increased enrollments. Furthermore, urbanization and metropolitanization may serve to facilitate the expansion of existing institutions. Thus, we allow for both rising student-institution ratios and a rising number of institutions as adaptive responses to changing enrollments. In any case, we treat enrollment as the key variable driving trends in the organization of higher education.

Elsewhere, we have taken some initial steps toward building a macrosocial indicator model of the occupational and labor force structure of the United States (Pampel, Land, and Felson, 1977; Land and Pampel, 1977). The model depicted in Figure 2-1 also takes the first step toward the future integration of the labor force and education sectors into a single model by endogenizing female labor force participation rates and mean occupational status.

To begin with, the educational trends that we have already traced produced larger numbers of instructional personnel, who are classified as professional-technical workers, the category scored with the highest occupational status. Therefore, we specified identities that define a primary and secondary teacher rate and a college faculty rate, which were then summed to provide a total instructor rate for the population in year t. These identities link the educational organization subsectors of the model to the labor force. The expansion of the proportion of the labor force involved in education is expected to provide for more professional jobs as teachers as well as for greater female labor force participation, since primary and secondary teachers are often female. In addition, the expansion of educational institutions provides jobs for librarians, secretaries, and other personnel who are often placed in "professional" categories of job classificatory schemes and who are more likely to be women than men, thus encouraging increased female labor force participation rates (see Felson and Land (1978) for equations supporting these assertions).

A Critical Note on the Initial Model

Since carrying out this research, we have gained additional modeling experience and insight into the flaws in our earlier efforts. Such rethinking is a normal part of structural equation modeling in a time-series context (e.g., in econometrics), with new models often reestimated and data improvements regularly made. Similarly, social indicator models need to be reworked from time to time.

Our initial model concentrated on educational enrollments and attainments but included only one indicator of trends in "quality"—the mean SAT score. We recommend that future models include more investigation of standardized test data, including data from earlier grades, college students, and Armed Forces Qualifying Tests (if sampling changes do not make comparison over time impossible), as well as disaggregation of test scores according to the skills or knowledge tested. Achievement test scores for specific subject matters (e.g., foreign languages) could also be compared.

Further development of models that make use of age disaggregation may reveal important information not captured by our initial model. For example, the military and civilian labor force competition with educational enrollment has different effects at different ages, which fact might emerge more clearly in such a model. Age, period, and cohort effects need to be examined and, if possible, teased apart. Disaggregation by sex is especially likely to be useful for understanding changes in college enrollment and high school graduation, since female and male trends differ in important ways. For example, the female college enrollment rate has increased even faster than the male rate in recent years and is less likely to be influenced by changing patterns of military activity.

The model presented earlier also lacks adequate linkage to models of educational finance as well as to models of the labor force. For example, the impact of educational expenditures on other segments of the economy—analyzable from an input-output perspective— requires further investigation, while the model of the impact of educational growth on female labor force participation and mean occupational prestige needs to be modified to include some important control variables. In particular, we need to evaluate the extent to which education affects the general shift toward more service employment, more bureaucratic work, and higher occupational skill levels.

While we believe that much could be done to elaborate and develop the current model, given existing theory and data, we nonetheless believe that such efforts will in a few years reach a point of diminishing returns. In the meantime, further development of theory and data is essential to model how education and its role in society change. The next sections take up some ideas for further development of such research.

Theoretical Needs to Specify Better Models of Education and Society

Perhaps the central conclusion from our initial modeling experience is that education is extremely vulnerable to changes in the larger society. Indeed, the SAT score equation seems to suggest that many of the changes in educational organization and methods occurring in the United States since 1960 may be more a response to changes in society (e.g., the age structure) than anything else. While the data presented earlier do not justify the conclusion that educational policies have no independent impact, *one begins to wonder whether educational institutions and policies have not been unfairly blamed for problems and credited for successes that are engendered primarily by other social changes.*

Figure 2-2 illustrates a general social indicators approach to investigating this question.

Five types of descriptive indicators are distinguished in the figure: educational policy instruments, other policy instruments, non-manipulable factors, educational outcomes, and side effects. An example of an educational policy instrument is a decision to have larger or smaller junior high schools. An example of a noneducational policy instrument that may influence education is a decision to build large public housing complexes for the poor that concentrate

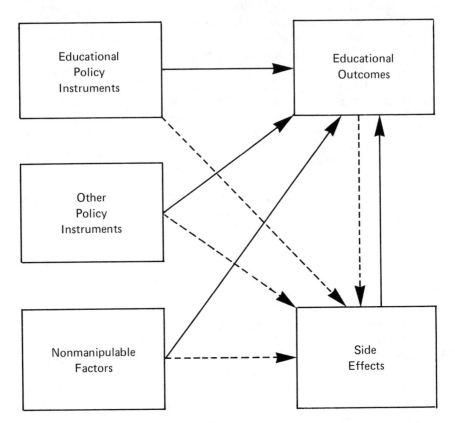

Figure 2-2. Thirteen types of descriptive and analytical indicators in a social indicator model of education in the context of a larger society. Descriptive indicators are contained in the boxes, and analytical indicators are depicted by arrows. Solid arrows are used for analytical indicators that directly affect educational outcomes, while dotted arrows denote analytical indicators lacking a direct impact.

children with fathers absent within a few school districts. Examples of nonmanipulable factors relevant to education are the changing age structure, the divorce rate, and the rate of geographic mobility. An example of a side effect is when school consolidation encourages white flight to the suburbs.

Besides the five descriptive indicators, the arrows indicate eight analytical indicators involving the interdependencies of the five descriptive indicators. For example, white flight to the suburbs (a side effect) may have a negative impact on quality of education.

Since this relationship itself may change over time, social indicators (e.g., correlations) may be gathered for this phenomenon.

Without denying the importance of educational theories and classroom policies, a variety of other public policies have significance for schools and vice versa. For example, housing and zoning policies, policies favoring the growth of suburbs, interest rates, locational decisions for public institutions other than schools— all these factors could severely influence educational outcomes. Similarly, schools and colleges may play a significant role in maintaining communities, providing jobs, facilitating or impeding labor force participation of mothers, providing health and social services to students, influencing residential location, and so forth.

The elucidation of the theory of educational linkages to the larger society would benefit greatly from the isolation of the minimal elements for "high quality education" to occur. For example, we suspect that these minimal elements would include a stable family, household, and neighborhood (sufficiently small units for affective social control); isolation from daily interference of nonstudents (including parents); regular attendance; and so forth. We note especially that models of this sort will need to specify statistical interactions among variables, since the absence of any of these minimal elements may be sufficient to prevent education from being carried out effectively. We also suggest that insofar as the whole is greater than the sum of its parts, a purely compositional analysis of districts, schools, and classes will not be sufficient to uncover these phenomena. Specifically, an improved theory of education and its interdependence with society would need to specify critical densities for certain properties of aggregates that cannot be reduced to individual students, parents, teachers, or administrators. For example, we suspect that there may be a theoretical critical number of "highly unmotivated students" whose convergence in a single social system (e.g., a single school lacking sufficient internal barriers to their interaction) will lead to a breakdown in effective education for other students as well. Indeed, we suspect that the absence of any of the minimal elements or the presence of greater than the threshold of any of the disruptive elements would be sufficient to undermine the system of education. We also suggest that while the details may differ at different ages and for higher education as opposed to secondary or primary education, it may be possible to develop an underlying theory of how the aggregation of persons of different types undermines or facilitates educational effectiveness.

Not only must educational theory cast a wide net in order to understand how schools and colleges operate in society, but learning outside of formal institutions needs to be linked to formal learning. The role of on the job training needs investigation, as does the role of family and peers in teaching not only knowledge and skills but also attitudes, norms, and other phenomena that schools are supposed to impart. Although developing new indicators depends on progress in the area of theory, we nonetheless begin to discuss some data worth collecting in the section that follows.

Data Needs to Specify Better Models of Education and Society

Ideally, models of education should be able to link educational processes at different levels of aggregation (e.g., for students, classrooms, schools, districts, regions, and the nation as a whole), should contain indicators for the behavior of various participants in the educational process (including students, parents, teachers, administrators, and anyone who supports or tampers with the process), and should facilitate linkage of educational processes to other institutional sectors of society (e.g., household, family, labor force, military, the criminal justice system, scientific research, and the community. Demographic accounting, while not guaranteeing that all such linkages and levels can be integrated perfectly, nonetheless offers a conceptual framework for designing a system of indicators of education as it functions in the larger society. Data on educational finance could also be linked to demographic accounting by classifying stocks and flows of persons through various categories of expenditures or taxation as these financial variables affect them.

A system of demographic accounts of education could probably do best by taking individual students as the basic unit of accounting, classifying them according to their exposures to teachers, schools, and the like. However, from time to time, one might wish to classify teachers, families, or other units within such an accounting framework. In general, we suggest that demographic accounts of education classify stocks and flows of students according to whatever experiences, roles, statuses, accomplishments, and problems they are involved in, as they change their position with respect to knowledge, household composition, school or teacher characteristics, labor force position, delinquency, and so on. Without such a system, we believe that multilevel, multiinstitutional analysis of education would degenerate into confusion. Even if such accounts cannot be fully operationalized immediately, the thinking required by their planning would help to guide macrolevel modeling efforts, as we demonstrated in our initial model.

The construction of such models is likely to be a piecemeal effort over several years, so we want to suggest some data priorities. We think that the integration of household and schooling data is the top priority for modeling education and its linkage to society. Specifically, we suggest quarterly measures of student experiences in school and household life, taking into account temporary absences of family members, complete family dissolution, changes in teachers and in peer group members, absences from school, and so on. At the same time, theoretical work needs to be done to isolate the minimal elements likely to support or disrupt successful education, combining both school and household factors. These minimal elements can then be used to classify stocks and flows of students in a social accounting scheme in order to assess the extent to which the necessary and sufficient conditions for education to succeed are being met.

Such inquiries would benefit especially from careful monitoring of time allocated to academic subjects and size and composition of the basic unit of daily interaction (whether the school or some segment of it), classifying students according to their daily community experiences as these shift over time. Such an accounting system should be designed to render comparisons across different education levels, among different areas of the United States, and among nations. Thus, higher education accounts in the United States might consider life in dormitory, fraternity, sorority, or other household equivalents that structure everyday experiences and hence facilitate or impede education, while high school accounts might consider composition of an entire school and of neighborhood youths not in school as the functional equivalent of a community for pupils in that situation. Students attending streetcar colleges and living in off-campus locations would have a very· different basis for their community, something that needs to be taken into account. In general, such accounts need to measure any spatio-temporal factors that facilitate or inhibit aggregations of motivated or unmotivated students and affect their ability to translate their motivation into action, taking into account the scheduling of school and work for other household members or persons whose actions impinge on the students. In other words, such accounts have to integrate various data to allow for significant short-run shifts in community life. These investigations should treat education as a collaborative social activity involving the presence of supports and the absence of likely overt or covert interferences. Such investigations need to begin with the most obvious and undebatable minimal elements necessary for education to succeed and should evaluate how community life brings these elements together.

It seems that such analyses would require massive data sets. Yet experience with victimization surveys shows that size of data sets and expenditures on them reach a point of diminishing returns. Moreover, the breadth of data is probably sacrificed to be able to afford larger sample sizes (e.g., 350,000 respondents). The victimization surveys are burdened by demands that they assess "true" crime rates for the nation as a whole, for all major offenses, and for each major community within the nation—tasks that require huge sample sizes. As an institutionalized endeavor, the victimization survey has all too little scientific flexibility, although a reevaluation and redesign phase is just beginning after many millions of dollars have been spent.

The consideration of "breakage effects," "school effects," "compositional effects," and so forth is an old topic in educational research. Our suggestion here is that much more detailed investigation is required and that much more precise theory must be developed about how these effects occur, taking into account short-term changes in household and school status and very specific conditions in both locations. Thus, data should be gathered on, for example, the extent of overt physical threats to students and the temporary absence of parents or teachers. Despite the major efforts to collect time-budget data for working men and women and for housewives, students are generally left out of such studies. Yet specific and detailed indicators of hourly activities of students—including students in early grades—as well as time-budget data on their parents and family members may provide a key to evaluating how and why they learn or fail to learn.

Moreover, cumulative impacts of various experiences over time need to be assessed, as experiences with small significance at any one time may have major impact over longer periods. We suggest that data on student experiences include some panel or recall data on changes in family and household composition over the past two years, as well as a history of changing school experiences.

While much educational data is collected witin educational institutions, all too little is collected outside. Although a number of surveys have considered how home environments influence education, we know of no uniform time series on these indicators, nor are we aware of any that consider directly the knowledge and skills of parents as these change over time. Except for a few Gallup polls, including short geography and spelling tests, trends in adult knowledge and skills are not known. Armed Forces Qualifying Test scores and industrial test scores could provide data for constructing a time series, but their samples are not drawn to represent the entire adult population. We have no direct way of assessing what proportion of Americans can type eighty words per minute, can operate a lathe, can spell "requirement," can multiply 46 by 38 correctly within one minute, and so on. Nor is there any organized evidence of trends in on the job training and experience, amount of time adults spend reading to children, amount of time children spend among peers, intellectual abilities of school teachers, and the like. Also, although we know trends in periodical subscription rates and book sales, we do not know how many persons read and understand these materials.

Finally, one needs to link community and school data to understand the effect of each upon the other. Not only are educational institutions affected by the support or interference of the larger community, but they themselves have a social and economic impact on the community, often influencing its stability. Thus community and neighborhood data must be coordinated with school data. Indeed, the school can itself be conceived of as a community characterized by its own population size, density, and heterogeneity and nested within a larger community. The relevant, hourly and daily shifts are strongly related to the interference of community problems with the school and vice versa.

We recognize that these ideas are not new. Many researchers have tried to investigate particular issues taken up here, not always successfully. In particular, the separation of "school" and "compositional" effects has long been a problem for educational researchers. We believe that the solution to this problem lies in further disaggregation of national education data, further consideration of rapidly changing social situations, and further linkage of school and household data. If social accounting were properly carried out, many of the good ideas of educational researchers would be more easily operationalized and would help us to learn more about trends and cycles in education in a complex society.

REFERENCES

Carr-Hill, Roy, and Olav Magnussen. 1973. *Indicators of Performance of Educational Systems.* Paris: Organization for Economic Cooperation and Development.

Cohen, Lawrence, and Marcus Felson. 1979. "Social Change and Crime Rate Trends: A Routine Activities Approach." *American Sociological Review* 44 (August): 588-608.

Duncan, Beverly. 1965a. "Dropouts and the Unemployed." *Journal of Political Economy* 53:121-34.

———. 1965b. "Family Factors and School Dropouts: 1920-60." Cooperative Research Project no. 2258, U.S. Office of Education. Ann Arbor: University of Michigan.

———. 1967. "Education and Social Background." *American Journal of Sociology* 72:363-72.

———. 1968. "Trends in Output and Distribution of Schooling." In *Indicators of Social Change: Concepts and Measurements*, edited by Eleanor B. Sheldon and Wilbert E. Moore, pp. 601-72. New York: Russell Sage.

Evers, Susan, and W.A. McIntosh. 1977. "Social Indicators of Human Nutrition: Measures of Nutritional Status." *Social Indicators Research* 4 (May): 185-206.

Felson, Marcus. 1976. "The Differentiation of Material Life Styles: 1925 to 1966." *Social Indicators Research* 3 (December): 397-422.

Felson, Marcus, and Kenneth C. Land. 1978. "Demographic and Economic Interrelationships with Changes in Educational Enrollments, Attainments and Organizations in the United States: 1947-74." In *Research in Population Economics: An Annual Compilation of Research*, edited by Julian Simon, vol. 1, pp. 93-125. Greenwich, Conn.: JAI Press.

Ferriss, Abbott L. 1970. "Forecast of the Supply and Demand for Faculty in Higher Education to 1975-76." In *Trends in Postsecondary Education*, pp. 197-218. Washington, D.C.: Government Printing Office.

Folger, John K.; H.S. Aston; and A.E. Bayer. 1970. *Human Resources and Higher Education*. New York: Russell Sage.

Fox, Karl A. 1974. *Social Indicators and Social Theory: Elements of an Operational System*. New York: Wiley-Interscience.

Galper, H., and R.M. Dunn, Jr. 1969. "A Short-Run Demand Function for Higher Education in the U.S." *Journal of Political Economy* 77, no. 5: 765-77.

Gross, Bertram M. 1966. "The State of the Nation: Social Systems Accounting." In *Social Indicators*, edited by R.A. Bauer, pp. 154-271. Cambridge, Mass.: M.I.T. Press.

Grubb, W.N., and Stephen Michelson. 1974. *States and Schools*. Lexington, Mass.: Lexington Books.

Harnischfeger, Annegret, and David E. Wiley. 1975. *Achievement Test Score Declines: Do We Need to Worry?* Chicago: CEMREL.

Hawley, Amos. 1950. *Human Ecology: A Theory of Community Structure*. New York: Ronald Press.

Hubert, J.J. 1977. "Bibliometric Models for Journal Productivity." *Social Indicators Research* 4 (October): 441-74.

Keefer, Louis E. 1966. "Urban Travel Patterns for Airports, Shopping Centers, and Industrial Plants." Report No. 24, National Cooperative Highway Research Program. Washington, D.C.: Highway Research Board.

Kinsey, Alfred C.; W.B. Pomeroy; and C.E. Martin. 1947. *Sexual Behavior in the Human Male*. Philadelphia: Saunders.

Koshal, R.K., L.E. Gallaway, and R.G. Akkihal. 1976. "Determinants of Male and Female Higher Education in the United States." *Social Indicators Research* 3 (June): 111-22.

Land, Kenneth C., and Marcus Felson. 1976. "A General Framework for Building Dynamic Macro Social Indicator Models: Including an Analysis of Changes in Crime Rates and Police Expenditures." *American Journal of Sociology* 82 (November): 565-604.

———. 1977. "A Dynamic Macro Social Indicator Model of Changes in Marriage, Family, and Population in the United States: 1947-74." *Social Science Research* 6 (December): 328-62.

Land, Kenneth C., and Fred C. Pampel. 1977. "Indicators and Models of Changes in the American Occupational System: 1947-73: Some Preliminary Analyses." *Social Indicators Research* 4 (October): 1-23.

Legaré, Jacques. 1972. "Methods for Measuring School Performance through Cohort Analysis." *Demography* 9 (November): 617-24.

McMahon, Walter W. 1970. "An Economic Analysis of Major Determinants of Expenditures in Public Education." *Review of Economics and Statistics* 52 (August): 242-52.

Munday, L.A. 1976. "Declining Admissions Test Scores." ACT Research Report No. 71. Iowa City: American College Testing Program.

Pampel, Fred C., Kenneth C. Land, and Marcus Felson. 1977. "A Social Indicator Model of Changes in the Occupational Structure of the United States: 1947-74." *American Sociological Review* 42 (December): 951-64.

Rivlin, Alice M. 1973. "Measuring Performance in Education." In *The Measurement of Economic and Social Performance*, edited by Milton Moss, pp. 411-27. New York: National Bureau of Economic Research.

Ruggles, Nancy, and Richard Ruggles. 1970. *The Design of Economic Accounts*. New York: National Bureau of Economic Research.

———. 1973. "A Proposal for a System of Economic and Social Accounts." In *The Measurement of Economic and Social Performance*, edited by Milton Moss, pp. 111-46. New York: National Bureau of Economic Research.

Samuelson, Paul A. 1974. *Economics: Introductory Analysis*. New York: McGraw-Hill.

Spaeth, Joe L. 1976. "Cognitive Complexity: A Dimension Underlying the Socioeconomic Life Cycle." In *Schooling and Achievement in American Society*, edited by W.H. Sewell, R.M. Hauser, and D.L. Featherman, pp. 103-32. New York: Academic Press.

Stone, Richard. 1971. *Demographic Accounting and Model-Building*. Paris: Organization for Economic Cooperation and Development.

———. 1975. "Transition and Admission Models in Social Indicator Analysis." In *Social Indicator Models*, edited by Kenneth C. Land and Seymour Spilerman, pp. 253-300. New York: Russell Sage.

Thonstad, T. 1969. *Education and Manpower: Theoretical and Empirical Applications*. Toronto: University of Toronto Press.

Zajonc, R.B. 1976. "Family Configuration and Intelligence." *Science* 192 (April): 227-36.

Chapter 3

The Efficient Use of Educational Data: A Proposal for the National Longitudinal Study of the High School Class of 2002

Bruce K. Eckland
University of North Carolina, Chapel Hill

PREFACE

In 1965 I attended a conference at the University of Wisconsin on longitudinal research in education at which William Sewell made the comment that what we really need is a study beginning at the birth of a cohort. No one, of course, took him very seriously, including myself. Sewell was concerned mainly with specification problems in causal models of the attainment process that cannot be resolved without time-series data, even though at the time we did not have a very good understanding of the nature of spuriousness and nonrecursive relationships. Duncan's introduction to path analysis had not yet appeared, and we knew virtually nothing about issues of underidentification or about how to deal with measurement error, among other things. We now know a great deal about most of these methods, but lack the data for using them. Quantitative methodologies, in Blalock's words, have gone far beyond our progress in data collection.

This chapter begins with an overview of some of the unresolved issues in educational research, at least as I see them. It ends with a proposal for a multipurpose longitudinal study of the high school class of 2002, but beginning in the first grade—that is, in 1990. In between the opening and closing sections, I take the reader on something of a personal journey through my experiences in the past several years as a consultant for the National Longitudinal Study (NLS) of the High School Class of 1972. My purpose in doing so is to note the kinds of methodological and management problems that are entailed in large-scale, federally sponsored survey research, so as not to minimize the significance and complexity of the undertaking that is being proposed.

My proposal for the high school class of 2002 has not had the benefit of much discussion other than the helpful suggestions made by participants at the Educational Finance and Productivity Center's conference in June 1978 and by my colleagues at the National Center for Educational Statistics (NCES) and the Research Triangle Institute (RTI). Nevertheless, I believe that the basic idea is one that has come of age. Sheldon and Land (1972), for instance, were quite serious several years ago when they recommended the establishment of a National Youth Panel covering ages ten to twenty-nine, with the respondents followed longitudinally until age thirty and replenished with a new sample from the youngest cohort in each survey period. But nothing came of it.

The most serious undertaking to data toward the actual development of a long-term longitudinal study of young children was initiated eight years ago by NCES. In 1970 a contract was awarded to the American Institute for Research (AIR) for identification of critical variables and instruments for a study of the impact of schooling on children, beginning with first graders and continuing for six or eight years. In 1972 another contract was awarded by NCES to the Purdue Educational Research Center for further development of the instruments and the design of the study. However, by 1974 the idea had fallen by the wayside, partly because NCES was by then heavily involved with the National Longitudinal Study of the High School Class of 1972.

In this chapter I have tried to illustrate the need for a longitudinal study design beginning in the first grade that gives simultaneous attention to life cycle, cohort, and historical change. There are other Finance and Productivity Center conference papers, however, to which the reader also should refer that provide a cogent and persuasive rationale for longitudinal studies. These include, among others, Rogosa's "Time and Time Again: Some Analysis Problems in Longitudinal Research" (chapter 4 in this volume) and Heyn's "Models and Measurement for the Study of Cognitive Growth" (Dreeben and Thomas, 1979).

THE STATE OF THE ART

The state of educational research in the United States is no doubt a hundred times better today in both quantity and quality than it was just a couple of decades ago. Educational sociology not long ago was about as low as one could go in terms of professional status in my field—sociology. Thanks, however, to the research of scholars like Riesman, Coleman, Sewell, Blau and Duncan, Jencks, and others, educational sociology how shares at least equal status with other specialties in sociological research. In terms of quantitative analysis, it is at the leading edge of many of the more advanced methodologies in the field.

However, the central issues in educational research are still going unanswered. The reason, as I will argue in the following pages, is because we do not have the right data. What we have cannot be used, no matter how efficiently, to answer the persistent questions before us about equality of educational opportunity and the enduring effects of schooling.

I will argue that the problem is not so much a question of applied versus basic research, of theory versus empiricism, of macro- versus microlevels of analysis, or the like, but of bringing the pieces together in an integrated model of the school as a social system in evolution and not having the necessary data to do so. A number of illustrations will be given of the kinds of unresolved design problems and data needs with which we are faced. Last, I shall review in this section some of the extant longitudinal studies and their particular shortcomings, which further serve to demonstrate the need for an alternative and markedly different solution to the problem.

The Proliferation of Educational Data and Research in the United States

Educational research in the United States almost defies description or quantification. The National Institute of Education (NIE) figures that about $506 million were spent on educational research and development in 1975 alone, most of which (about $470 million) came from the federal government (NIE, 1976).

This includes only sponsored research. The actual level of all educational data collection is probably several times larger than this if we were to count every person and agency involved in collecting information about our schools and colleges, including those who do not receive special support or who routinely collect data as part of their jobs. Take, for example, all the unsponsored research being conducted by faculty and doctoral students in those thousands of departments of education, teachers colleges, psychology departments, and similar places where researchers are observing classrooms, testing students, interviewing teachers, or in other ways systematically gathering information. Add to this the huge archives being created in each of the fifty states, where educational bureaucrats are busy collecting their own facts and figures about students and schools. Indeed, almost everyone associated with the schools, except the students, is involved in the business of collecting and using educational data, including probably every principal and teacher in every school and college in the country, if we mean by this the systematic collection of factual information about some aspect of schooling or students for any purpose.

It could be argued, of course, that all of this activity is not really educational research, and most of us probably would agree. Yet it is part of the data resource potential of the nation. The skeptic, though, might still ask, How useful is it? The answer obviously depends on the nature of the specific research question. Nevertheless, a general response might be, "Not very," and the reasons are many. For one thing, there are serious measurement problems. Many of the descriptive data, even at the state and federal level are not very reliable. To cite just one example—although migrant workers are heavily concentrated during the winter in California, Florida, and the Southwest, most states provide special services to their children under the Title I Migrant Program. In order to qualify for funds, the children have to be counted. Because these children do indeed move about so frequently, a central records system was created a number of years ago in Little Rock, Arkansas, to keep track of them. The government, however, still does not know how reliably the migrant children are being counted, especially by the individual states, and a massive study is currently being undertaken to find out. Few believe that the records are very accurate, since there are many known cases of overreporting.

Problems of this kind make many potentially useful comparisons between schools, districts, or larger political units suspect if it is necessary to rely on figures provided by the participants. There are, of course, exceptions. Another problem is that many of the educational data in the United States, at least that collected on individuals, are protected by privacy acts and therefore are not accessible to the investigator. (This is true, for instance, of the migrant data noted above.) And probably few of the data on students or schools, in any case, are sufficiently complete or continuously collected over time to make them very useful for answering the kinds of questions in which many investigators are interested. As a consequence, there unfortunately is constant pressure to go out and collect more data.

The deluge of requests by researchers for access to our schools reached a point some years ago where teachers and school principals were already protesting against the onslaught. Now even the federal government has difficulty obtaining consent from the schools to do research. The approval of numerous local agencies and national associations is required to conduct any large-scale research in the schools, even when it is simply a matter of collecting facts and figures. One of the most influential of these groups is the Chief State School Officials (CSSO), a tightly knit voluntary association composed of state educational officials. There is no major national study in education today that does not solicit help from this group if it wishes to insure school cooperation.

CSSO's position, which exemplifies the state of the art of access, is quite simple. Teachers and principals, they say, have been inundated with surveys that take time away from instruction, and they wish to reduce this burden on the schools. As the unofficial watchdog of the system, CSSO will advise their members and constituents not to cooperate with the researcher, including the federal government, if in their opinion they themselves have not been properly informed, if the reason for collecting the data cannot be justified, if sufficient lead time is not given to the schools, if all reasonable effort is not made to reduce the response burden of the study, and if the chief state school officer in each state is not contacted before the researcher goes to individual schools.

To the best of my knowledge, CSSO has in most cases been fairly reasonable about its demands. Perhaps this is because the liaison officers representing CSSO are typically themselves members of the research community, because the study or project directors (at least in NCES and the U.S. Office of Education [USOE]) do in fact listen to them, and because, under the implicit threat of CSSO's sanctions, their advice is generally heeded.

Despite the best efforts of CSSO and other groups, probably no one believes that data collection and school studies will actually stop. The idea is to slow down the growth of such studies and to stop some of those that are least relevant. Faculty and graduate students will still find their way into the schools and so will state and federal bureaucrats. However, the accountability movement, exemplified most recently by minimum competency testing, continues to gain steam, the problem could worsen.

In addition, the field of educational research and the data being generated are a hodgepodge of largely unrelated studies, ranging from the small, isolated experiment in a classroom, to massive large-scale surveys like Project TALENT, to the occasional public opinion poll. Relatively few of these data, in my opinion, are useful much beyond the original purpose for which they were collected.

Take one of the worse examples—namely, opinion poll data. About a year ago, the College Entrance Examination Board commissioned John Reed, a sociologist, to search the archives of American opinion and survey data to identify changes since 1960 in public attitudes toward education (certainly sounds like a useful way to use data). Several hundred relevant items were located in the Gallup, Roper, and Harris polls, as well as in various National Opinion Research Center (NORC) surveys. Reed found, however, that almost all were worthless for describing trends over time simply because the pollsters had changed question wording from one survey to another.

I will have more to say later about the uses of extant data. Let me conclude at this point that there are mountains of extraordinarily rich data out there for historians of education to mine for years to come. However, it is my impression that, with few exceptions, they are an unlikely resource for dealing with the kinds of research questions in education that continue to remain unanswered because we do not have the proper data. What kinds of questions and data am I talking about?

The Central Research and Policy Issues

As a means of setting the background against which I will later argue the need for a major new step or dimension in educational research, it is necessary to describe at least briefly what I think the central research issue is. It is not applied versus basic research, but the integration of the two. It is not theory versus methods or allowing one to wholly determine the other, but using the best of each. It is not micro- versus macrolevel analysis, but designing formal models of the education process that use both. It is not interpretive research (ethnomethodology, symbolic interactionism) versus quantitative methods, but recognizing that one type of method can complement the other. It is not normative or functional theory versus conflict theory, but the synthesis of the two. And it is not discipline-oriented versus interdisciplinary research, but maintaining the integrity and utility of both approaches. All of the above, I believe, are false dichotomies, even though each has its advocates.

I believe the central research issue in education today is developing a synthetic study design that uses the best of these different perspectives and approaches in an integrated analysis of the internal processes of education combined with the structural analysis of educational organizations, including the family and the larger political and economic structures that penetrate the school. Irrespective of their particular theoretical position, I doubt that any sociologist would disagree that what goes on in the school—including the tacit, invisible act called learning—cannot be fully understood without considering the social structure of the school and the broader community and society in which the school resides. I suppose this is a sociological truism. Nevertheless, it needs to be repeated because, despite our best intentions, our approach to the problems of education for the most part, whether we are psychologists or sociologists, has been segmented. Most educational psychologists investigating the cognitive or socioemotional development of the child, for example, seldom give more than lip service to the social structure of the school or to the learning environment of the home from which the child comes, even though evidence consistently indicates that the latter is more important than the former. On the other hand, few sociologists studying the social organization of schools or the educational attainment process ever get down to the level of school pedagogy or individual differences in learning. This is usually left to the educationist or psychologist to figure out. Few scholars have been able to bridge this gap comfortably, and as J. Alan Thomas (1977) convincingly argues, the need to do so is inescapable if we are ever to adequately understand educational productivity or any other important aspect of schooling. The efficient use of educational data almost seems to require such an approach.

One of the more outstanding examples of an integrated analysis of social structure and the internal process of learning is found in the work of Basil Bernstein. His studies of sociolinguistics and class structure have led to the now well-known thesis that what partly accounts for the low scholastic performance of children from working-class homes is that they are linguistically deprived. Unlike the middle-class child, who develops an "elaborate code" oriented to the communication of highly differentiated and individuated meanings, the lower-class child uses a more "restricted code" based on the shared identifications, expectations, and assumptions of the working-class family (an excellent summary and review of Bernstein's formulation of the problem is given in Karabel and Halsey [1977:62-71]). Bernstein's work is noteworthy not only because it points the way toward how micro- and macrolevel research might be linked together, but also because it shows how easily theoretically oriented research bears on social policy. In this case the policy is compensatory education, which Bernstein argues is a confrontation between the common middle-class culture of the school and the particularistic meanings and linguistic codes that the working-class child brings to the school. Finally, Bernstein's work is also exemplary because it leads us to the main policy question in education today—the enduring issue of social equality.

As ambiguous as the meaning of the term is, the overwhelming policy emphasis within HEW at all educational levels is on providing equal educational opportunity. On behalf of the National Center for Education Statistics, Ernst W. Stromsdorfer (1977), an economist, recently compiled a list of the policy objectives of the federal government from various sources, including the Congressional Budget Office, and used budget allocations as an index of priorities among the competing educational programs. In the area of elementary and secondary education issues, he found that of the nearly $6 billion appropriated by Congress in fiscal year 1977, 76 percent fell under the heading of "promoting equality of educational opportunity" to disadvantaged, handicapped, language-limited, American Indian, and racial minority children. Another 9 percent went to "improving the quality of education," and 12 percent went for "promotion of employment and career preparation." Likewise, most funding for postsecondary education, which totals another $4.5 billion, went for the same purpose, mainly in the form of direct aid to students.

Barring a national or world catastrophe, it is extremely unlikely that the major policy objectives of the federal government in education will change very much before the end of the century and probably not for years after that. Stratification and inequality will outlast all of us. As a consequence, it should not be surprising that most government-sponsored research in education is also likely to deal in one way or another with equal opportunity, however defined. And as I will note in a moment, the answers to the kinds of specific issues that fall in this area will ultimately require a new dimension in educational research. One side of the new dimension, as already noted, is combining levels of analysis and, in the process, the theoretical perspectives of psychologists, behavior geneticists, and educationists, on the one hand, and sociologists, economists, anthropologists, and historians, on the other. The other side is developing the kind of research design that could accomplish this task.

Unsolved Data Problems

The central methodological problem, I believe, is primarily a matter of data collection and not one of statistical methods or structural models for the integrated analysis of individual and group data. This is not to say that all such issues, like dealing with different units of analysis or treating the simultaneity problem in structural equations or disentangling period and cohort effects, have been resolved. They have not. Nevertheless, we simply do not have longitudinal data on school populations and the schools students attend for a period of time sufficient to answer many of the questions about the origins of inequality in which we are interested. As a general rule, the impetus for developing more refined or new ways to analyze data, at least in my experience, comes from having the data in hand and then searching for ways to use it most efficiently and not the other way around. In any case, the issue is somewhat beside the point, which is that, irrespective of the state of our analytical tools, we do not have the data. What kind of data? Let me offer some examples.

The Effects of Schooling on Cognitive Growth. One of the unsolved issues is what kind and how much of an effect schooling has—not schools necessarily, but schooling. The emphasis here is to give recognition to the strong possibility that schools, in the aggregate, do not vary much in their resources and that what actually counts is how they use them (this is the thrust of Thomas's [1977] argument and of a recent paper by Charles E. Bidwell and John D. Kasarda [1977]). After all, most of the variance in student performance, as the Coleman Report (Coleman et al., 1966) and other studies have documented quite clearly, lies within and not between schools, which leads to the possibility that we have been looking in the wrong place. It is the individual teacher and the individual student that count, assuming that something in the educational process does.

Answering a question of this kind, especially if the goal is to address public policy concerning the equitable distribution of community or federal resources, requires data on several levels of analysis with repeated measures over time. Even assuming a population of students that remains intact (no attrition or movement between schools), time-series data are necessary to document changes in whatever the dependent variable might be—for example, achievement test scores, self-esteem, locus of control, or career aspirations. Incidentally, this statement holds true whether the research design is experimental or simply involves working with the natural variation found in the classroom or school environment. The outcome variable(s), in turn, should be examined in relation to the nature of student-to-student and student-to-teacher interactions (and I mean "interactions" in the sense of describing outcomes in terms of the effects not only of teachers on students but of students on teachers); in relation to the organizational properties of the school, such as ability grouping, open classrooms, and tracking; and ultimately in relation to the community, school district, and state where politics and social class set many of the basic parameters by which all else operates. Finally, the findings in the long run should be generalizable to the total population and to important segments of the population, such as minority groups, and not restricted to an isolated experiment. There are few, if any, past or current studies in education that would even come close to meeting these data requirements.

Equal Opportunity or Early Socialization. Let me give a second and more concrete illustration of what I am talking about. One of the important issues in equity theory that remains unsolved is, I believe, the question of distinguishing the structural causes of inequality of educational opportunity from the learning process itself. The latter, in this instance, includes not merely cognitive skills but also the attitudes, values, and other predispositions that lead some students but not others to reach an educational objective. By structural causes I am referring to the organizational properties of the school or college through which the students pass, including the social structure of the classroom. It is not easy to obtain the kind of data needed to draw reliable conclusions about whether the source of differences in the educational achievement and attainment of students is indeed "institutionalized discrimination" or otherwise located in the "opportunity structure" or is instead a consequence of earlier socialization and learning. Feminists, I think, are still going around in circles on this issue, as both types of factors are no doubt involved in any explanation of why females continue to be so heavily underrepresented in traditionally male professions. Yet no one seems to know which is more important. The problem, I believe, is mainly a methodological one of being able to sort out (if the proper data are available) the various determinants of inequality over time in such a manner as to be able to draw unambiguous conclusions.

In the same context, let me give an example from the National Longitudinal Study of the High School Class of 1972, about which I will have much more to say later. Controlling for social class background and aptitude, it was found that black high school seniors were more likely to have been enrolled in a college preparatory curriculum and to have actually gone to college than were whites. Moreover, even from an early age they were more likely than whites to have been planning to go to college. But there are other surprises, too. Using the same set of controls, blacks were also more likely to have been encouraged by their teachers to go to college; they received better grades in high school; they had higher self-perceptions of their academic ability to do college work; they were more likely to have received individualized instruction in high school, and more likely to have taken a greater number of math, science, and foreign language courses than whites of the same socioeconomic background and measured ability (see Thomas, Alexander, and Eckland [1979]; also Lindsay [1978] and Thornton [1978]).

How these particular findings should be interpreted is open to very serious question, however. For one thing, some researchers will challenge the specification of the analytical model and argue that it does not make good sense to introduce the controls for class background or ability since they are so strongly correlated with race. (The majority of blacks indeed fall into the lowest quartile on both measures.) However, one could argue on the other side that both empirically and theoretically it is important to try to isolate the "race effect" from socioeconomic status (SES) and that this can be done easily enough since numerically there are more whites than blacks in the lowest SES and ability quartiles. Therefore, what one is essentially doing when introducing these controls is comparing blacks and whites with roughly the same social and personal resources for schooling. Nevertheless, the specification problem can be resolved only by the availability of time-series data, by more reliable measures of the background variables themselves, and by measuring them at a much earlier time period.

Another problem with the above findings is that one does not know whether to interpret them as evidence of reverse discrimination or, if one prefers, of affirmative action. It is quite conceivable that the consistent black advantage found independent of social class, as documented, is wholly an artifact of the research design—which, remember, is a sample of high school seniors. It could be hypothesized that the personal resources of blacks who stayed in school to the twelfth grade are not really comparable with those of their white counterparts because of selective or differential attrition rates within or between these populations. To answer this question, however, requires a study that starts much earlier than the senior year and that follows the students through secondary school, including the dropouts, with repeated measures of the key variables at different times.

The example just given should make several things clear. One is that theory and quantitative analysis are intimately related. The specification of one's analytical model always rests on theory (even if it is only implicit); and theory is always arguable, although some theories are more supportable by the data than others. It also shows the numerous kinds of variables that might have to be measured in order to sort out the causal role of the personal attributes that students bring with them to any given situation, such as aspirations and measured ability, from the structural properties of the school, such as curriculum tracking; each of these has quite different implications for equity theory and policy. But more important for my purpose, the example shows just how necessary it is to have the proper data. In this case, the problem is one of having an appropriate sample design and longitudinal data over the correct period of time, without which there is a danger of drawing conclusions from the NLS that could be both misleading and harmful.

The Study of Period Or Social Change. Another kind of question about education that is constantly being posed, especially by policymakers, is not necessarily how things happen the way they do, but whether they are changing, usually meaning for better or worse. Social scientists have few answers, mainly because the intercohort or cross-sectional data needed for addressing such questions, except at a very gross level of generality, are usually not available and when they are they are often inadequate for the purpose. We have even weaker data for explaining those trends that can be documented, which in the long run is the more important research task.

Typically, questions about social or period change require large national samples because local and even state samples of students are almost invariably subject to misinterpretation due to selective migration between time points. The data archives of the Bureau of the Census, including the Current Population Surveys (CPS), certainly contain one of the largest single bodies of national statistics on education, but it is severely limited in content. The only very useful information on education, even in the CPS, is simply that on educational attainment and the current enrollment status of respondents. The National Center for Education Statistics, on the other hand, collects hundreds of different types of statistics on education. in the United States, some of which go back many years. These include data on enrollments by level and type of institution, size of instructional staff, retention rates and degrees earned, income as related to years of schooling (from the CPS), educational expenditures by level and type of institution, and so forth.

Much less, however, is known about the students themselves or about the changing quality of education in the United States.

It was for exactly this reason that the National Assessment of Educational Progress (NAEP) was inaugurated a number of years ago. NAEP uses household surveys to periodically test national samples of four different age groups (nine, thirteen, and seventeen year olds, and young adults aged twenty-six to thirty-five) on such subjects as social studies, mathematics, and reading skills. Results are reported by age level, region, sex, race, parental education, and community size. For example, broken down by region, the results show that adults in the Southeast score lower on all tests, whereas there is very little difference between other parts of the country. Broken down by year, the reading scores for nine year olds showed a slight rise between 1970 and 1974 (NCES, 1977). The NAEP data, while probably reliable for documenting any significant trend in test scores and for doing so by any of the classification variables mentioned above, do not provide an adequate resource for analytical studies of social change in education. For one thing, there is no way to relate the test scores directly to the specific school(s) the respondents attended. Whatever work might be done with the NAEP data would have to be at a very gross level of aggregation. Furthermore, since new samples are selected each year, as in a census survey, the data have only limited use for developmental studies of individual or group differences in cognitive performance.

Although it too has certain limitations, the only national study other than NAEP (at least so far as I am aware) that has ever been able to directly compare the test scores of two separate national cohorts over time was completed only in 1977 (Beaton, Hilton, and Schrader, 1977). It is, in my opinion, a classic in ingenuity and serves to show just how worthwhile quantitative research in intercohort or period analysis in education can be. In response to the growing pressure for answers to the SAT score decline, investigators at the Educational Testing Service (ETS) compared the reading scores of 20,000 twelfth grade students in Project TALENT from 1960 with the scores of the total NLS sample of the senior class of 1972, along with the SAT scores of those in both groups who were college bound. The central issue was whether or not the score decline could be attributed to changes in the demographic characteristics of students taking the test, rather than to changes in curriculum, teachers, parental influence, or the number of hours students spend watching television or being doped out on drugs. There was a strong possibility that the students taking the test now represent a different segment of the population than they used to. After all, not only had attrition rates been going down and the percentage of high school graduates going on to college been increasing over these years, the percentage of college goers taking the SAT had been increasing even faster. These facts alone could possibly account for some of the decline. But proving it and calculating just how much, if any, of the score decline could be attributed to population change at first looked like an impossible task—until it was recognized that some of the test scores taken by the TALENT and NLS students, the only two large-scale national surveys of high school seniors to have been conducted over the period of the decline, could be equated.

The first step was to administer the tests from both surveys (only the reading comprehension tests were used) to a group of students. A stratified national sample of about 1,700 seniors in eighty-eight high schools in 1976 was selected for the purpose; the tests were administered (i.e., each student took both forms) and then were directly equated such that any given score on the TALENT test could be interchanged with a score on the NLS test. Using these data, along with the SAT scores and information on age, sex, parental occupation and education, and family configuration, the researchers were able to show, I think irrefutably, that between two-thirds and three-fourths of the SAT score decline between 1963 and 1972 was due to changes over these years in the high school population, but even more importantly to changes in the percentage of high school seniors at various ability levels who chose to take the SAT.

Since no comparable data are available after 1972, what accounts for the continuing decline on the SAT in more recent years is a completely open question. In any case, the policy implications of the ETS findings are obvious. So too, I believe, is the importance of intercohort studies that have sufficient depth and breadth of content to be able to answer questions of this kind. Again, the efficient use of educational data points to large-scale survey research that is comparable from one period of time to another.

Other Outcomes of Education. My final illustration of some of the unsolved issues in education for which new and better data are needed concerns studies of the noncognitive outcomes or consequences of education, such as citizenship, changing values, and the socioeconomic returns of schooling. I would also include here the advancement of students from one station in life to the next as a consequence of prior schooling, such as the transition from high school to college. Unlike the economists, who have developed elaborate models for estimating the economic returns of education, most of us in sociology talk about how important schooling and college are for everything ranging from who mates with whom to who votes in any given election. However, almost all of this is speculation, in my opinion, because it rests mainly on comparing educational levels of the population with the hypothesized outcome of interest. There are remarkably few studies that have introduced adequate controls to rule out the strong possibility of spuriousness. This is particularly true in the case of studies on differences in values and attitudes that might be attributed to schooling where it is absolutely essential to have before and after measures. I could offer many examples from the literature, but I suspect that most readers are familiar with at least some of them. Thus, I will briefly report an example that involves some of my own work and that has only recently appeared in print. The topic deals with the consequences of school desegregation for blacks, and once again, it comes from the National Longitudinal Study of the High School Class of 1972.

Robert Crain and Rita Mahard (1978) at the Rand Corporation recently completed under contract with NCES a study of the effects of high school racial composition on achievement test performance and college attendance, using the NLS data, which contains about 1,300 schools, including 484 attended by blacks. Schools were the unit of analysis. The results showed mainly negative effects of enrollment in a predominantly white high school on college attendance for blacks in the South and positive effects in the North. I have examined the same data and produced different results (Eckland, 1979). The negative consequences for blacks of attending a predominantly white high school are not on college attendance but on high school grades and curriculum placement. Moreover, the deleterious effects of school desegregation not only appear in the North but are actually more severe there than they are in the South. What explains the difference in findings is that I have used the standardized test scores as a control variable, whereas Crain and Mahard did not.

We find that neither measured ability nor social class are related to the racial composition of the schools that blacks attend in the South, but that both are in the North. Assuming, as Crain and Mahard did, that the test scores are a consequence of secondary schooling leads to one set of results. Assuming, as I do, that the scores mainly measure the academic competencies that students had on arrival leads to an almost completely different set of results of the effects of school desegregation in the North. I do not claim to know the final answer, but I do wish to point out that the data are inadequate to resolve the issue, which could be resolved if earlier measures of cognitive performance were available. What needs to be ruled out is the self-selection or recruitment hypothesis, which states that the positive relationship between the test performance of blacks and desegregation is spurious because of the common dependency of both variables on the characteristics of those (both whites and blacks) who end up in desegregated schools.

As with other problems in education, the outcomes of education cannot be understood without longitudinal data, beginning in the early grades and with repeated measures over time on the critical variables. Until we have such data, we will continue to grope in the dark for answers.

The Utility of Extant Data

The data needs as outlined above all point strongly to longitudinal studies and large-scale studies that do not encounter the pitfalls of attrition and migration of the very respondents most likely to be subject to the social forces around which the research question revolves. Cross-sectional surveys, such as the Coleman Report, serve useful purposes in much the same way that "social indicators" do, but they can produce misleading results. District level and state surveys, on the other hand, have the inherent problem of dealing with the fact that people do move, which creates similar limitations.

Nothing has been said up to this point about the use of "meta-analysis," which I am reluctant even to acknowledge. The term was coined recently by Gene Glass (1976) in an article in which he argues for aggregating the results of as many different studies as one can find on the same question to come to a summary conclusion about the existence and strength of a particular relationship. (He uses the correlation between SES and achievement as an illustration.) In my opinion, meta-analysis is one of the most dangerous practices that I can imagine a researcher undertaking. It virtually ignores, as Glass himself encourages, distinctions between a good study and a poor one on the basis of such criteria as sample size and design or problems of data measurement. Worse yet, it ignores both the theoretical and the methodological models employed in the analyses from which the findings are obtained. As I have already pointed out in looking at the effects of school desegregation, differences in the analytical approach alone led to totally different results using the same data. Meta-analysis would ignore such differences and, therefore, in my opinion is plainly irresponsible. This does not mean that every past study in education is worthless or should be scorned (although probably a lot of them should be) or that literature reviews are unimportant. However, meta-analysis, as described by Glass, is certainly atheoretical and distorts the integrity of educational research.

Small-scale empirical studies continue to pile up, while questions of broader theoretical and policy interest remain unanswered. But not all of the past research has been small scale. Some studies, in fact, have been extremely ambitious. In the remaining pages of this section, I would like to review a few of these, simply to point out their main strengths and weaknesses. I will restrict my attention to what I believe have been the more important large-scale longitudinal surveys in secondary and higher education in the past twenty-five years.

Two of these I have already referred to: Project TALENT and the NLS. Since I will be discussing the NLS in depth in the next section I will skip doing so here. The TALENT data bank is indeed unusual. It is the granddaddy of longitudinal studies in the United States, if not for originality at least for size. The original sample design, which included 400,000 participants enrolled in the ninth through twelfth grades in 1960, called for following up each grade group one year, five years, ten years, and twenty years after graduation from high school. (The ten year follow-up was later changed to eleven years, which I assume was because of delays in meeting the first scheduled ten year follow-up in 1970.) The first three follow-ups for each of the four grades have been completed, and the first twenty year follow-up is scheduled in 1980. The data are extremely rich in content (some of the follow-ups even contain information on smoking habits) and are valuable for purposes of both longitudinal and cross-sectional analysis. Most of the work has been funded by USOE, although it is privately conducted and controlled by the American Institutes for Research (AIR).

The major weakness of the project has been its notoriously poor response rates, particularly in the later follow-ups. For example, in the second follow-up of the first senior class in 1965 (five years after high school), the response rate was only 32 percent. Despite available sample weights derived from a separate resurvey of a 4 percent representative sample of nonrespondents, I know some researchers who are still reluctant to use the follow-up data strictly because of the response problem.

A second weakness, which is not entirely AIR's fault, is the lack of base year information on the race of the respondents. Moreover, subsequent efforts to obtain racial identity have been hampered by the low response rates in the follow-ups. As I say, AIR really cannot be blamed, because in the 1950s, and early 1960s it generally was impermissible for researchers (especially if supported by the federal government) to ask people about their race. (Some readers may recall that the only way the Bureau of the Census got around this was for interviewers to judge for themselves by looking at the respondent to see if he or she was black or white.) As it stands, the TALENT data are not useful for detailed studies involving racial miniorities. Today, of course, you can hardly do a study unless you ask about race, and if it is under a federally funded contract, there is a special classification scheme that the Office of Management and Budget (OMB) requires.

There also are several other major longitudinal studies in the past two decades that have dealt with young people in the transition from high school to college or beyond. In my opinion, only three or four have had a significant impact on our knowledge base and the related literature. These are the Wisconsin study, Bachman's Youth in Transition, the ACE study, and the NORC follow-up of the college seniors of 1961.

William Sewell's Wisconsin study does not suffer from sample size or low response rates, but it is a one state sample. About 10,000 high school seniors who were originally contacted in 1957 were followed up in 1964 and again in 1975. Aside from the problem of the typicality of Wisconsin (which I can accept), the 1964 follow-up data (though not the base year data) are severely limited in scope, consisting basically of information on only educational, employment, and marital status. The later follow-up, in contrast, obtained a wealth of information, but much of it was retrospective. Nevertheless, these data, more than any other in the field of educational research, have been used by Sewell and his associates to establish many of the basic parameters of the general educational attainment model, including the social psychological mechanisms of schooling that affect both educational aspirations and achievement.

Jerald Bachman's follow-up of the high school sophomore class of 1967 was a national longitudinal study of adolescents. Over 2,000 students were included in the original sample, and the study was conducted by the Institute for Social Research at the University of Michigan. The students in the sample were followed up in 1968, 1969, and 1970; and the study obtained response rates of 73 percent in the last wave. It was, moreover, a nationally representative sample of eighty-seven high schools. However, it was limited to public schools and to males.

Alexander Astin's nationally representative ACE sample of some 60,000 first time enrollments at 248 institutions of higher education in 1961 is one of the largest of its kind. The follow-ups were conducted by the American Council on Education in 1962, 1965, and 1971. Although the data are weighted in most published reports, low response rates could be problematic (60 percent in 1965 and 41 percent in 1971). No public release tapes are available.

The NORC survey is a base year study and follow-up of the 1961 graduating class of a national probability sample of 135 colleges and universities. About 41,000 students were resurveyed in 1962, 1963, and 1964, and a 30 percent subsample was resurveyed in 1968. The response rates for the first three follow-ups were 76, 71, and 60 percent, respectively. Both weighted and unweighted data are available.

All the studies cited in this brief review have limitations. In the case of Project TALENT, it is response rates. In another case, one of the most intensively used, it is a one state sample. In another, the sample is restricted to males. Another also obtains poor response rates. And the last begins too late in the educational cycle to have more than limited use in the study of inequality of educational opportunity, which begins well before students ever graduate from college.

THE NATIONAL LONGITUDINAL STUDY
OF THE HIGH SCHOOL CLASS OF 1972

Given the limited utility of extant educational research for answering the kinds of questions that many of us—including, I believe, some of the bureaucrats in Washington—literally lose sleep over, what can be done about it? More longitudinal studies? Exactly. But aren't they costly? Yes, but I would argue that in the long run, one good longitudinal study is worth ten or more cross-sectional surveys. Don't they take a long time to produce answers, which we needed yesterday? Yes, but you will never get the answers any other way. Who would support them? The federal government; it is already in the business.

To illustrate some of these points, I would like to share with you my impressions of a federal project with which I have been associated for some years—the NLS. In doing so, I will concentrate on the data collection and management problems and not on the conceptual framework or the research hypotheses, although I will have something to say about them too. The NLS is, I believe, exemplary and could be just the beginning of a new era in longitudinal research.

Background of the Study

The current National Longitudinal Study, which at the outset was guided largely by the practical everyday information needs of several federal agencies, is a prime example of interagency cooperation. The program represents a major investment of federal resources for research in education, mostly from the budget of the National Center for Education Statistics, which conducts the study (the bill will run well over $10 million before the end of this decade). I will begin by reviewing its background and current status. The NLS, incidentally, is not to be confused, as it often is, with the ongoing Parnes study supported by the U.S. Department of Labor, which samples age cohorts in household surveys but is also longitudinal and bears the same initials as the NLS.

At the outset, let me also note that the NLS differs in administration and design from its forerunner, Project TALENT. Although both projects are federally funded, TALENT was directed from the start and continues to be controlled mainly by one private institution (AIR); project management of the NLS, in contrast, has remained in the hands of the federal government, with various tasks divided among several private contractors but closely monitored by NCES. TALENT was a one shot effort begun in 1960, with a commitment to follow up the participants for twenty years; the NLS is a program of longitudinal surveys in which new cohorts are to be selected about every eight to ten years, while maintaining contact with the members of each cohort for a period of up to ten or twelve years. And unlike TALENT, which obtained very low response rates in its follow-ups, NCES has invested sufficient funds in the follow-up activities of the NLS, including funds for personal interviews, to insure its success.

The beginning of the NLS goes back to the late 1960s when several agencies within USOE were concerned about the need for information that would allow researchers to relate the educational experiences of students to later career outcomes. The kind of data that they wanted required longitudinal studies, which they knew were expensive, and as a result, the idea of cost sharing came up early when the agencies recognized that they had similar needs. A formal meeting of prominent educational administrators and researchers both inside and outside government, called the Mayflower Conference, was held in April 1970 to discuss the idea of a "School Output Study," as it was being referred to at the time. After this conference and more planning, the high school class of 1972 was selected as the first of an intended series of national longitudinal surveys. Also, after the Mayflower Conference, the title of the project was changed to "Longitudinal Study of Educational Effects." Before the project was actually implemented, however, the name was changed once again, this time to the more innocuous "National Longitudinal Study of the High School Class of 1972." Despite changes in the title, the central objective of the study remained the same—namely, to assess post–high school experience of individuals in reference to their educational experience. At least one reason for the last name change may have been that a number of persons at NCES were still smarting over the flack that they had taken from the Coleman Report and insisted that this was not going to be another "school effects" study.

Although NCES controls and supervises the study, guidance and support originally came from several different agencies in USOE. These included the Office of Planning, Budgeting, and Evaluation; the Bureau of Postsecondary Education; the Bureau of Occupational and Adult Education; and the Bureau of Programs for the Handicapped. Some financial support also came from the Department of Defense, which was interested in students going into military service.

In addition, four different advisory committees provided guidance during the planning stage of the base year survey. One committee was composed of academic researchers and the representatives of various educational organizations; two other committees were made up of officials of state education agencies; and the fourth, an internal USOE users committee, represented the data needs of the various offices and bureaus of HEW. Although there have been several planning conferences since the study was implemented, except for the USOE users committee, none of the above groups has remained intact. In all fairness to NCES and the individuals who attended these meetings and conferences, it is my opinion that they were used mainly to gain interest and cooperation rather than to obtain real advice on content or research design. Seldom did committee or conference members come to any definite conclusions or recommendations about the course of the NLS, and if they did, they tended to be ignored by NCES (often with good reason). There are some important exceptions that will be noted later.

Survey Operations. Field trials for the NLS began in 1971 with the administration of tests and questionnaires to 900 seniors in a stratified national sample of seventy-four high schools. This field test sample served as the population for evaluating all instruments, both base year and follow-ups; for testing monetary and other incentives to increase response rates; and for evaluating various tracking devices. Preliminary to the second follow-up, for example, twenty-four different experimental conditions were included in the field test.

The full-scale base year survey was initiated in the spring of 1972. A national probability sample of 18,143 seniors from 1,070 public, private, and church-affiliated high schools participated. The sample design may be described as a deeply stratified two stage probability sample with schools as first stage sampling units and students as second state units. The population consisted of all 1972 twelfth graders enrolled in all public and private schools in the fifty states and the District of Columbia. The first stage sampling frame was constructed from computerized school files maintained by the Office of Education and by the National Catholic Education Association and was stratified into 600 final strata based on type of control, region, twelfth grade enrollment, proximity to institutions of higher learning, percentage minority enrollment, income level of the community, and degree of urbanization.

In order to increase the number of disadvantaged students in the sample, schools located in low income areas and schools with high proportions of minority group enrollments were sampled at approximately twice the sampling rate used for the remaining schools. Eighteen students per school were sampled, with equal probabilities within schools. Because some schools could not participate in the base year survey owing to the lateness in the school year when the field work was done, further attempts were made to secure their participation at the time of the first follow-up survey. The result was to increase the total number of participating schools to 1,300 and the number of participating students to 22,654. Since it was deemed desirable to obtain unbiased estimates of the total population, student weights were calculated to adjust for nonresponse and the purposive oversampling to some school districts. These adjustments involved partitioning the entire sample into weighting classes, which are groups of students homogeneous with respect to the original survey classification variables.

At the time of the base year survey, five separate instruments were administered. Each student completed a questionnaire containing 104 items dealing with family background, education, and plans and aspirations for the future. In addition, each student took a sixty-nine minute test battery measuring verbal and nonverbal ability, consisting of six subtests designed by the Educational Testing Service; and a student School Record Information Form was completed for each student by the school. The appropriate school staff completed a School Questionnaire and a Counselor Questionnaire, designed to collect detailed data on teacher, school, and counselor characteristics.

The first step in data collection for the first follow-up survey in fall 1973 involved an intensive tracing operation to update name and address files. The major mailing of over 22,000 questionnaires was followed by a sequence of reminder postcards, additional questionnaire mailings, and reminder mailgrams to nonrespondents. Active mail return efforts continued from October through December 1973 and achieved a 62 percent return. The names and addresses of those who failed to mail back their questionnaires were then turned over to the Bureau of the Census for personal interview. The personal interview phase continued through March 1974 and brought the overall response rate to 94 percent.

The second follow-up began in October 1974 and was completed by April 1975. Similar procedures were used, and this time the mail return was 67 percent and the personal interviews pulled the total response rate up to 93 percent. The third follow-up took place two years later, in October 1976, approximately four and one-half years after the original base year survey. At this time, most students who went on to college immediately after high school and continued on schedule would have graduated and entered either the labor force or postgraduate programs. This time 74 percent returned completed questionnaires by mail and personal interviews brought the total to 92 percent.

A fourth follow-up was begun in October 1979, and it is anticipated that a fifth follow-up will be conducted in 1983 or 1984. Preliminary results from the third follow-up indicate that four years to a college degree may not be the norm at all. As a matter of fact, as of October 1976, the number of persons still enrolled as undergraduates was larger than the number who had obtained bachelor's degrees (Eckland and Wisenbaker, 1979). Moreover, only 21 percent of the college graduates had gone on immediately to graduate or professional school, a figure that is expected to double in time. What this means is that when the fourth follow-up is completed, although most of those who are likely ever to obtain bachelor's degrees probably will have done so, there will be a substantial number still working toward advanced degrees. Given the current and probable future emphasis on continuing and adult education, not even a fifth follow-up in 1984 will find that all persons will have completed their course of studies, although the bulk certainly should have. In any case, it will not be until about 1984 that any broad statements can be made concerning the impact of education on entry to work for the entire high school class of 1972.

Response Rates.   A few comments about the follow-up question-naires and return rates are in order here. First, it will be noted that responses to the mail surveys increased each year from 62 to 67 to 74 percent, thus alleviating some of the cost of personal inter-views. This occurred despite the increasing length of the follow-up questionnaires, which rose from twenty-four to twenty-eight to thirty-four pages in length. The difference in questionnaire length between the first and second follow-ups is accounted for mainly by the introduction of a large number of items on the adult roles of respondents as citizens, consumers, spouses, and parents—items that could be thought of as nonvocational outcomes of schooling. The increase between the second and third follow-ups was due mainly to the fact that two years rather than only one had passed between follow-ups, which required asking for information about enrollments and jobs for two October dates. Irrespective of when the questionnaires were completed, which was generally between October and April, most items were consistently referenced to what the respondent was doing the first week of October of each year, including any intermediate year between follow-ups.

The increase in mail returns is probably explained by two factors. One is that in the third follow-up a monetary incentive was intro-duced to achieve a higher return rate. The incentive had been tested during a field trial and was shown to increase response rates by several percentage points. A $3 check was subsequently included with the third follow-up questionnaire in the first mailing. The other factor is the likelihood that over time the reluctant respondents who had to be interviewed in the early follow-ups realized that if they did not respond by mail, then within a month or two someone would be knocking on their door. Out of guilt or distaste for per-sonal interviews, they may have decided to respond by mail. In any case, the mail response rate went up twelve percentage points be-tween the first and the third follow-ups, and it will probably remain high for the fourth follow-up. (It might also be noted that continued contact has been maintained with the original participants through periodic newsletters and postcards.)

High response rates are not unheard of in longitudinal studies, although most do not achieve this kind of success. Money and the capability of following through with personal interviews do make a big difference. In a ten year follow-up of college freshmen from a large state-supported university in the Midwest that I conducted in 1962, a 94 percent return to a sixteen-page questionnaire was achieved only after much persistence, including telephone calls and certified letters (Eckland, 1965a). Later, in a fifteen year follow-up of a national sample of high school sophomores, I obtained only a 60 percent return after expending an equivalent amount of time and effort (Alexander and Eckland, 1973). However, the questionnaire in this study required respondents about three hours on the average to complete, and there were no personal interviews. Sewell, in his seven year follow-up of the Wisconsin high school class of 1957, obtained a 91 percent mail response. His questionnaire consisted of a return postcard and did not require contacting the student directly, since the card could be completed by the parent. The point that I would like to make is that longitudinal studies, especially of the size and scope of the NLS, do require vast resources and institutional support if they are to be successful. And one of the most important measures of success is beyond question the response rate (Eckland, 1968; see also, Eckland, 1965b).

Handling Incomplete Returns. Another complexity of conducting longitudinal research is the handling of missing data or incomplete returns. The problem is much more serious in panel studies than in cross-sectional research. While a 5 to 10 percent missing data problem even on critical items can probably be tolerated in a one time survey, when the same questions are asked on each resurvey, the percentage missing one or more times on a parallel item may quickly double or triple. This is because those failing to pass the edit check on a particular item in one follow-up are not necessarily the same persons who fail the next time. A substantial amount of time, therefore, is consumed in editing returns and in reducing the amount of missing data, unless, of course, the investigator is willing to take shortcuts.

In the fifteen year follow-up survey just mentioned, 33 percent of all respondents had left one or more pages blank (the questionnaire consisted of thirty-six pages). In every instance, new questionnaires were mailed and the respondents were asked to complete the parts that they had left undone. Seventy-five percent complied with the request. In the NLS, the procedure was more elaborate. About twenty key items were selected as critical to the follow-up surveys, and if a respondent failed edit checks on any of these, he was contacted by telephone for the appropriate information. Thus far, after three follow-ups, about three-fourths of the NLS sample has been personally contacted either for reasons of non-response or for failing to pass the edit checks.

In my opinion, an important principle to remember in the efficient use of survey data is not to invest major resources in longitudinal research unless an adequate commitment and investment is to be made in obtaining high response rates and fairly complete data. The only exception that I can think of is if the investigator's research design actually calls for obtaining data primarily from sample members who may have a personal interest in the study and are therefore likely to respond, as in the case of polling members of an organization on some policy issue where the researcher is really interested only in the opinions of those who most strongly identify with the organization. This is not the objective, however, of most studies, particularly longitudinal ones. In fact, the problem is usually just the opposite. The subjects of most interest in the NLS, as is typically the case whenever the subject matter has anything to do with schooling and inequality, are likely to be the dropouts and other deviants—that is, those least likely to identify with the organization and therefore least likely to respond or to give complete answers.

The New 1980 Cohorts. As indicated earlier, the NLS is a program of longitudinal studies, meaning that the high school class of 1972 will not be the last to be followed by NCES. NORC recently won the opening contract for the next series of studies, called "High School and Beyond." This will follow the senior high school class of 1980. In addition to replicating the 1972 NLS base year and follow-ups, the study will include high school sophomores. The sophomore cohort contains, of course, many students who will never enter the senior year of high school, and therefore the sample is much more representative of the total age cohort. Besides increasing the generalizability of the results, the earlier starting point for this group provides an unusual opportunity for studying the effect of schooling on cognitive growth and social development. The sophomores also broaden considerably the base population for examining the economic, social, and organizational characteristics of the schools that may affect the different paths that students take into the world of work, college, marriage, or the ranks of the unemployed.

Aside from the many advantages that the new sophomore cohort provides, the replication study of the senior class of 1980 will provide new challenges. Panel studies like the NLS that contain repeated measures on the same subjects over time are still somewhat unusual in themselves, and we are only beginning to develop the analytical tools for dealing with time-series data and cross-lagged models. The anticipated follow-ups of the 1980 NLS seniors will allow us to address an entirely new set of theoretical and policy-oriented questions about social or period change over the eight years separating the 1972 and 1980 cohorts. The replication study will also introduce a new set of methodological problems, in particular those of conceptualizing and developing quantitative models for intercohort analysis and of devising appropriate methods for uniquely allocating the separate effects of periods, cohorts, and age levels. Demographers have been faced with the problem for some years and have had little success. However, I suspect the main reason is that the data that demographers typically have to work with are seldom anything like the NLS data. Most of the census surveys are not longitudinal but are repeated cross-sections of the population, making it difficult if not impossible to separate period from age or cohort effects. The few major longitudinal studies that have been done, like the National Fertility Study, have not yet been replicated, making it difficult to separate cohort and age effects from period effects. In educational research, aside from the NLS, no major longitudinal study has ever been done that gives us these new capabilities. Thus, the efficient utilization of educational data in the future will be likely to require the simultaneous development of new kinds of methodological tools needed to analyze them. The impetus for doing so, however, is not likely to come about until the data are available.

The NLS Data Archives

In 1975 the first public release files and a supporting users manual were released by NCES to the general research community, containing the base year (1972) student survey and the first follow-up (1973) survey data. A year later, the 1976 public release file, which contained all the information in the first files plus the second follow-up (1974) data, was released. In 1978, the third public release file added the data from the third follow-up (1976). The sheer size of these files makes them somewhat inaccessible to the causal user because of the computer costs associated with using them. The total number of characters on the NLS tapes increased from 46 to 92 million between the first and second release files and to 174 million characters in the third release file.

Besides the sheer size of the files, they are exceedingly complex and cannot be used efficiently or effectively without a strong technical background and some familiarity with the data base and its documentation. There are two reasons for the complexity of the release files. The first is that the questionnaires and other documentation are themselves complex; the second is that NCES purposively made no effort to reduce the complexity when preparing the tapes.

Take the third follow-up questionnaire, for example, in which there are fifty-five routing or skip patterns that either implicitly or explicitly directed respondents around various questions in the instrument. There is simply no way to avoid this kind of complexity entirely, especially in the construction of lengthy mail questionnaires. There are other complexities built into the release files as well, such as the numerous sample weights for various combinations of the data sets and variables. In addition, there are eight different types of error and missing data codes, plus a complicated system of scores identifying the different routing errors that the respondents could have made.

The level of detail of the data files could have been reduced by inputing scores for some missing data and by making more use of constructed variables. However, early on NCES took the position that the integrity of the files should be preserved and that the data should be released in exactly the form in which they were obtained. While this allows data users to make their own decisions about how to handle missing or inconsistent responses, it also causes many headaches and adds considerably to the costs of using the files. These and other problems are discussed in an RTI document based on an informal survey of the reactions of over 120 NLS data base users between September 1976 and March 1977 (Levinsohn and McAdams, 1978).

Measurement Problems.   One of the problems inherent in large, multipurpose data banks is the number of ways that the same basic theoretical constructs may end up being defined by different users. All survey researchers sometimes have problems defining their variables. Ideally, our variables should be measured in such a manner as to reflect as closely as possible whatever underlying theoretical construct they are intended to measure. Longitudinal surveys like the NLS, however, create new measurement problems for us, two of which are discussed here. One is related to the complexity of the instruments and the longitudinal aspect of the research design. The other has to do with the fact that data users often define the same construct differently, and some users take greater care than others.

Each of the NLS questionnaires contains so much information and detail that in some instances one finds it possible to define the same general construct in half a dozen or more different ways.

Take what would normally seem like a rather straightforward question: Who went to college? Do you mean immediately after high school or do you include the delayed entrants; and if the latter, where is your cutoff point, since you know that the number will not be exhausted until the cohort dies? Also, by college do you mean going to any kind of postsecondary school, including proprietary schools, or are you referring just to two and four year college enrollments? If the latter, are you including only those in academic programs or those in vocational programs too? After all, many students attending two year "colleges" take only technical courses to prepare for immediate employment. A few of the published reports from the NLS using college enrollment data unfortunately do not give the reader sufficient information to know how the investigator would answer some of these questions. However, the problem is much more complicated than this.

If the object is, for example, to restrict the definition of college enrollments to first time entrants in undergraduate (academic) programs in two or four year institutions in October 1972, we have a reasonably precise definition, but it is not easy to construct this variable from the data. In fact, it requires over fifty steps involving seven different items in the first follow-up questionnaire.

The general problem is not only that several different items often have to be used to form the desired variable, but also that in some cases the researcher has several options from which to choose. For example, in determining who the postgraduate students are from the third NLS follow-up questionnaire, there are three questions in reference to October 1976 that ask (1) whether the person was enrolled in a graduate or professional school, (2) whether the respondent was classified by his or her school as a graduate or professional student, and (3) whether the respondent was studying for a master's, Ph.D., or first professional degree. The total for these three items were 922, 683, and 786, respectively. What then does the researcher do, other than flip a coin? He or she obviously digs deeper into the data by, for example, finding out exactly what kinds of programs the students had enrolled in and whether or not they had gotten bachelor's degrees (which, by itself, does not help much since some students enter professional programs, like medicine, without degrees). My point is that the definition of some of the most basic variables in the NLS, and in other complex surveys, can be exceedingly complicated and still not as precise as one would like.

Moreover, the fact that the research is longitudinal makes matters worse, since sometimes items are changed from one follow-up to the next for reasons that usually seem justified at the time but may have adverse effects later. Complicating the situation still further is the fact that the NLS is also a data archive being used by over a hundred different researchers and organizations. How do different researchers deal with the same measurement problem? Certainly not all in the same way. The general lack of standardization in variable measurement will be a continuing problem in the efficient use of the NLS, with data users possibly going in as many different directions as there are different users.

NCES has not been totally insensitive to the problem. In preparing the first release tape, about half a dozen constructed variables were included. Some of these, such as socioeconomic status and ability, were composite scores, each based on multiple indicators or several tests. The constructed variables have been widely employed by the NLS data users. With each new follow-up, NCES has been adding more constructed variables to the release tapes.

Sample Depletion.   A totally different problem, unique to longitudinal surveys, is depletion. By this I mean that there are so many different roles and paths that respondents eventually follow that as the survey progresses, the number in any particular group of interest may decline to a point where the standard errors of measurement are so large that making generalizations is useless. The size of the subsamples, of course, depends on whether the investigator is interested in unbiased estimates of the marginals or simply in testing hypotheses involving a difference between groups. But even if the latter, which generally does not require quite as many cases as the former, the samples still cannot be too small unless the hypothesized differences are very large—which in social research is seldom the case.

The NLS began with over 22,000 participants. Even if it had begun with 122,000, the number for some purposes still would not be enough. The matter, of course, depends on the nature of the questions being addressed. The original purpose of the NLS was to examine the educational and vocational careers of a national sample of high school seniors. The follow-up surveys, therefore, have focused heavily on the progress of the class of 1972 through college. However, now that a substantial number of respondents have graduated and gone on to advanced studies, the numbers in some subgroups of interest have become so small that it is difficult to obtain reliable estimates. For example, sample depletion almost entirely rules out drawing generalizations about specific fields of study or occupational groups, except a high level of aggregation.

Depletion of the sample as respondents move along different paths also affects some important subgroup comparisons. In the case of blacks, for instance, it probably would be misleading to generalize about the impact of higher education today on the socio-economic achievement of black college students without examining separately those in desegregated institutions and those enrolled in traditionally black colleges, which still enroll nearly half the black undergraduate population in the South. Even though disadvantaged school districts were sampled at twice the rate of other districts in the NLS sample design, it turns out that the base year survey contains only about 130 blacks from the South who attended traditionally black colleges, about 150 southern blacks who attended other colleges, and a total of 215 northern black college students, only 15 of whom enrolled in traditionally black colleges. If the research question is simply access to college, the numbers are adequate, since they are derived from a substantially large pool of black high school seniors. However, if the research question shifts, as it more recently has, to the continuing progress of these students in college and beyond, the numbers are obviously going to dwindle down to almost nothing. In fact, the current NLS (third and fourth follow-up surveys) will be very limited in what it can say about the transition from college to graduate school for blacks and other racial minorities.

The sample design for the 1980 cohorts fortunately calls for some improvement. Current plans are to insure that approximately 30 percent of the final follow-up sample of seniors are black (a substantially higher proportion than in the 1972 cohort, which turned out to be only 14 percent) and that at least 25 percent of them be above the population median in academic ability. These requirements should yield considerably more blacks than in the 1972 study.

Management and the Users

The organization of large-scale survey research involves the interplay of many different actors and groups. In the history of the NLS, the actors have changed, new ideas have come along, and new problems have arisen. The NLS, in some respects, can be viewed as a project in evolution and still in search of an intellectual framework.

The Contractors. There are probably less than a dozen private, nonprofit firms in the United States with the capabilities for conducting a study of the size and scope of the NLS. Many have bid for one or more phases of the study, and five have won contracts. UCLA's Center for the Study of Evaluation won the first contract, which involved an intensive background review of selected major longitudinal studies pertinent to the NLS. At about the same time, the Research Triangle Institute was contracted by NCES to test a number of alternative field procedures and to help develop the general research design for the study. Westat, Inc. concurrently won the contract to develop the sample design for selection of the high school seniors. And the Educational Testing Service conducted the base year survey in 1972.

The field test for the first follow-up was conducted by the U.S. Bureau of the Census. RTI, however, won the contract for the first full follow-up mail survey and all other follow-ups to date. This includes separate contracts for developing and field testing all instruments related to the follow-ups, except the first, and using its own national field staff for interviewing the nonrespondents to the mail surveys. Once the personnel were trained and a routine established for conducting the follow-ups, it obviously would not have been practical for NCES to change contractors each time a new follow-up was scheduled. Consequently, they retained the contract with RTI after the first follow-up and did not open later contracts to competitive bidding.

The cost of such data collection, however, is obviously and unavoidably high. This has placed considerable pressure on NCES to be fair in letting contracts and to insure the proper management and performance of the contractors. For this and other reasons, NCES was required a few years ago to organize a site visitation panel to evaluate both the contractor and the contractee. The panel consisted of fifteen outside educational administrators and researchers who spent four days in the summer of 1975 investigating RTI's and NCES's performance, from the management of the NLS to the technical soundness of the project. The review seemed routine, and RTI and NCES came out with a reasonably clean bill of health.

The Function of Advisory Groups. As noted earlier, numerous groups had provided guidance for the general design and priorities of the NLS. With the exception of USOE's federal users group, however, there has been little continuity over time in the composition of and therefore the direction provided by these advisory groups. For example, when an eight member panel of outside consultants was created by NCES and met for three days in October 1975 to provide advice and guidance for the third follow-up survey, only one member of the panel had attended the original Mayflower Conference, and only one other had any previous contact with the NLS. As a consequence, much time was lost simply in educating the panel about the project.

Lack of overlapping membership between most of the various panels and meetings that NCES has held over the years leads to the criticism that these groups were little more than window dressing. The criticism may have some truth behind it. The role of any group of outside consultants is, of course, strictly advisory to the federal government, which must take final responsibility for the conduct of the project. Nevertheless, by reconstituting these panels and advisory groups each time they met, NCES clearly avoided having to be responsive to the advice of any of them. I am not saying that the conferences were not useful, for in some ways they were. Yet until recently, NCES has managed to avoid any pressure to defend its decisions before any group outside the government that has kept tabs on what was going on.

The New Planning Committee. To correct this situation, or at least with an eye toward correcting it, NCES established a new "National Planning Committee" for the NLS that met for the first time in August 1977. The eight member committee is composed primarily of educational researchers, half of whom have had some previous contact with NLS, and all of whom are from outside the government. According to the Request for Proposals (RFP) for the 1980 base year surveys, the contractor, NORC, is to keep the committee informed of the progress of the project (this was never done in the past), and it is to meet with the committee at critical stages when research priorities are being set, design alternatives are being discussed, instruments and forms clearance statements are being developed, analysis pans are being formulated, and technical reports are being developed and reviewed. NCES intends to keep the membership of the committee stable and to call upon it to provide the overall professional guidance for the development and conduct of the NLS in the future.

NCES is in the business of collecting educational data, not of conducting basic research in education. There is an important difference here, and it is apparent in the composition of the professional staff at NCES, most of whom are statisticians and administrators. Few have a vested interest in the substantive issues of basic research. (The exceptions do not prove the rule.) Even those who attend the federal users group, which represents several different agencies in USOE and has a strong influence on the content of the questionnaires, are mostly junior level federal administrators or their delegates and have no particular expertise in the substantive questions or in how the data would be analyzed. As a consequence, priorities guiding the NLS have tended to be insensitive to some of the more basic issues that the general objectives of the study were intended to address, thereby leading to inefficiencies in data acquisition, particularly in content, that could have been avoided if outside consultants had been more effectively employed early on.

The Prerogatives of Federal Bureaucrats.   Let me illustrate just how the parochial views of federal administrators can affect the conduct of a study like the NLS. In doing so, I am not generalizing to all or even to the majority at NCES. I am referring to the idiosyncratic behavior of a few individuals who were strategically located when certain decisions were being made.

It is obvious to social scientists that family variables are as important as, and in some instances more important than, either education or work variables for understanding what happens to students after they leave high school. Familial, educational, and work roles are all intricately woven together and cannot be adequately understood apart from each other. After high school, for example, marriage and childbearing certainly have an important effect on continuing education. Several important family-building items were excluded from the follow-ups over the objections of the contractor.

One of these incidents involved the second follow-up instrument. After clearance from OMB, and when the instrument was in final (galley) form, NCES dropped one and only one item. It was a question asking respondents how many children they expected to have. The entire questionnaire had already passed the judgment of several review committees. To the best of my knowledge, the reason for deleting the item had nothing to do with the research design or with the substantive issues that were being addressed but was solely a matter of personal discretion by one NCES director who did not understand or refused to believe that educational attainment might have something to do with family planning.

In another case, some of the staff at NCES insisted when the first follow-up questionnaire was being developed that it was inappropriate to ask respondents how many children they had unless they were married. As a result, the instrument contained the usual question on marital status and if the respondent was never married he or she was skipped around the question dealing with number of children. After considerable efforts at persuasion by the contractor and others, NCES reversed its position when the second follow-up questionnaire was constructed. In order to prevent anyone from becoming too suspicious that the federal government was asking information about illegitimacy, the items dealing with marital status and number of children were separated by two pages in the questionnaire.

The results in the second follow-up proved rather interesting for certain subgroups. For example, among blacks, more women reported having children than reported being married, a not inconsequential finding when it comes to explaining race differences in educational attainment. In any case, the data on fertility in the first follow-up are virtually useless. In order to correct the situation, NCES has introduced a question in the fourth follow-up that will ask respondents to provide the birth dates of all natural and adopted children.

I personally doubt that either one of the above incidents would have occurred had NCES been more open to the external constraints and advice of an outside planning committee during those formative years. In the absence of a strong advisory group, NCES understandably had no recourse but to avoid or delete questions that they believed might be unwarranted or constitute an invasion of privacy.

Other Federal Agencies.   It is somewhat surprising that a project of the size and scope of the NLS has not attracted more attention from other agencies of the federal government, especially when the data could obviously serve their purposes. A few additional items of special interest to researchers in the National Institute of Child Health and Human Development (NICHD) or in a half dozen other agencies outside USOE certainly would not have added that much extra cost. But can multimillion dollar surveys be all things to all people? Let me give a concrete illustration of how this question once came to bear on the conduct of the NLS.

As most readers are aware, all federally funded research that involves collecting data from ten or more human subjects requires clearance from the Office of Management and Budget. In the past, the clearance packages for the NLS went through as a routine matter, usually without a question being raised. In fact, when the first follow-up questionnaire went to press, so many changes had been made that it hardly resembled the pretest instrument. Yet OMB raised no objections. Nor did they raise objections when the pretest instrument for the third follow-up was cleared in 1975.

The trouble came a year later, in 1976, just before the third follow-up survey was ready to go into the field. The official claim was, as OMB saw it, that NCES and its contractor were not sufficiently responsive to the needs of other agencies in the federal government that could profit from findings of the NLS. They had in mind economists in the Department of Labor. As a result, they held up approval of the clearance package for the field test and assembled a group of economists in Washington to deal with the problem. Although the outcome of this exercise led to only a few changes in or additions to the survey instrument, it certainly momentarily distracted the staff at NCES as well as the contractor.

If there is a lesson to be learned from this (aside from the fact that clearance statements are in fact sometimes given careful review by OMB), it is that the larger the costs, the more people are likely to be involved and the greater will be the pressure from other agencies within the federal government to share the data, which may mean their having some impact on the design of the instruments. The practical question is, How far can this process go before the survey becomes entangled in bureaucratic red tape and the length of the questionnaires so burdensome that response rates begin to suffer?

Many at NCES, as well as other sponsors of the NLS, have been concerned for some time about the length of the questionnaires. With every new follow-up, the instrument has gotten longer. And every time management wonders if it has gone beyond the "limits" of the respondents' tolerance, which no one has yet been able to define. In the field trials of the third follow-up in 1975, in fact, two separate questionnaires were pretested, one thirty-two pages and the other forty-eight pages in length. There was very little difference in response rates. Yet everyone assumes that there is a limit somewhere. The issue is not an idle one, since the number of different kinds of data needs a longitudinal study can serve is directly related to questionnaire length.

Moreover, most federal agencies are concerned to some extent about the response burden on individuals. That is, quite apart from whether respondents are willing to cooperate, should the federal government be asking them to do so? This is particularly a problem in the schools and is likely to have a serious effect on the conduct of the 1980 base year survey when NCES plans to ask about 72,000 students to participate in the base year tests and about 24,000 to commit themselves to completing a series of lengthy questionnaires over the next ten years or more. The response burden also argues for paying respondents for their time, which now is being done in the follow-ups.

Questionnaire length is not the only factor likely to limit the collection of data that may be utilized for more than one purpose. Certainly the more agencies involved in the funding and review process, the more cumbersome the administrative process becomes. As it is, both NCES and the contractor have sometimes found it extremely difficult to meet deadlines for the NLS because of outside interference. It also is my impression that, like most federal agencies, NCES tends to guard jealously the funds it receives from Congress. The NLS represents a major commitment of resources that it naturally is not apt to chance forfeiting by allowing the project to become a data base for everyone in the government. NCES will, of course, respond to outside pressure, such as that exerted by OMB in 1976.

Moreover, some agencies outside USOE that might gain most by contributing to the survey have been reluctant to become involved. The Department of Labor, for instance, provides no budgetary or other support to the NLS even though a very substantial part of the project deals with employment and career development. These agencies would probably argue that they are supporting their own longitudinal studies that better satisfy their needs.

Thus, large-scale data banks such as the NLS are likely to continue to be more limited in use than perhaps they should be, serving primarily the needs of the federal agency that sponsors them. In some ways this is good. Competition tends to generate a great deal of research and data. On the other hand, it is obviously wasteful. Moreover, it tends to cut out the smaller groups within the federal research establishment that cannot afford to mount such costly projects on their own.

The Users. The NLS was designed primarily to provide statistics on the educational progress and outcomes of a national sample of students for the government—that is, the various user groups in USOE. From the beginning, however, it was also intended for use by the general research community. And as time goes by, the latter has played an increasingly important role in helping to guide the direction that the new 1980 cohort studies are likely to take. This may partly be explained by the fact that NCES on its own initiative has begun to involve researchers from the academic community in more active roles. I believe, however, that it is mainly because the more active users of the NLS data tapes over the past several years have been university and privately based researchers, some of whom have been working under contract with NCES.

Although a fair amount of work on the NLS data has been completed since the study began in 1972, most of the work is very recent, and much of it is in progress. According to an RTI survey of the data users (Peng, Stafford, and Talbert, 1977), the number of completed reports issued each year increased as follows: 1973, eleven; 1974, seventeen; 1975, thirty-eight; 1976, fifty-eight; 1977 (by March 15), twenty-seven. Many of these (seventy-two) were grant or contract reports, and some (twenty-four) were Government Printing Office reports. The results are just beginning to appear in professional journals, and it is assumed that the number of published reports and articles will increase quite markedly as work in progress is completed and the number of users increases.

NCES has also been attempting to increase the involvement of outside researchers by providing contracts through the issuance of RFPs on topics of both academic interest and policy relevance. Several such contracts were made over the past five years in conjuction with the first three follow-up surveys.

Nevertheless, the level of activity is not overwhelming for an educational data resource that is as large and as versatile as the NLS. This is probably due in part to some of the problems mentioned earlier, such as high users' costs and the reluctance of NCES to involve university-based researchers more directly at the outset. However, I suspect the main reason is simply that dissemination of the release tapes takes time; it takes still more time to apply for grant support and even longer to get the work done and published. As of March 1977, there were already over 120 known users outside of NCES and RTI, the majority of whom are located in university settings, including UCLA, Johns Hopkins, Columbia, Purdue, Pennsylvania, Maryland, Yale, Emory, Connecticut, Indiana, Wisconsin, Arizona, Harvard, Missouri, Chicago, Rochester, Michigan State, Brown, Pittsburgh, and Vanderbilt.

Compromising the Objectives. "The NLS is a major national resource that lacks direction." This has been one of the most often stated criticisms of the project. Even after eight years in the field, NCES does not have a clear conceptual framework of what the NLS is about, other than to collect a body of broadly useful data for the policy purposes of various federal programs and the basic research interests of a loosely defined group of academicians covering the early life histories of a national sample of high school students. There is no conceptual framework of the kind that spells out each research question or hypothesis and elaborates either its theoretical significance or its significance for educational policy. Actually, it may be unreasonable to expect that a conceptual framework uniformly acceptable to NCES and its clients could ever be developed.

NCES has obviously been forced to compromise in choosing between a multipurpose data base that might be useful to somebody (though this is an overstatement) and a well-focused study with more limited goals. Their dilemma was never any clearer than when the RFP for the 1980 cohort pretest and base year contract was released in the spring of 1978. One of the contractor's first tasks, according to the RFP, was to develop "the overall intellectual framework" for the survey, taking into account the statements of major purpose of the study (all of which were loosely given), the research hypotheses to be addressed (NCES itself has never stated any), statements of the detailed questions that the study will attempt to answer (the contractor would have to make them up largely on its own), and so forth. Yet at the same time that the contractor was given "wide latitude for creativity" in performing its task, it was also to be handed on the day the contract was signed the "final draft copy of all instrumentation" for the new study. Even the most naive among us will sense that there was something basically wrong here.

Admittedly, NCES was caught in a time bind. They had to either get the RFP out when they did or postpone the new cohort surveys until 1981. But before an RFP could be prepared, so much time had elapsed that they had to move ahead with the instrument development on their own. There would not have been sufficient time after the contract had been signed. This is, of course, really no excuse. It is simply a matter of priorities, which at NCES are clearly to get the job done on schedule and to do it well technically. The contractor was assigned the task, after the fact, of developing a conceptual framework to fit the instruments, which it had some (limited) latitude to modify.

This, I believe, only serves to reinforce the view that the central task of NLS is to accumulate a large longitudinal data bank, guided by the immediate priorities of a federal users committee in Washington and the research interests of a panel of outside consultants and individual social scientists. I am convinced that this has been and still is the true objective of the project and that, indeed, it may be one of its primary virtues.

Obviously the NLS does not totally lack direction. Various individuals and groups have been giving it direction since its inception, although not always reaching agreement on priorities. Each person, of course, sees something different in the NLS, and some have been more persuasive than others in seeing that their interests are represented, particularly in the development of the instruments. These inputs came from psychologists, economists, sociologists, and even behavior geneticists, among others, along with the policymakers. If the study had very specialized goals and a strong protocol for achieving them, I seriously doubt that the research interests of so many different people could have been accommodated.

The political process that has led to the current status of the NLS is obviously, then, a compromise between the interests of many different policymakers and the diverse interests of the research community. NCES has been the broker (and in my opinion a fair one), negotiating conflicting needs and differences of opinion. I think that it is fortunate that NCES is conducting the program and not NIE or any other agency in USOE. NCES is a service organization, and its only real mandate is to collect and disseminate statistics related to the state of education in the United States. Almost no other organization in the federal educational bureaucracy could so easily serve so many different interest groups.

NCES and its contractors will continue to search, as they should, for a theoretical or conceptual framework and a set of well-formulated questions. However, I believe that these are implicitly built into the research design itself and into the main priorities of both the federal government and many academic researchers. The issue, as stated earlier, is equal educational opportunity. The NLS, above everything else, is a program of longitudinal panel studies designed to trace the basic organizational properties and events that affect the life chances of adolescents as they move through the educational system and into adult social roles. The methodology is geared to assess both developmental (cohort) processes and period (intercohort) change and in addition to assess in quantitative terms the impact of various social, personal, and demographic factors in the lives of these young people. The content of the NLS questionnaires largely reflects these concerns, as well as the numerous policy questions of interest to government officials in charge of federal loan programs, work-study programs, talent search, manpower development and training programs—and the list could go on. And herein lies the conceptual framework of the NLS. It is a multipurpose national data archive, and this is its greatest asset.

THE HIGH SCHOOL CLASS OF 2002

By now it should be abundantly clear that answering the persistent policy questions of HEW and of the educational community requires viewing the organization and the process of education from a much broader perspective than we have ever done before. The kinds of segmented studies that most educational researchers have been doing seldom take into account and measure more than a few elements of the ecology of the schools and the communities of which they are a part. Hardly ever is the behavior of the same students or groups examined in different social settings and at different times in a manner that would allow us to draw unambiguous conclusions about the effects of schooling on either their cognitive or their socioemotional development or about the effects of educational selection (certification). Instead of viewing the behavior of different participants such as teachers, parents, student, and counselors simultaneously as members of a social system, we typically examine these elements only one at a time. And in studying school outcomes such as academic or socioeconomic achievement, we have largely ignored something so simple and telling as the developmental processes and organization of the schools that lead some students to drop out the first chance they get. It is no wonder that educational research has borne so little fruit in the way of definitive conclusions and broader understandings of how the system works.

We have to begin to be much broader in our manner of thinking about the problem and bolder in our approach. For years social scientists have been accused by natural and physical scientists of not thinking big enough.

The proposal that follows is for a multipurpose national data archive based on a continuing series of longitudinal studies beginning in the year 1990 in the first grade with resurveys (follow-ups) in each school and of the same cohort approximately every other year through high school and beyond. As I will discuss shortly, the program would be sufficiently flexible to allow add-on samples for special purpose studies of other students, a school, an entire school district, or a state, including participant observation studies in the classroom. The core sample itself would be selected in the opening month of school and would represent a national probability sample of all public, private, and parochial elementary schools and first time enrollments in the fifty states. The natural variation in the school, home, and community environments would make up the "experiment," but in other respects the research design would be nonexperimental. No planned manipulations of the students in the core sample would be allowed, except those that arose of their own accord in the natural environment of the school system. If the first cohort started in the fall of 1990, the first group to graduate from high school would be the class of 2002—exactly thirty years behind the NLS class of 1972. New cohorts would be selected about every ten years, with a continuous series of replications.

Before discussing some of the substantive issues that the research could conceivably address, and ultimately the design and management problems, let me state why I think that such a study is feasible. First, and more important than anything else, it seems to me that we are slowly moving toward a study of this kind anyway, but unfortunately with no conscious plan. The impetus is coming from two directions. That is, at the same time that the age of the target populations for many federally funded projects is being lowered to meet the objectives of studies on secondary and higher education (like the NLS), the length of time that we invest in following up very young children is being raised to meet the objectives of studies on elementary education (like Follow Through). At some time when the two—perhaps inevitably—meet, we will be in a position of having longitudinal data on several overlapping cohorts of students from preschool through graduate school. This represents a huge waste of resources for educational research. The studies, if current trends continue, would still be nothing more than an agglomeration of unrelated projects, unmatched samples, and information that would be virtually useless for anything much beyond the original and usually narrowly defined goals of each study. All of the long-range advantages of replications for intercohort analysis and for the study of individual development through the life cycle would be lost.

I mentioned earlier that one of NCES's new cohorts in 1980 will begin two years earlier than the 1972 NLS—that is, moving the starting point from the twelfth to the tenth grade. It was largely a matter of practicality and not desirability that prevented them from going back to, say, the ninth grade. One of the new objectives of the 1980 cohort studies is to be able to say something about the post-secondary school experience of school dropouts, and NCES is fully aware that they will miss some dropouts by starting in the sophomore year. If, however, they were to start with ninth graders, they would have to deal with both junior and senior high schools instead of only with the latter and then have to track all those students who advanced from junior to senior high the very new year. (Transfers will be a problem anyway, because NCES has to track all the sophomores who move from one school to another before graduating.) Each year that one goes back in time, the logistics of the situation become more complicated. This, of course, raises a serious problem for the study being proposed here. Is the focus on schools or students or both? (The school data on students who transfer at later stages, for instance, may not be as complete as for those who do not transfer.) My answer is, both; and the only resolution to the problem may be an occasional re-survey of some schools to pick up the incoming transfers and new surveys of other schools with heavy concentrations of members from the original core sample.

In any case, my point is that there is a persistent pressure for studies of secondary education to move back earlier in the educational cycle not only to obtain data more representative of a total age cohort but to better study the effects of schooling and the factors involved in why some students obtain the necessary credentials for college and others do not. Concurrently, larger and longer longitudinal studies are being initiated at the point at which children enter the educational system. These, almost wholly, have been research and development studies of compensatory education. One example is the evaluation study of Follow Through, which started with baseline data in 1972 on students in several hundred schools whose progress is still being followed. The intent is to measure the enduring effects of various alternative programs in early elementary education that were funded by the Office of Economic Opportunity in the early 1970s.

Perhaps the most ambitious and costly study of elementary school children ever undertaken by USOE, however, is the Study of Sustaining Effects (SSE), currently under contract with Systems Development Corporation in Santa Monica. The main objective is to assess the effects of compensatory education on the cognitive performance and social emotional development of about 120,000 students in 343 schools in grades one through six in the fall and spring for three consecutive years, beginning in 1976. Data on teachers' practice of instruction have also been obtained in the hope of relating student growth to the kind of instruction a student receives. Several different populations are contained within these numbers, including a representative sample of all public schools having grades one through six, a nominated sample composed of schools reputed to have unusually effective programs for low-achieving students, and a comparison sample composed of schools located in depressed areas but receiving no special funds for compensatory education. The SSE study represents major investment in federal research dollars, as have most earlier studies of compensatory education. What is important to note here is that, while they began at the Head Start level, the evaluation studies of compensatory education are moving upward in grade level.

In looking just at the two main studies I have mentioned, the distance between the sixth grade, where SSE ends, and the tenth grade, where the 1980 NLS will begin, is not very great. There are several reasons why the gap is likely to close in the future. One is that both proponents and opponents of compensatory education are unlikely to be satisfied with short-run answers about the "enduring effects" of early education programs, and I think they will continue to press for long-term studies, possible extending into adolescence. Another is that various kinds of compensatory and remedial education programs can now be found at almost every level of education, including postgraduate school. Each program has its advocates, and many are conducting or have conducted their own evaluation studies. Moreover, each new study usually requires a control or comparison group, and often this means a large representative national sample of students at a particular grade level. I do not have the figure, but I would be surprised if less than a dozen large, multimillion dollar, national surveys of elementary or secondary schools were not in progress at this moment. Think of the duplication of effort and the waste. And I mean waste not just in the sense that one good longitudinal study could satisfy a large part of the specific data requirements of several different federal projects but that the resulting data would be eminently more useful than anything that has been available before.

A long-term national longitudinal study of elementary school children would obviously be very costly and would require extensive planning and the cooperation of many groups. However, such an undertaking is not entirely unheard of. In Sweden, for example, several investigators have been tracking since 1961 the educational and vocational progress of a 10 percent sample of all Swedes born in 1948 (Harnqvist, 1977). When the study began, most of the children were already in the sixth grade. The British have been conducting an even longer term study, beginning with the birth of a cohort—that is, all children born during a one week period of March 1958 in England, Scotland, and Wales. The first follow-up of about 16,000 children was carried out when they were seven years old.

It could also be argued that another good reason for a core longitudinal study of the educational process from beginning to end is that we need to learn much more about the natural variation of human performance within the naturalistic setting of the schools before a new bandwagon of experimental and innovative programs starts up. Given the public's current mood and the apparent desire to go "back to basics," perhaps it is a good time to take stock of what programs do indeed work and for whom, as well as to find out why so many children seem to succeed in school despite all the criticism of their teachers, problems of discipline, and the like. We may learn far more from a well-designed long-term longitudinal study of the individual student and the extant learning environment than from continuing to fiddle with the system and altering it in ways that invoke radical designs and raise false hopes. It seems to me that we need to know how education works (what it is) before we can answer questions about what it can or ought to be.

The Research Agenda

If one drew a random sample of educators, educational psychologists, educational sociologists, and economists and asked each of them to list a hundred questions that they would like to see contained in a base year survey of first graders whom they knew would be followed up for the next twenty years or more, how much overlap would there be? In terms of the general nature of the questions (in other words, forget about the exact wording), I would anticipate a great deal of overlap. Most of the basic parameters or elements of the school environment and learning process are well known if not well understood and so too are most of the problems. A large number of these in one fashion or another no doubt fall under the general heading of equality of educational opportunity, as discussed earlier.

At the individual and classroom level, it would be hard to imagine a longitudinal educational study today that did not contain a good test battery (including tests of reading comprehension, vocabulary, and mathematics); information on the student's academic progress as measured by grade performance or some other form of evaluation; information about the student's social behavior, aspirations, values, and attitudes toward self and others; information on family background (including, if possible, parent interviews or home observations); information about the teacher (including assessments of performance, training, etc.) and, if possible, about the teacher in interaction with the student in the use of time and resources; information about the social and organizational structure of the classroom as a learning environment; and information about the school, its resources, and how they are used. The list could go on, but not too far, because I think we would quickly run out of common elements.

At the school or district level, the data needs would be of a different kind, but no doubt would include detailed information about the school's staff (especially the conduct and professional style of the principal), the reward structure and the distribution of power and authority, the curriculum and special programs, school finance and expenditures, the manner in which problems of discipline are handled, the community, the involvement of parents, and the school board. Again, the list could go on, but not too far.

It probably would not be until after the first hundred items or so that debates would start about relevant and irrelevant data needs. But this problem is not new to either scholars or politicians, and there are ways of managing it that I will come back to later. An equally important problem that is likely to arise concerning the agendy and add-ons, particularly given the long-term costs of the proposed project, would be, for example, someone in the Department of Labor telling OMB that the study should focus more on career training, including out-of-school and summer jobs (particularly as the cohort approaches adolescence); or someone at the National Institutes of Health wanting to give all the children routine physical examinations each year in order to study the impact of environmental pollution on physical growth and development; or someone in the Population Studies Center at NICHD wanting to study teenage pregnancies and unwed parenthood. I, in fact, would argue that most such requests, if they represent legitimate research interests of the federal government and have the backing of the research community, could and should be accomodated.

There is no reason why the study would have to be narrowly defined in terms only of educational (learning) objectives. The rise of mass education in this country cannot be separated from the industrial and technological revolution, the decline of the functional importance of the family, and, more recently, the civil rights movement. America has been changing in ways that place an ever-increasing burden of responsibility on our educational institutions. We expect the schools not only to teach the three Rs but to teach our children to mind their manners (because they do not seem to be disciplined in the home) and to respect the rights of others (particularly if the others are black or red). The schools also seem to have taken on the job of sex education, as well as of checking Johnny's teeth, his hearing, and his vision (I presume because parents cannot be relied upon to do so).

I do not mean to overdo the point, but it should be made very clear that we have thrust upon the schools many of the responsibilities of parenting. Given these new obligations for the upbringing and socialization of children, it seems to me that the taxpayers have every right to see whether they are getting their money's worth. A multipurpose study of children growing up in America today, therefore, should deal with violence in the schools and problems of classroom discipline (and not ignore the problem as most studies do). It should investigate the development and containment of racial prejudice and bigotry (which is the only sensible reason for desegregation). It should learn, if privacy acts do not interfere, as much as it can about how rules of sexual conduct are learned and assess the effects of sex education on teenage pregnancies (about one-third of which are out of wedlock). And it should open the doors for a long-term evaluation of medical screening (and probably genetic screening as well). And last but not least, the study should investigate the development of sex rule stereotypes in early childhood and find out how and if such stereotypes are reinforced by the social organization of the classroom, the content of the curriculum, or the teachers themselves. These are all legitimate and important research topics, and each serves as another reason for studying longitudinally the experiences of a cohort beginning in the first grade.

The high school class of 2002, of course, should not be the only cohort. The study should be replicated at least every ten years. The objective would be twofold. On the one hand, replications are necessary to test the generalizability of basic findings involving social, economic, psychological, and educational theory. On the other, they are absolutely essential for studying period change. A succession of cohorts would illuminate the extent and direction of changes in educational practice and the structure of opportunities. In fact, it would be possible to pinpoint rather precisely where (i.e., at what grade levels) social change has been more rapid or slow. Moreover, only with successive studies would it be possible to distinguish changes between cohorts, a problem I alluded to much earlier in a discussion on disentangling period, age, and cohort effects.

Given all these reasons for a new step in educational research, and knowing the tendency for questions to proliferate in a multipurpose study as well as the need for limiting the inquiry in certain respects at least, let me move on to the proposed research design.

Research Design

It would be naive not to assume that major impediments to the proposed study of the high school class of 2002 are costs and the time it would take before the final results were in. On the other hand, I would argue (1) that the project could actually be cost efficient considering the many data needs it would serve, even if it only replaced some of the current data being collected by the federal government; and (2) that the project would produce immediate and continuous results from the start and would not need to replace the NLS until the first cohort reached adolescence, at which time it would replace the NLS. Instead of money or anything related to the payoff of the study, the real problems have to do with research design and management.

The Base Year Sample. The probability sample in the first NLS (1972) contained about 1,300 senior high schools and 22,000 students; the second NLS (1980) will contain almost the same number of schools (although they will be a different sample) and 76,000 students in the base year (36,000 sophomores and 36,000 seniors). A total of 1,225 schools and 400,000 students constituted the probability sample of TALENT in 1960. Thus, the number of elementary schools in the class of 2002 study would probably have to be on the order of 1,200, since this is about the minimum number required to obtain appropriate sampling estimates (at least it was in the NLS, which contained 600 sample strata). Given the substantially larger number of elementary schools in the nation, however, the figure could be somewhat higher, particularly if additional strata are introduced into the sample design.

Half a million students, as in the TALENT survey, is far more than the number required. Probably around 100,000 is sufficient for the base year survey (and not all of these students would have to be followed up every year). One kind of trade-off that enters into the question of student and school sample size is the practical problem of probability sampling within schools (in this case within grades within schools) against including the entire class or grade in each school. The 1972 NLS, it will be recalled, took random samples of eighteen students within each school (a number that will be doubled in 1980 in each class), while TALENT included all students in each grade in their school sample. The latter approach is in some ways more efficient, although it tends to generate more data than necessary for most (but not all) purposes and increases the overall response burden. The problem would certainly require careful consideration, and one would have to take into account possible information needs for studies in which either classrooms or schools (or both) are the units of analysis. Let us assume, at this point, that we are talking about a sample of about 1,200 elementary schools and 100,000 first grade students, beginning in 1990.

The Core Sample. The base year survey would probably contain more students than it would be necessary to follow up systematically until the twelfth grade and beyond. Considering the problems of sample depletion discussed in regard to the NLS (i.e., the splintering of the cohort into different subpopulations of interest as the study progresses), the core sample would probably require somewhere between 20,000 and 30,000 students. Up to 50 percent of them might be members of racial minorities, which is one reason for the particular size of the core sample itself. It is this sample, not the full base year sample, that would be routinely followed up.

Aside from any add-ons or augmented samples, the core sample should remain intact for the duration of the study. A critical data base should be developed consisting of test and survey items that are repeated in each follow-up survey. A secondary data base could also be developed containing items of information that it might not be critical to ask each year but perhaps every other year or so. Moreover, there should be room for short-term information needs that may be required at only one or two points in the entire course of the survey. All of this, of course, would require careful planning and as much as possible should be done in advance while still allowing for some degree of flexibility as new problems and substantive issues arise.

The core sample should not only meet the data requirements of the study itself, but should also include sufficient information to be useful as a national control group against which separate compensatory education studies and other research on specific kinds of educational programs can be compared and evaluated. This would mean, in other words, giving careful thought to and anticipating the general data needs of program evaluation research—such as the capability of equating test scores across studies—when designing the instruments for the core sample.

The Follow-ups. A very high level of participation would have to be maintained in the follow-ups. The response rate to the first follow-up of the NLS (a year and a half out of high school) was 95 percent; it dropped to 94 percent one year later and to 93 percent two years after that. If one assumed that following young children beginning in the first grade would be an equally difficult task, one might anticipate a 93 percent retention rate by the end of the fifth grade. And if the number continued to decline by 1 percent each year, the rate by the twelfth grade could be down another seven points to 86 percent, with perhaps a drop to 80 percent by the time those in the cohort who remained on schedule graduated from college.

I suspect, however, that the problem would not be quite this severe. For one thing, young school children, although they probably move more frequently, should be somewhat easier to track, to maintain contact with, and to retain the cooperation of than adolescents graduating from high school and leaving home for the first time. Moreover, while the NLS achieved remarkably good results, even those results could be improved upon. Last, it is my understanding that in most survey research, even household surveys, an 85 percent response rate is considered generally acceptable. Thus, it would appear that obtaining a reasonably high level of participation over the twenty or twenty-five years of the study is indeed an achievable goal.

There will be tracking and participation problems, however, that will affect the study in other and probably more important ways. Nationally, about 5 to 10 percent of the parents, and therefore their children, move out of a school's attendance district during a school year. Most short-term residential mobility in the United States involves intracity changes of address, however, and although in the process the child may be forced to move to another school, it is likely to be within the same school district. Nevertheless, in the long term, many students (and no one knows the exact proportion) may be expected to make a residential move that places them in a different town and school district before reaching the twelfth grade. Conceivably, by the time all moves are counted, over half the school districts in the country could at one time or another have enrolled a member of the base year survey.

There should be no major problem in tracking these students, and of course, at least those in the core sample should be tracked, and some of the essential data on the schools to which they transfer should be acquired. The study, after all, is not only about schools but about students. In my opinion, the ETS decision not to follow the students who left the schools that formed the sample for their 1961 Growth Study turned out to be unfortunate. The Growth Study is one of the very few national studies that have attempted to measure over time the cognitive growth and vocational development of a school sample of adolescents. The study began in 1961 with the testing of about 32,000 students in grades five, seven, nine, and twelve in seventeen communities chosen to provide a range in geographic location, size, and socioeconomic status (Hilton,

1971). By 1963, when the sample was retested, ETS had lost 8 percent of the original respondents, and they lost another 7 percent two years later. In the case of the 8,939 fifth graders in 1961, only 63 percent were left in the core sample eight years later when they were retested as seniors. Because no effort was made to follow the students who were not enrolled at the time of the retests, it is not known how much of the loss was due to students who dropped out of school altogether or to students whose families moved to a new location. However, given the size of the loss, and if attrition rates were about 20 percent, almost half of the loss had to involve students who transferred elsewhere. In other words, ETS made a practice of testing all students and only those in the relevant grades in the same schools each year. Interestingly enough, this led ultimately to testing about 13,000 students who were not in the original sample but were added as a result of new students transferring into the school system.

Much can be learned from the Growth Study because it not only illustrates the attrition and out-transfer problems when students in the middle years are not tracked, but also shows that when schools are the unit of analysis, there is a constant flow of new students at all levels being admitted into the system, which raises the question of whether or not they should be tested. Something else might be learned from the study, too, since it also had to contend with another problem—the movement of students from elementary to junior high and from junior to senior high school. Fortunately, it is probably still true in most places that the "graduating" class of a particular elementary school remains intact when it moves into junior high, and the same may be said about the transition from junior to senior high. But to the extent that senior and junior highs do not obtain the bulk of their students from the same set of feeder schools, more complications could arise and would have to be investigated.

Augmented Samples. I would recommend that during the course of the study, "augmented samples" of the high school class of 2002 be added at key transition points, such as when the core sample reaches the seventh, tenth, and twelfth grades. This would involve either drawing new samples in the same schools or districts where the bulk of the core sample was still enrolled or testing all students in the relevant grade level in these schools (as ETS did)—the choice depending on the original sample design.

In any case, there would be two reasons for these augmented samples. One, as mentioned above, is that by the seventh grade, for example, many of the students in the core schools would not have participated in the base year because it was only later that they moved into these schools. The second is that some students may skip a grade, while others may not be promoted and as a consequence can fall a year or two behind their original classmates. This involves another tracking prolem and also means that some of the students who eventually graduate with the high school class of 2002 will not have started with them in the first grade in 1990. Thus, when the core sample reaches the twelfth grade, some procedures for augmenting the sample would have to be developed to produce unbiased estimates of the twelfth grade population that would make the study directly comparable with the current NLS studies (which this study should eventually replace).

Decisions would also have to be made as to whether all, some, or any of the members of the augmented samples would be included in the subsequent follow-ups. Presumably they would be, but how many might depend on their numbers. Based on the figures from the Growth Study, the increase in sample size could be 40 percent or more if the size of the augmented portion of the study were to be directly comparable with the size of the core sample. Depending on exactly what the augmented sample would be used for, however, the actual number would probably not have to be nearly as large as this.

Add-on Samples. Augmented samples serve the primary function of retaining the ability to generalize about the population at any critical grade level that the core sample passes through, and they are of secondary importance otherwise. The study, however, should retain over its entire course, if possible, the flexibility of adding on other samples of various types for different periods of time.

One form that these add-ons could take is as follows. Let us assume that the base year survey contains data on 100,000 first graders and that only about one-fourth of them are selected as members of the core sample that would be followed up in accordance with the master plan. It would be possible, and probably quite desirable, to select a half dozen or so additional groups for follow-up, each for a specified length of time or for as long as there was interest in doing so. More than likely these would be "deviant" groups in the sense that they might represent only a small fraction of the total population. Such groups might be the physically or mentally handicapped, twin pairs, children of migrant workers, those from single parent households or households where nonstandard English is spoken, and those enrolled in any one of a number of different compensatory education programs. Any cr all of these groups could constitute separate add-on samples for special study or follow-up and could be identified in the original base year survey.

Moreover, to increase the flexibility of the research design in this respect, it might be desirable (and it would be comparatively inexpensive) to continue to track all 100,000 students (or whatever the base year number turned out to be) at least through the sixth grade, even though no information other than school record data was being obtained as time went on. This would provide a unique opportunity to identify subpopulations of special interest in the middle years for more intensive study. For example, I think most people expect that minimum competency testing will be a permanent part of the scene before the turn of the century, but I suspect that we will still be arguing over its merits. An untapped pool of students in the middle or high school years for whom first grade test scores and other background information were available could be drawn upon to address the issues that are likely to develop.

Maintaining at least some contact with the entire base year cohort could also serve as a back-up if it became necessary to find replacements for the core sample, which could conceivably happen if certain types of individuals more than others were lost or refused to cooperate. Most surveys do not worry much about replacements except in the original sample design (where it now is done almost routinely). Given the length of the follow-up, it would probably be a good idea to have a pool from which replacements could be drawn at least through the sixth grade, if not later.

Special State or District Supplements. There are other types of add-ons that do not depend directly on the base year sample and that place few constraints on the survey. A particular state or school district, for instance, might have a specific data need or might simple wish to augment the sample in order to generate unbiased estimates of a particular ecological unit. A very much larger school sample than currently envisioned would probably be required to provide unbiased estimates for each of the fifty states. The practice of add-ons, however, is not uncommon and has yielded mixed results in the past. When NIE conducted the Safe School Study in 1976, to my knowledge only one state (Indiana) "piggybacked" its own survey onto NIE's (Eckland, Bayless, and Bannon, n.d.). On the other hand, probably about one-third of the states have conducted state assessments directly parallel to the National Assessment of Educational Progress. NCES, moreover, plans to invite the states to augment the samples when the 1980 NLS goes into the field, but no one expects that there will be many takers. Another way in which a state or even an individual school could be allowed (and encouraged) to obtain some specially needed information would be to reserve a limited amount of space in the survey instruments for items of local interest.

Participant Observation and Related Studies. One of the more important but easily forgotten provisions that the study must make is to create a research setting in the sample schools for intensive study of the behavior of children in interaction with teachers and with each other. Survey researchers typically seem to run in and out of the schools as quickly as they can. In fact, in some national surveys they do not even set foot in the school, but rely on an untrained teacher, counselor, or school secretary to administer the tests and instruments. This study must be different.

There is no reason why a series of reasonably self-contained participant observation studies could not be incorporated into the research design. Special purpose samples might be required in some cases, unless all children in a particular grade or classroom were included in the base year or follow-up surveys. However, this is certainly manageable. Provisions and funding for special purpose studies of the classroom could be made by one or another of the sponsoring agencies, with an open competition for proposals based on their policy relevance and scientific merit.

The proposals could also include family- and community-oriented studies, some of which might require testing the parents over time or periodic observations of the home environment or studies of children in interaction with their parents. Someone else, on the other hand, might propose a study of a particular community in stress in which one or more of the sample schools are located. Anthropologists could team up with the survey researchers in an attempt to measure, for instance, the influence of whatever it is that is happening in the community or in the streets on the socioemotional development or degeneration of the children in a before and after design.

There is no obvious reason why any of the above-mentioned studies should adversely affect the survey. On the contrary, they could greatly enrich it. However, all such proposals would have to be screened carefully in order to maintain the nonexperimental design of the study and to prevent any Hawthorne effects from creeping in.

Field Trials. One way to safeguard the core sample is to require that all instruments, special purpose samples and studies, observational methods, and the like be pretested and evaluated before being introduced into the main survey. This is a matter of routine in survey research, but it is even more critical in this survey because the dollar value is so high and flexibility is so desirable.

You may recall that in the first NLS a sample of seventy-four schools and 900 seniors in 1971 was used to pretest the instruments for the 1972 base year survey and that the same group was tracked for the purpose of pretesting the follow-up instruments. Similar procedures would have to be employed in this study, although I would strongly recommend starting two years rather than one year ahead of the 1990 base year survey. In other words, the pretests should begin with the entering first grade class in 1988 (that is, less than ten years from now). One year, as I think NCES would agree, is simply not enough time to analyze and evaluate properly the results of field trials, to perfect the final instruments, and to move the final clearance package though all the users' groups and, lastly, OMB.

Project Management

If the NLS can be used as an example, there are enormous management problems that would have to be dealt with before such a project got underway. It is partly for this reason that I have proposed a 1988 starting date for the field tests. Conceivably, if there is any significant expression of interest in the idea, it might take several years to obtain funding and several more to work out the research design to everyone's satisfaction. Another reason for my choice is that one of the main selling points of the survey is that it would be a natural extension of (or replacement for) the current NLS, in which the cohorts are slated to run about a decade apart. The 1980 NLS studies are already underway. In order to design a survey of the first graders who would reach the twelfth grade by 1992, the field trials would have to have been in the field in the fall of 1978. In other words, the high school class of 2002 is about the earliest feasible date, and I think the century mark should be avoided.

As stated in my earlier discussion of the NLS, ultimate control of a federally funded project of this kind must be retained in Washington. For the various reasons given, it would be unwise to relinquish control of the project to any individual or private institute, as was done with TALENT. And the scale of the project is certainly beyond the reach of any present group of scholars and of most foundations. Some of us, moreover, will not even live long enough to see the class of 2002 graduate.

Although final control would probably be retained by NCES, a strong planning and advisory group would be essential. This might mean establishing or identifying some intergovernmental agency that could work in conjunction with NCES and in cooperation with the National Research Council (or some other well-respected group that would represent the research community) in order to secure funding and to protect the interests of all groups involved. Some of the governmental agencies in USOE with known research priorities in child and adolescent development include the Bureau of Education for the Handicapped; the Bureau of Elementary and Secondary Education; the Office of Bilingual Education; the Office of Career Education; and the Office of Planning, Budgeting, and Evaluation. Some of those outside USOE, in addition to NCES, that share many of the same interests are the National Institute of Child Health and Human Development; the National Institute of Drug Abuse; the National Institute of Education; the National Institute of Mental Health; the Assistant Secretary for Planning and Evaluation; the Office of Child Development; the Office of Youth Development; the Department of Labor; and the Law Enforcement Assistance Administration.

A very broad constituency, therefore, might be involved; at least I am reasonably certain that this is how OMB would see it, and OMB itself would probably represent that constituency if necessary to insure that the maximum amount of information possible is gained from the study for federal users. There should be assurances that the academic community be well represented— and not "after the fact," when all the critical design decisions had been made. The National Research Council or the Social Science Research Council might be persuaded to help in this regard. It is vitally important that academic researchers be represented by some official or quasi-official body instead of a group of outside consultants chosen by NCES and instructed to meet at its discretion, as is now the case.

Aside from cost sharing and coordinating the activities or interests of all these groups, there would be numerous data management problems. I have spoken about some of them in my discussion of the NLS and will not go over them again here. For the most part, the problems will merely be more complex. One potential innovation that I shall mention, though, is the possibility of establishing a tracking and retrieval system patterned after the Migrant Student Record Transfer System (MSRTS). The MSRTS consists of about one hundred teletype terminals connected to a computer in Little Rock and over the past ten years has been used for tracing the movement and transferring the school records of about 400,000 children of migratory agricultural workers and fishermen as they move from one state to another.

Other systems also ought to be explored to insure the dissemination and efficient utilization of the data after they are collected. This should not be left wholly to the government, as NCES at present does not have a service-oriented data bank center of its own. The Inter-University Consortium for Political and Social Research is one possible depository. But there are better models than this to follow, such as the TALENT data bank and the little-known Twin Registry at the National Research Council.

There are many other issues that I have hardly touched on. They include the whole area of instrumentation and test development, although a good deal of the groundwork here has already been done by NCES (NCES, 1973). Questions concerning the administration of tests and other field work--such as the desirability of both early fall and late spring testing during the same school year—also require careful consideration. This would no doubt make it easier to link gains in cognitive performance more directly to their hypothesized sources in the classroom.

The matter of tracing a single cohort for so many years deserves to be thought through carefully in the light of any adequate alternatives. For example, a combination of cross-sectional studies and follow-ups of shorter duration but spanning the entire school-aged population might prove more feasible. It may also be less costly and lead to as many suggestions for policy and practice as might come out of a true longitudinal study. On the other hand, it might not. Another alternative is smaller but more closely spaced cohort samples that could be pooled when period effects were not relevant to the researcher's problem.

The exact starting point of the project should also be considered carefully. I have proposed the first grade on the grounds that it is the earliest grade at which one can be certain that almost all children in the age cohort are enrolled. Yet even though some areas of the country do not have kindergartens, it might be desirable to start earlier anyway and to augment the sample later. An earlier start could mean, too, picking up three or four year olds in Head Start programs. Or it could mean beginning with a cohort at birth. The only real problem with this suggestion is that by the time the sample reaches the first grade, it would already be dispersed some distance from the starting point and probably across several thousand elementary schools. The idea nevertheless should not be ruled out without giving it more thought. This applies, of course, to the entire proposal. My intent here is to stimulate—not to exhaust—our thinking on a project whose time, I believe, has come.

REFERENCES

Alexander, Karl, and Bruce K. Eckland. 1973. "Effects of Education on the Social Mobility of High School Sophomores Fifteen Years Later (1955-1970)." Final Report for the National Institute of Education. Educational Resources Information Center, ED 084-207.

Beaton, Albert; Thomas L. Hilton; and William B. Schrader. 1977. "Changes in the Verbal Abilities of High School Seniors, College Entrants, and SAT Candidates between 1960 and 1972." Appendixes to *On Further Examination*, pp. 1-92. New York: College Entrance Examination Board.

Bidwell, Charles E., and John D. Kasarda. 1977. "Conceptualizing and Measuring the Effects of Schools and Schooling." University of Chicago. Unpublished.

Coleman, J.S.; E.Q. Campbell; C.J. Hobson; J. McPartland; A.M. Mood; F.D. Weinfeld; and R.L. York. 1966. *Equality of Educational Opportunity*. Washington, D.C.: Government Printing Office.

Crain, Robert L., and Rita E. Mahard. 1978. "School Racial Composition and Black College Attendance and Achievement Test Performance." *Sociology of Education* 51 (April): 81-101.

Dreeben, Robert, and J. Alan Thomas, eds. 1979. *The Analysis of Educational Productivity: Issues in Microanalysis*. Cambridge, Mass.: Ballinger Publishing Company.

Eckland, Bruce K. 1965a. "Academic Ability, Higher Education, and Occupational Mobility." *American Sociological Review* 30 (October): 735-46.

———. 1965b. "Effects of Prodding to Increase Mail-Back Returns." *Journal of Applied Psychology* 49 (June): 165-69.

———. 1968. "Retrieving Mobile Cases in Longitudinal Surveys." *Public Opinion Quarterly* 32 (Spring): 51-64.

———. 1979. "School Racial Composition and College Attendance Revisited." *Sociology of Education* 52 (April): 122-25.

Eckland, Bruce K., and Joseph M. Wisenbaker. 1979. "National Longitudinal Study: A Capsule Description of Young Adults Four and One-Half Years After High School." Washington, D.C.: Government Printing Office.

Eckland, Bruce K.; David Bayless; and Margaret Bannon. N.d. "Indiana Safe School Study Report." Indianapolis: Indiana Department of Public Instruction.

Glass, Gene V. 1976. "Primary, Secondary, and Meta-Analysis of Research." *Educational Researcher* 5 (November): 3-8.

Harnqvist, Kjell. 1977. "Enduring Effects of Schooling—A Neglected Area in Educational Research." *Educational Researcher* 6 (November): 5-11.

Hilton, Thomas L. 1971. "A Study of Intellectual Growth and Vocational Development." Final Report, Department of Health, Education, and Welfare. Educational Resources Information Center, ED 056-063.

Karabel, Jerome, and A.H. Halsey, eds. 1977. *Power and Ideology in Education.* New York: Oxford University Press.

Levinsohn, Jay R., and Katherine C. McAdams. 1978. "The NLS Data Base Design: A User Survey." Research Triangle Park, N.C.: Research Triangle Institute.

Lindsay, Paul. 1978. "The Effects of Quantity and Quality of Schooling." Ph.D. dissertation, University of North Carolina.

National Center for Education Statistics (NCES). 1973. "Longitudinal Study of Elementary School Effects: Design, Instruments, and Specifications for a Field Test." Final Report, Purdue Educational Research Center. Educational Resources Information Center, ED 100-945.

———. 1977. *The Condition of Education.* Vol. 3, pt. 1. Washington, D.C.: Government Printing Office.

National Institute of Education (NIE). 1976. *The Status of Educational Research and Development in the United States.* Washington, D.C.: Government Printing Office.

Peng, Samuel S.; Cecille E. Stafford; and Robin J. Talbert. 1977. "Review and Annotation of Study Reports." Research Triangle Park, N.C.: Research Triangle Institute.

Sheldon, Eleanor Bernert, and Kenneth C. Land. 1972. "Social Reporting for the 1970's." *Policy Services* 3 (July): 137-51.

Stromsdorfer, Ernst W. 1977. "An Outline of Research Issues and Priorities." In *NLS Classes of 1980 and 1982: Planning Conferences.* Research Triangle Park, N.C.: Research Triangle Institute.

Thomas, Gail E.; Karl L. Alexander; and Bruce K. Eckland. 1979. "Access to Higher Education." *School Review* 87 (February): 133-56.

Thomas, J. Alan. 1977. "Resources Allocation in Classrooms." Chicago: Educational Finance and Productivity Center, University of Chicago.

Thornton, Clarence. 1978. "The Effects of High School Context upon Black and White College Attendance." Ph.D. dissertation, University of North Carolina.

Chapter 4

Time and Time Again: Some Analysis Problems in Longitudinal Research

David Rogosa
The University of Chicago

INTRODUCTION

The intent of this chapter is to survey present knowledge and practice in educational research concerning
methods for analyzing longitudinal data. Ideally, the
chapter would successfully address the following questions: What
kinds of methodological advice on longitudinal research are being
published? Is this advice any good? Is anybody listening to this
advice? What areas and orientations need more attention?

These questions are considered with varying emphasis and varying
success. We focus on the analysis of longitudinal panel data for
two reasons. First, large amounts of longitudinal panel data have
been collected in many well-known studies in educational research.
Second, analysis procedures for longitudinal panel data are not
as well known or well developed as are analysis procedures for
time-series data. Longitudinal panel data consist of observations

The research assistance of David Brandt and Michele Zimowski is gratefully
acknowledged. Data from the Berkeley Growth Study were provided by the
Institute of Human Development, University of California, Berkeley. Portions of
the research reported in this chapter result from research in the Educational
Finance and Productivity Center, University of Chicago performed persuant to
contract no. 400-77-0094 with the National Institute of Education. Contractors
undertaking such projects under government sponsorship are encouraged to
express freely their professional judgment in the conduct of the project. Points
of view or opinions stated, therefore, do not necessarily reflect official NIE
position or policy.

on a relatively large number of individual cases over a few (two or more) time points—that is, observations on n cases at T time points or waves. At each time point measurements on one or more variables are obtained. Longitudinal panel data may be thought of as a collection of n short time series or as composed of T replicated cross-sections. One distinguishing feature of longitudinal panel data is that the number of occasions, T, is too small for the application of conventional time-series methods.

Two distinct literatures on methods for the analysis of longitudinal panel data exist, one for the analysis of discrete or qualitative outcome measures, the other for the analysis of continuous or quantitative outcome measures. Because longitudinal panel data in educational research are predominantly of the latter type (e.g., measures of academic achievement), and to provide some continuity in the exposition, we do not discuss methods for analyzing qualitative longitudinal data. A companion paper on the analysis of discrete longitudinal data would be valuable; in fact, a number of recent surveys in statistics and econometrics on the analysis of discrete panel data serve this function.

Issues of statistical estimation, such as comparisons of the statistical properties of competing estimators, are not given much attention because the primary issues in educational research applications appear to be those of problem formulation and of identification of the key parameters in models for the longitudinal panel data. The principal question is how to use longitudinal panel data effectively, and this question takes precedence over questions of statistical efficiency. Also, not much is said about the design of longitudinal panel studies, although many important design issues, such as criteria for the number and spacing of waves of observations, remain far from settled.

Longitudinal data and their analysis present two major kinds of opportunities for empirical research: the first, and more limited, is to provide better answers to questions often addressed by cross-sectional research; the second, and not as well understood, is to inform about the process of change, a function that cross-sectional data usually cannot serve.

As a partial review of present practice in educational research, this chapter gives much space to the first function of longitudinal research, which is itself often inadequately understood and unsuccessfully executed. The second function is sometimes featured in recommending future directions for methodological and empirical work. Potential applications of methods, primarily from econometrics and statistics, are sketched and unexplored areas noted.

Some procedures that are commonly used to analyze longitudinal panel data are simply borrowed from the arsenal of methods developed for analyzing associations among variables in cross-sectional data. Other methods, typically less venerable and well known, are specific to the analysis of longitudinal data, such as models for rates of change.

Along with these opportunities, longitudinal data also pose special difficulties for data analysis that are not usually encountered in analysis of cross-sectional data. In part, these difficulties are due to the more complex structure of longitudinal data, especially dependencies over time. The complexities of longitudinal data that present problems in many analyses are often those features of longitudinal data that represent information not obtainable from cross-sectional data. But extracting this additional information may be very hard work.

Perhaps the principal cause of difficulties encountered in analyses of longitudinal data is the attempt to address more difficult and sophisticated questions than are attempted using cross-sectional data. And often such questions are more difficult than the data can support. This situation is summarized by an "uncertainty principle" discussed by Griliches: "The amount of information in any one specific data set is finite and, therefore, as we keep asking finer and finer questions, our answers become more and more uncertain" (1977: 13). For example, research questions concerning reciprocal causal effects require more information that is available in cross-sectional data, and researchers have attempted to exploit the additional information in the longitudinal data in order to address these harder questions. However, recent research and methodological debate concerning reciprocal causal effects clearly illustrate that sound answers are far from guaranteed even with the collection of longitudinal panel data.

An attempt is made in this chapter to feature areas of educational research where the additional information in longitudinal panel data may prove of great worth and to exhibit concern and caution in areas where it seems that longitudinal panel data are too crude to answer "finer and finer" questions. To provide some perspective on the recent surge of interest in longitudinal research in education, it should be remembered that longitudinal data are not a panacea for all research problems and that the relative advantages of longitudinal data over cross-sectional data are sometimes overstated.

The second section, "Comparing Cross-Sectional and Longitudinal Analyses," reviews the comparisons in the educational research literature between analyses based on longitudinal data and analyses based on cross-sectional data. Critiques of some of these empirical and numerical comparisons are presented. The third section, "Understanding Longitudinal Hierarchical Data," presents a formulation of longitudinal panel data that takes into account the hierarchical structure (e.g., student within class within school) of many educational data. Alternative regression analyses for hierarchical longitudinal data are described and illustrated.

Models for the process of change are described in the section "Modeling Change: Methods and Applications." The application of a continuous time model for the rate of learning to research on school effects is discussed. The assessment of reciprocal causal effects, such as those presumed to exist between student self-concept and academic achievement or between teacher expectancy and student achievement, is the subject of the fifth section "Investigating Causal Feedback and Reciprocal Causal Effects." Structural regression models, dynamic change models, multiple time-series models, and the method of cross-lagged correlation are compared, and research applications of these methods are presented.

COMPARING CROSS–SECTIONAL AND LONGITUDINAL ANALYSES

In recent years educational researchers have become sensitive to some limitations inherent in analyses of data from cross-sectional designs. A number of authors have concluded that cross-sectional data are not adequate for the assessment of the effects of educational programs and processes—"longitudinal data have been recognized as the *sine qua non* of good evaluation in nonexperimental settings" (Marco, 1974: 225). Interest in longitudinal data was at least partially motivated by two unpleasant research findings in the 1960s—schools do not make a difference (e.g., the Coleman Report) and educational innovations do not have much effect (e.g., the Head Start evaluation).

One criticism of the Coleman Report (Coleman et al., 1966) is of its cross-sectional design; critics such as Dyer (1972) contend that the relation of school and teacher variables to student achievement can be accurately assessed only through analyses of longitudinal data. The use of temporal variation to identify causes and effects is seen as an attractive strategy in much of social science:

> When variables are observed at two or more points in time, additional information exists beyond that obtained in cross-sectional data. This is

information which, if used properly, can indicate what factors bring about change in a variable. These changes will, of course, create or maintain the relationships that may be found in cross-sectional data, and thus provide information about the dynamics of a system beyond that provided by cross-sectional data. (Coleman, 1968:475)

The analysis of quasiexperiments using analysis of covariance and other types of regression adjustments has suffered repeated criticism, beginning with the Campbell and Erlebacher (1970) critique of the Westinghouse analysis of Head Start. One result of this controversy was the recognition that with nonequivalent groups neither cross-sectional nor simple pretest-posttest designs are adequate for the assessment of the effects of educational innovations. Some researchers have turned to more extensive longitudinal designs for better evidence on the functioning and effects of educational innovations—for example, models of individual growth (Bryk and Weisberg, 1976, 1977), and time-series intervention designs (Glass, Willson, and Gottman, 1975; Hibbs, 1977).

A third impetus for the collection of longitudinal data arises from attempts to study educational and psychological processes that are assumed to involve reciprocal causal influences. Examples of causal feedback relations in educational research are those between self-concept and academic achievement and between teacher expectancy and academic performance. The limitations of cross-sectional designs for the analysis of reciprocal causal effects have been noted in many contexts (e.g., Purkey, 1970; Rogosa, 1979a). The method of cross-lagged correlation is currently enjoying great popularity in education and psychology for the assessment of reciprocal causal influences.

Although many researchers understand that longitudinal data are highly desirable and perhaps essential for any assessment of educational effects, the cost and practical difficulties of obtaining longitudinal data diminish their attractiveness. And regrettably, the importance of longitudinal data in educational research is not even always acknowledged; in Pedhazur's (1975) review and critique of statistical methods used in school effects studies, no mention whatsoever is made of the usefulness of longitudinal data.

The educational research literature does not provide much guidance on the design and analysis of longitudinal research. This literature contains only a few methodologically oriented papers that compare results that might be obtained from analyses of cross-sectional data with those from analyses of longitudinal data (some of these are examined below). However, in other areas of social science, a number of comparisons and reviews of longitudinal and cross-sectional data analyses are available. Kuh (1959) presents some very clear comparisons of regression analyses of firm investment behavior on profits and capital stock using data from time series and from cross-sections. The regression estimates are found to vary markedly, and Kuh provides some cogent explanations based on economic theory and on statistical considerations. In life-span psychology the classic example of the problems with the interpretation of cross-sectional data is the often-cited decrement in adult intelligence as a function of age reported in cross-sectional studies (see Nesselroade and Baltes, 1974). This decrement is actually a consequence of an interaction between age and generation effects rather than a result of age effects. Damon (1965) and Kuhlen (1963) provide additional empirical documentation of the differences between the results of analyses of cross-sectional and longitudinal data.

Freeman and Hannan provide an excellent discussion of possible distortions from cross-sectional studies in the context of organizational growth and decline in school districts:

> Repeated cross-sections from a panel of organizations which are out of equilibrium will ordinarily produce estimates varying considerably from cross-section to cross-section. . . . It should be apparent that, if the processes of study are not symmetric in growth and decline, cross-sectional analysis mixing growers and decliners will obscure the processes of interest. (1975:216)

The dynamic models of organizational change over time formulated by Freeman and Hannan are discussed in the final section of the chapter.

One way of justifying the use of a cross-sectional design is to assume that the cross-sectional data will yield the same conclusion that longitudinal data would. To the extent that this assumption is violated, the cross-sectional data can be considered an inadequate proxy for longitudinal data. The discrepancy between the results of a cross-sectional study and those obtained from longitudinal data could be termed the temporal bias in the cross-sectional analysis. The notion of temporal bias would address the question, When cross-sectional data are used to investigate longitudinal effects or temporal change, how misleading are the results likely to be?

The relationship between analyses based on cross-sectional and those based on longitudinal panel data can be described through a decomposition of a datum X_{jt}, which represents an observation on the attribute X for individual j ($j = 1, \ldots n$) at time t ($t = 1, \ldots T$). The decomposition expresses each longitudinal observation in individual j as the sum of the mean for that individual over the T time points and the deviation of X_{jt} from that mean at time t:

$$X_{jt} = \overline{X}_{j\cdot} + (X_{jt} - \overline{X}_{j\cdot}). \qquad (4.1)$$

The mean over time, $\overline{X}_{j\cdot}$, can be viewed as a cross-sectional component in that $\overline{X}_{j\cdot}$ contains no temporal information; the $\overline{X}_{j\cdot}$ are temporally aggregated data in the extreme. The $\overline{X}_{j\cdot}$ term contains information on differences among persons. The $(X_{jt} - \overline{X}_{j\cdot})$ term contains information on the within person deviations from a person's average value over time.

The decomposition in equation (4.1) parallels the decompositions employed in studies of the analysis of hierarchical data (persons in groups). The term "aggregation bias" is used in that literature to represent differences among the results of analysis conducted on data at different levels of aggregation, especially between analyses based on group means and analyses based on data from individuals (see Hannan and Burstein, 1974). Temporal bias, representing the difference between cross-sectional and longitudinal analyses, is seen through equation (4.1) to be analogous in form to aggregation bias. The notion of temporal bias may be pursued as the difference between results from analyses that ignore temporal variation (as in cross-sectional data where that information is not available) and results from analyses that incorporate longitudinal information. For example, using an outcome variable Y and a decomposition like equation (4.1), the regression of $\overline{Y}_{j\cdot}$ on $\overline{X}_{j\cdot}$ is a regression that ignores temporal variance. And a characterization of temporal bias in such a regression analysis is the difference between the slope from the regression of $\overline{Y}_{j\cdot}$ on $\overline{X}_{j\cdot}$ and the regression slope of Y_{jt} on X_{jt}. Further discussion of these topics and of the complications arising from the presence of both temporal and hierarchical aggregation is presented in a subsequent section in the consideration of the analysis of hierarchical longitudinal data, such as longitudinal panel data on student learning in schools.

Before turning to those issues and to other topics in the analysis of longitudinal panel data, we will briefly survey the educational research literature on comparisons of cross-sectional and longitudinal data and their analysis. Empirical analyses in three areas involving longitudinal panel data on school learning are presented below.

Cognitive Growth

Hilton and Patrick (1970) present an extensive analysis of data from the Educational Testing Service (ETS) Growth Study, in which four waves of achievement test scores were collected on 32,000 students at two year intervals starting in 1961 when the students were in the fifth grade. Their comparative analysis of three types of data obtained from the Growth Study—matched longitudinal, unmatched longitudinal, and cross-sectional—were designed to address the question, "To what extent can one accurately describe student academic growth on the basis of either cross-sectional data or longitudinal data?" (1970:15).

The distinction between matched and unmatched longitudinal data arises from considering the school (or other level of grouping) to be the unit of sampling; the school mean may be computed from the scores of all students attending the school at each data collection time (unmatched) or from only that core of students who have data for all collection periods (matched). Clearly, associations among individual-level variables can be computed only from matched longitudinal data. However, associations among group means may be computed from either matched or unmatched data. This distinction appears in many other discussions and analyses of longitudinal data; in this chapter we focus almost exclusively on matched longitudinal data. In life-span psychology, unmatched longitudinal samples, obtained from random sampling with replacement of subjects at each wave, are advocated as a device to avoid problems such as test-retest effects (Schaie, 1965; Baltes, 1968).

Hilton and Patrick (1970) investigate selection effects, cohort effects, and age effects, along with other phenomena, in the three types of data. The matched longitudinal data yield the highest mean levels of achievement, probably because of the greater mobility and incidence of dropouts of lower ability students. As pointed out in other contexts (e.g., Schaie, 1965), all three kinds of data are subject to serious distortions in some settings.

Goulet (1975) also discusses possible shortcomings of longitudinal and cross-sectional designs with specific reference to studies of educational attainment. He gives much attention to the effects of chronological age (CA), arguing that because of the confounding of CA-related and school-related influences on development, longitudinal data will often yield estimates of growth that exceed those obtained from cross-sectional data using within-grade contrasts. Goulet advocates a time-lag design, in which subjects with different birth dates are tested at the same chronological age. This design requires that nonoverlapping random samples of students be tested at different times in the school year. Using data from such a design, he obtains estimates of the effects of school experiences independent of other CA-related factors.

Designs such as this time-lag design and the related cohort-sequential design (Nesselroade and Baltes, 1974) are longitudinal panel designs with many observations missing by design. In the statistical and biometric literatures, these designs are termed mixed longitudinal or linked cross-sectional designs. The statistical analysis of data from such designs through multivariate analysis of variance models with incomplete data is described in Woolson, Leeper, and Clarke (1978).

Residuals as Measures of School Effects

A series of papers related to the performance index (PI) first proposed by Dyer (see Dyer, Linn, and Patton, 1969) incorporates comparative analyses of cross-sectional and longitudinal data in investigations of school effects. The notion of a PI is based on the argument that residuals from a regression of achievement measures on prior achievement and individual and community background variables are a useful measure of school effectiveness. That is, schools having achievement levels greater than those predicted on the basis of input measures may be regarded as effective schools. Robert Klitgaard (e.g., Klitgaard and Hall, 1977) has extended and applied procedures for the detection of these residuals. He argues that searching for average effects through correlational studies of achievement, school inputs, and student background characteristics is unlikely to detect effects of schooling. Looking for unusually effective schools by their deviation from the norm may be more productive. Certainly, such procedures require longitudinal data to accurately reflect the effects of varied inputs on educational outcomes.

Dyer, Linn, and Patton (1969) compare the results of regression analyses to form the school residuals using four types of data: (1) regression of individual-level output on individual-level inputs for a matched longitudinal sample; (2) regression of school-district-level output on school-district-level inputs (district means) on the same matched longitudinal sample; (3) regression of district-level output on district-level inputs for an unmatched longitudinal sample; and (4) regression of district-level output on district-level inputs for a cross-sectional sample. They assert that type 1 data are superior for computing the residuals. But because the cost of data collection and analysis decreases from type 1 to type 4, the discovery of a less expensive proxy for the individual-level matched longitudinal data would be extremely useful.

The originial data for type 1 and type 2 are identical. In type 2, however, district means are computed from the data on individuals, and the regression analysis is then conducted at the district level. Choices between individual-level and group-level analyses are pervasive in educational research because of the hierarchical nature of the educational system—where students receive instruction in classrooms, which are located in schools, which are grouped into school districts, and so on. The analysis of such longitudinal hierarchical data is the topic of the next section.

The data used by Dyer, Linn, and Patton (1969) contained over 10,000 individual scores for over sixty districts for pretest and posttest measures of achievement collected on fifth and eighth graders. No measures of student background characteristics were available. The achievement measure was the Iowa Tests of Basic Skills; the composite score and some subscores were analyzed. The most striking result is the large difference between the cross-sectional and longitudinal analyses. The correlation of the residuals from the individual-level matched longitudinal regression (type 1) with the residuals from the cross-sectional data (type 4) was nearly zero; the correlation based on the composite score was -0.12, and the median correlation over the subtests was -0.07. The individual-level and district-level residuals (type 1 and type 2) had a correlation above 0.90, and the correlations of both type 2 and type 3 with the cross-sectional residuals were nearly zero. Dyer, Linn, and Patton conclude that "measures when based on matched longitudinal samples are the ones most likely to provide valid measures of system effectiveness" (1969:605).

Convey (1977), Klitgaard and Hall (1977), and Marco (1974) propose, and investigate by numerical example, other residual indexes of effectiveness at various levels of analysis. Analytic comparisons of some of these indexes would be very useful in addition to analytic comparisons of results from analyses of cross-sectional and longitudinal data.

Analyses of Artificial Data on School Efffects

Luecke and McGinn (1975) provide one of the most elaborate numerical demonstrations of the problems with interpretations based on analyses of cross-sectional data. Having set out to "explore the limitations of cross-sectional data for educational policy research" (327), they conclude, "Our results are consistent with the position that cross-sectional data can tell us little about how a dynamic system has worked in the past, or how it could be made to work in the future" (347). Two sets of results based on their artificial data are presented—comparisons of correlations among variables within cross-sections over different time periods and comparisons of some methods previously employed in studies of school effects. Their paper is worth examining in detail for both its methodological import and its links to the school effects literature.

The analysis strategies investigated by Luecke and McGinn are based on the correlation between educational inputs (S) and student achievement (A), with student background characteristics (F) often partialed out. The sample partial correlation $r_{AS \cdot F}$ is the correlation of the residuals $A \cdot F$ and $S \cdot F$. The Dyer-Klitgaard methods investigate the magnitudes of residuals such as $A \cdot F$. The partial correlation will detect school effectiveness when $A \cdot F$ is systematically related to the variable(s) that are used to represent school input. However, this partial correlation may be distorted toward zero in the presence of unusually effective schools.

Luecke and McGinn generated artificial repeated cross-sections that loosely corresponded to data from a school effects study; their particular example is the Coleman Report and its relatives. Their purpose was to compare longitudinal and cross-sectional results. The data consisted of an individual Achievement outcome measure for the ith student (A_i), the Family background measure (F_i) for that student, and School quality (S_i) and Teacher quality (T_i) measures relevant to that student. Five waves of observations were generated.

Different data sets were generated that conform to four distinct structures for the data. These structures, composed of different posited relationships among the variables, are shown in Figure 4-1. For example, in the DATIND variation, F, S, and T are constrained such that each has an independent effect on A, but no effect on each other. In the DATALL variation, F is the only exogenous variable; all other possible influences are included. Luecke and McGinn speak of causal structures and draw the conventional causal arrows but then discuss correlations between variables within time periods as "direct effects." They are often not precise in distinguishing between the causal structure built into the artificial data and the observed associations that result from the operation of that causal structure over time (see, e.g., their Fig. 2, 1975:337).

Correlations within Cross-Sections. Table 4-1 presents the correlation matrices for the first and last (fifth) time periods. This evidence is the sole basis for the numerical demonstrations. Purely on the basis of these matrices, Luecke and McGinn state, "The underestimation of School over the five time periods would be

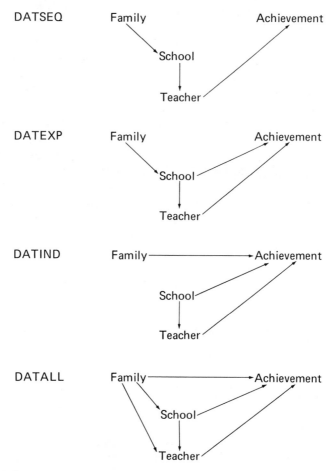

Figure 4-1. Causal relations built into each variation of the model.

Source: Luecke and McGinn, 1975. © 1975 by President and Fellows of Harvard College. Reprinted by permission.

largest if reality conformed to the DATALL model. . . . The direct effect of Family on Achievement would be exaggerated most were reality like either the DATIND or DATALL models" (1975:336). Underestimation in what sense?

The partial correlation $r_{AS \cdot F}$ is a common measure of the association between school quality and student achievement in school effects research. This partial correlation addresses the question, What is the association between School and Achievement over and above their associations with Family? For the DATALL model, where the effect of School is "underestimated," the partial corre-

Table 4–1. Correlation Matrixes at Time 1 and Time 5.

DATSEQ

	Time 1					Time 5			
F	1					1			
A	−0.01	1				0.06	1		
S	0.38	0.08	1			0.15	0.07	1	
T	0.15	0.16	0.23	1		0.08	0.14	0.25	1

DATEXP

	Time 1					Time 5			
F	1					1			
A	0.12	1				0.18	1		
S	0.39	0.29	1			0.12	0.33	1	
T	0.15	0.24	0.23	1		0.07	0.17	0.22	1

DATIND

	Time 1					Time 5			
F	1					1			
A	0.24	1				0.44	1		
S	−0.01	0.24	1			0.01	0.24	1	
T	−0.02	0.15	−0.04	1		−0.01	0.11	0.04	1

DATALL

	Time 1					Time 5			
F	1					1			
A	0.32	1				0.52	1		
S	0.38	0.38	1			0.12	0.33	1	
T	0.22	0.27	0.24	1		0.18	0.24	0.20	1

Source: Luecke and McGinn (1975).

lations are 0.29 and 0.32 at time 1 and time 5, respectively. The partial correlation actually increases slightly from the first cross-section to the last. Similarly for DATIND, where Family is supposedly "exaggerated," School seems to hold its own: $r_{AS \cdot F} = 0.25$ at the first cross-section and 0.26 at the last cross-section.

There are two serious problems with Luecke and McGinn's attempt to compare the effects of schools estimated from cross-sectional and longitudinal data. The first, as indicated in the previous paragraph, is that their artificial data do not support their conclusions. The second is that they offer no comparisons that include actual longitudinal data; within-time correlations at a later time are not equivalent to correlations between inputs at one time and educational outcomes at a later time. Judgments of the efficacy of longitudinal data and of underestimation or exaggeration should be based on the latter correlations.

Comparisons of Analysis Methods.   Luecke and McGinn present detailed numerical results obtained using three analysis strategies for cross-sectional data found in the school effects literature—that used in the Coleman Report (Coleman et al., 1966), that used in a reanalysis by Mayeske et al. (1973), and that used by Jencks and Brown (1975) in a reanalysis of the Project TALENT data. The three methods differed in ways that are unrelated to the major problem of using cross-sectional data in place of longitudinal data: the Mayeske method aggregated the family variable to the school level, and all three methods differed on the exact definition of the teacher variable and the deletion of students who changed schools. The differences among these methods illustrate that the complexities of dealing with hierarchical data in these contexts are too often overlooked.

In comparing the multiple regression analyses that correspond to the three strategies, Luecke and McGinn do begin to use the longitudinal nature of the data they generated. They employ what they call an All Information analysis—the regression of Achievement at time 5 on the five previous waves of School and Teacher measures and the initial Family measure, with eleven predictor variables in all. All Information does not appear to be the most cogent longitudinal analysis strategy. Various estimators for regression parameters when lagged independent and/or dependent variables are employed have been proposed and evaluated in the econometric literature; Luecke and McGinn used the problematic method of ordinary least squares in the All Information method. Also, the regression coefficients from All Information are somewhat difficult to interpret as only an average coefficient is reported for Teacher and School.

Differences among the three regression analyses are evident but not spectacular, and the differences are not extremely systematic. Luecke and McGinn relate the regression analyses to their "direct effect" correlations at time 1. Even the results from the longitudinal All Information method do not receive their consistent approbation. But generally All Information (and often Talent) yields results that are not inconsistent with the ordering and causal structure depicted in Figure 4-1. They conclude that statistical analyses can be highly misleading and that better data on educational processes in classrooms and schools are probably the most essential ingredient in making research more useful for educational policy decisions.

The ambiguities and difficulties in Luecke and McGinn's analyses make their work less than a clarion call for sound longitudinal analyses. A clear comparison of a longitudinal analysis with cross-sectional analyses on data with a predetermined structure would be an effective pedagogical device. Additional analyses and explication of Luecke and McGinn's data might prove useful. However, analytic results are a more useful guide for sound research practice.

A second example of analyses of artificial data on the effectiveness of schools is found in Richards (1975). Richards was interested primarily in comparing the performance of various psychometric measures of change in two-wave data (see Rogosa, 1979d) for the assessment of the correlates of change. Comparisons of cross-sectional and longitudinal analyses arise in his results by virtue of his including the simple posttest score in the comparisons of the measures of change.

To summarize the comparison, the cross-sectional data were accurate for detecting the relative effectiveness of schools when the simulation model had students assigned randomly to schools. When reality was approximated by a nonrandom assignment of students to schools of differing quality, the cross-sectional analyses were far less adequate (by Richards's measures) than any of the longitudinal methods for detecting the relative impact of schools. Richards considers measures of change computed at both the student and the school level.

Again, these results are far from definitive, and the analysis contains serious limitations and flaws. Analytic comparisons of the measures of change should have been attempted. Trustworthy results, not tenuous recommendations, should be the goal of investigations of methods for analyzing longitudinal data.

UNDERSTANDING LONGITUDINAL HIERARCHICAL DATA

Longitudinal panel data on student learning in schools have a special character. Because the educational system is structured so that students are nested within classrooms, classrooms within schools, and schools within school districts, longitudinal panel data in educational research consist of a combination of time-structured and system-structured components. Longitudinal hierarchical data is the term we use to describe data having this dual structure. The temporal and hierarchical structures are sufficiently intertwined that both temporal and areal aggregation and disaggregation need be taken into account in any successful data analysis strategy. Previous methodological and substantive research has, with few exceptions, either ignored this joint structure or dealt with it incompletely and unsuccessfully.

In this section we attempt to make some progress toward understanding longitudinal hierarchical data. We explore the structure of these data, discuss some approaches and alternatives in their analysis, and present some examples of the analysis of longitudinal hierarchical data in educational research settings.

The Structure of Longitudinal Hierarchical Data

We will consider data of the form X_{ijt}, which denotes a measurement on an attribute X made at time t $(t = 1, \ldots T)$ on person j $(j = 1, \ldots n_i)$ who is a member of group i $(i = 1, \ldots I)$. For the discussion we take the group to be a school.

A temporal decomposition of X_{ijt} that is analogous to equation (4.1) is

$$X_{ijt} = \overline{X}_{ij\bullet} + (X_{ijt} - \overline{X}_{ij\bullet}). \qquad (4.2)$$

This decomposition expresses each longitudinal observation on person j in school i as the sum of two uncorrelated components— the mean of the scores for the individual over the T time points and the deviation about that mean of the score of that individual at time t.

The standard decomposition up on which the analysis of hierarchical data is based proceeds from equation (4.2):

$$X_{ij} = \overline{X}_{i\bullet} + (X_{ij} - \overline{X}_{i\bullet}). \qquad (4.3)$$

The decomposition of X_{ij} into a school mean and a deviation about the school mean leads directly to between-school and within-school analyses (e.g., Cronbach and Webb, 1975). Since $\overline{X}_{i\cdot}$ and $(X_{ij} - \overline{X}_{i\cdot})$ are uncorrelated, equation (4.3) shows that the variance of X_{ij} may be partitioned into between-school and within-school pooled components. The between-school component ignores the within-school variance of the individual scores.

Similarly, in multivariate hierarchical data, covariances may also be partitioned, and within-group and between-group regressions can be identified. Relations among these regressions depend on the intraclass correlation of the group means (see Hannan and Burstein, 1974). Under the heading of "aggregation bias," much attention has been focused on the difference between the regression slope computed from the individual-level data (the total line) and the between-groups regression slope.

In equation (4.2), $\overline{X}_{ij\cdot}$ represents the complete temporal aggregation of X_{ijt}. Components analogous to between-group and within-group moments may be identified from the decomposition of the longitudinal data X_{ijt} in equation (4.2). A cross-sectional component can be identified by thinking of the average over time $(\overline{X}_{ij\cdot})$ as containing no temporal information. In multivariate data with an outcome variable Y, the decomposition $[Y_{ijt} = \overline{Y}_{ij\cdot} + (Y_{ijt} - \overline{Y}_{ij\cdot})]$ and equation (4.2) show that the regression of $\overline{Y}_{ij\cdot}$ on $\overline{X}_{ij\cdot}$ is a regression that ignores temporal variance, just as the between-school regression resulting from the decomposition in equation (4.3) ignores within-group variance.

Investigations of temporal aggregation and its effects on statistical analyses, which can be found in the economics literature, focus on partial temporal aggregation, as in the aggregation of monthly statistics to quarterly or annual data (see Hsiao, 1977; Laub, 1972). The temporal data are aggregated part of the way toward a cross-section, with a portion of the temporal variation retained. In cross-sectional educational data an analogous partial aggregation would be aggregation of individual student data into classroom averages. A class-level analysis preserves some within-school variation. (See Hannan [1971: ch. 3] for further discussion and examples from quantitative geography.)

The two decompositions in equations (4.2) and (4.3) are linked by identifying $\overline{X}_{ij\cdot}$ in equation (4.2) with X_{ij} in equation (4.3). The nesting of longitudinal observations which are replications of observations on individual students within observations on students which are replications of observations on schools is illustrated by the sequence of these two decompositions. This double nesting gives rise to additional approaches to longitudinal hierarchical data. For example, both individual and temporal observations can be considered replications of observations on schools. Replication by individuals is indicated in equation (4.3); replication by time point can be represented by considering observations over time on school means or school-level attributes, the $X_{i.t}$, which has within-school variance over time but not within time. A decomposition for the temporal replications on school-level variables is $X_{i.t} = X_{i..} - (X_{i.t} - X_{i..})$.

An important aspect of the structure of longitudinal panel data is the nonindependence of observations, whether they be replications over time or replications within a group. Measures on the same individual over time are not likely to be independent; autocorrelations are an intrinsic property of longitudinal data. In the same manner, students within the same school are probably more alike than are students in different schools, because of demographic factors, school policies, educational effects, and the like. The complexity of longitudinal hierarchical data arises from the interaction of these two types of nonindependence of observations.

The nonindependence of students within a group is reflected in an intraclass correlation among the X_{ij}; intraclass correlations are formally identical to autocorrelations when the longitudinal data are mapped into the hierarchical data formulation. The autocorrelation can be considered a measure of the redundancy in the longitudinal observations; an autocorrelation of one indicates no within-school, over-time variance. Intraclass correlation measures the redundancy of students with the group; perfect redundancy (intraclass of one) is the situation: If you've seen one kid (within a school) you've seen them all.

Approaches to the Analysis of Longitudinal Hierarchical Data

Two features of longitudinal panel data complicate their analysis—the multiple forms of aggregation and disaggregation that these data can assume and the complex structure of the nesting of the temporal and hierarchical components. In this section we sketch some formulations for incorporating the structure of the data into regression analyses; in the next section we present empirical examples of alternative analyses based on different decompositions of the longitudinal hierarchical data.

Pooled cross-section models facilitate the representation of the formal similarities between longitudinal panel data and hierarchical cross-sectional data and provide an approach to the analysis of longitudinal hierarchical data. Specification and estimation of pooled cross-section models for longitudinal panel data have been the focus of much technical discussion in the econometric literature (e.g., Maddala, 1971; Nerlove, 1971a, 1971b; Wallace and Hussain, 1969). Hannan and Young (1976) sketch some equivalences between hierarchical and longitudinal models which are pursued below.

We start with a standard pooled cross-section regression model for longitudinal panel data with no hierarchical structure. An individual-level model for data with an outcome variable Y and predictor variable X is:

$$Y_{jt} = \alpha + \beta X_{jt} + u_{jt}. \tag{4.4}$$

Nerlove (1971a) explicitly considers X a lagged measure of Y.

The structure of the residuals is the distinguishing feature of the model:

$$u_{jt} = \mu_j + \tau_t + \nu_{jt}, \tag{4.5}$$

where μ_j represents the time invariant effects for individual cases; τ_t represents the time-specific, case-invariant effects; and ν_{jt} represents the remaining, assumed random, disturbance. The μ_j, τ_t, and ν_{jt} are assumed to have mean zero, to be identically and independently distributed, and to be mutually uncorrelated. In much research on this model the time-specific term, τ_t, is omitted. The autocorrelation, ρ, is due to the invariance of the μ_j over time: $\rho = \sigma_\mu^2/\sigma^2$; $\sigma^2 = \sigma_\mu^2 + \sigma_\tau^2 + \sigma_\nu^2$. The μ_j may be thought of as being composed of relevant factors (constant over time) that are omitted from the model.

Hannan and Young (1976) consider a model for hierarchical data Y_{ij} and X_{ij} identical to equations (4.4) and (4.5). The τ_i are identified with causal factors that vary only between schools, and the μ_j are identified with individual factors that vary within, but not between, schools.

Estimation of these pooled cross-section models by generalized least squares (GLS) and by alternative procedures is considered by Nerlove (1971a, 1971b), Maddala (1971), Hannan and Young (1977), and others. The GLS estimation procedures can be thought of in terms of the decomposition in equation (4.1), in that the cross-sectional and longitudinal information are weighted by the quantity ρ (the measure of redundancy) in their combination. In a certain sense the GLS estimation is a combination of the two analyses indicated by the decomposition in equation (4.1).

A major analysis issue is the structure in the covariance matrix of the u_{jt}. This matrix is block-diagonal, with each block having diagonal elements equal to 1 and off-diagonal elements equal to ρ.

For the hierarchical data this error structure depicts the situation of cases within a group as being more alike than cases from different groups. The structure of this error covariance matrix is also a key quantity in the longitudinal models. This error covariance matrix reflects the lag structures presumed to operate over time. The lag structure in the pooled cross-section models is quite simple: auto-correlations are assumed constant over various time lags. More complex lag structures would undoubtedly be more realistic in many applications. Unfortunately, in most educational panel data the number of waves is rather small; consequently, complex lag structures cannot be substantiated or justified empirically.

Analyses of hierarchical longitudinal panel data require a more complex structure for the error covariance matrix. The decompositions in both equations (4.2) and (4.3) need be taken into account in constructing a model for the disturbances. This model could then be incorporated into a GLS estimation procedure of the appropriate parameters.

Pooled hierarchical cross-sections are formally equivalent to multilevel cross-sectional data. Analytic results for multilevel data—such as relations among regression parameters at many levels of analysis or bounds on grouping effects for various degrees of aggregation—could be applied directly to the relevant parameters in the pooled hierarchical cross-section model. Unfortunately, results for more than two levels of analysis are almost nonexistent. These results would also be useful for purely cross-sectional data, since multilevel structures (e.g., kids/classes/schools) are ubiquitous in educational data.

A major function of this formulation of hierarchical longitudinal data is to argue that longitudinal data cannot be profitably analyzed or interpreted without explicitly taking into account their hierarchical structure. Also, this formulation may yield important results on the distortions introduced into data analyses by the use of aggregated data. Perhaps directions of bias under plausible research settings or bounds on expected effects for temporal or hierarchical aggregation can be obtained. Analytic work is needed to explicate these issues better.

The need for such analytic work is seen from the variety of analyses that can be and are carried out on the same longitudinal hierarchical data. Analyses based on the X_{ijt} may be contrasted with analyses based on X_{ijt} averaged over time or over individuals within groups. If the X_{ijt} are aggregated to the school level over individuals, the within-school variance of individuals is ignored, and the longtiudinal data are the school means, $\overline{X}_{i.t}$. Alternatively, the temporal variation in the X_{ijt} may be discarded by averaging over time; $\overline{X}_{ij\cdot}$ are computed from the X_{ijt} and are analogous to cross-sectional data on individuals within groups. Further aggregation of the $\overline{X}_{ij\cdot}$ yields $\overline{X}_{i\cdot\cdot}$, which are analogous to cross-sectional data on schools.

Illustrations of the Analysis of Longitudinal Hierarchical Data

The empirical examples presented here illustrate the forms of longitudinal hierarchical data and the multiplicity of analyses possible with these data. The examples are drawn from two empirical approaches to the identification of school effects.

Residuals From What Line? As previously discussed, residuals from a regression of school outcomes on student background characteristics may be used as a measure of school effectiveness. Large positive residuals are taken as evidence of program effectiveness, and those schools possessing large positive residuals are deemed effective schools (Klitgaard and Hall, 1977; Dyer, Linn, and Patton, 1969). The hierarchical structure of the data gives rise to three possible regression lines for the computation of these school residuals—the between-school line, the overall student-level regression line, and a within-school pooled regression line. Examples of all three approahces are found in recent analyses.

The California Assessment Program (CAP) (California State Department of Education, 1977) uses residuals from between-school and between-district prediction equations to identify schools and districts that are either above expected performance, within a range of expected performance, or below expected performance. The CAP data are longitudinal and include information on school and district background variables and on achievement measures in mathematics and reading. These data are similar to, but more extensive than, the Michigan data analyzed by Klitgaard and Hall (1977).

As described earlier, Dyer, Linn, and Patton (1969) and Marco (1974) compare school residuals computed from school averages with those computed from individual scores and then averaged within a school. High correlations are found among these alternative measures, but Forsyth (1973) raises serious questions about their stability.

The third regression analysis strategy, that of computing individual-level residuals from a within-schools pooled regression and then averaging these residuals within a school, is found in the Jencks and Brown (1975) analysis of the Project TALENT data. Jencks and

Brown use the variability of these "mean residual" scores over schools as a measure of the differential effects of schools on student learning.

As a footnote to our consideration of these methods we should note that least-squares regression methods are not appropriate for the computation of these residuals. The adage that "least squares eats outliers" is not even comforting as a conservative bias in such methods because in being strongly affected by outliers least squares can also make "normal" data points appear to be outliers.

Mixing Levels of Analysis. Often in studies of school effects, resource and school input measures are not available for each student and can only be obtained as a school or school-district aggregate. But background and achievement measures on individual students are usually available. The hierarchical aggregation of some variables but not others is an additional twist in the variety of forms for hierarchical longitudinal data.

A common analysis procedure for assessing the effects of educational resources on student achievement is to perform a regression of individual achievement (A) on an individual background measure (B), and an aggregate measure of school resource ($\overline{S}$), commonly the school mean. The regression equation is

$$A = \beta_0 + \beta_1 \overline{S} + \beta_2 B + u.$$

The regression slope for $\overline{S}$ is used to indicate the importance of educational inputs on student achievement. Bidwell and Kasarda (1978) argue that use of $\overline{S}$ instead of an individual-level measure of school resources is incorrect conceptually and also serves to bias downward the estimated effect of resources on achievement. Rogosa (1979c) presents some analytic results to support this claim, at least in certain circumstances. Conditions were derived for the inequality $\beta_{AS \cdot B} > \beta_{A\overline{S} \cdot B}$ in terms of the grouping of students into schools. The conditions for the above inequality were seen to be plausible in many educational settings.

MODELING CHANGE: METHODS AND APPLICATIONS

One approach for utilizing longitudinal data for the analysis of the process of change is to model rates of growth or decline directly. These dynamic models of change, usually represented as a system of differential equations, express the rate of change as a function of the variables presumed to influence change. The parameters of these continuous-time models have direct interpretations in the explication of the process of change. Solutions of these differential equation models yield equations of the general form of distributed lag regression equations. As the parameters of these regression equations are (nonlinear) functions of the parameters of the dynamic change model, estimates of the parameters of the underlying dynamic change model may often be obtained from the estimates of these regression parameters.

To illustrate the formulation and interpretation of dynamic models for change, we consider an example of their application to research on school learning and school effects (Sørensen and Hallinan, 1977). In a later section, an additional example of the application of models for change is discussed which is taken from research on the organizational structure of school districts (Freeman and Hannan, 1975). In each of these studies, dynamic change models are formulated on the basis of substantive arguments, and solutions of the models yield regression equations, the parameters of which can be estimated from the data. Other applications, such as the dynamic change models for mother-child interaction developed by Thomas and Martin (1976), illustrate the usefulness of these models in psychological research.

Models for the Process of Learning in the Study of School Effects

Sørensen and Hallinan argue that conceptual issues in the definition and establishment of school effects have been underemphasized in past research: "The emphasis has been on establishing relations among variables, not on specifying the mechanisms that would produce such effects" (1977: 274). They formulate a dynamic change model for school learning in an attempt to specify the causal mechanisms that produce learning in schools. The basic premise of such a model is that "learning is a process in time: the amount of learning achieved can be registered as change over some time interval in an individual's knowledge" (275). Variation in student learning is assumed to be influenced by two broad sets of individual variables—those that determine ability and those that determine effort. The third central component in the production of learning is identified as the opportunity for learning: "Learning only takes place if there are opportunities for learning present. Variation in such opportunities will produce variation in learning independent of the abilities and efforts of the children" (276).

From these premises a model is constructed in which the rate of change in academic achievement (rate of learning) is a linear function of the ability and effort of the student (s) and the level of achievement obtained by time t, $Y(t)$. The quantity representing the ability and effort of the student is assumed to be a linear function of individual characteristics (X_i) such as IQ or family background:

$$s = a_0 + \Sigma a_i X_i. \tag{4.6}$$

Specializing to just two X_i for convenience, the continuous time model is:

$$\frac{dY(t)}{dt} = a_0 + b Y(t) + a_1 X_1 + a_2 X_2. \tag{4.7}$$

"The model mirrors a mechanism where growth in academic achievement is constrained by opportunities for learning" (Sørensen and Hallinan, 1977: 280). The central parameter in the substantive development of this model is b, a characteristic of the teaching that takes place in a school. Because b is defined as the negative reciprocal of the total amount of material covered in a period of time, variability in b over schools reflects different opportunities for learning. Sørensen and Hallinan posit that variation in this parameter over different schools determines how much inequality in achievement will be generated by schooling.

Important restrictions are built into the dynamic change model in equation (4.7). The parameters are assumed to be identical for all individuals and to be constant over time. Student characteristics (X_i) are also assumed to be constant over time. In addition, the relation in equation (4.7) is presumed to be nonstochastic; no disturbance term is included. While Sørensen and Hallinan do present some more general continuous-time models with many of these restrictions relaxed, this simple model serves to illustrate the basic features of the dynamic change model.

Since rates of change are not observable, it is necessary to solve the differential equation (4.7) in order to estimate the parameters of the model for change in learning. The solution is obtained by integrating the differential equation over time. The solution has the form (Coleman, 1968):

$$Y(t) = \alpha_0 + \beta Y(0) + \alpha_1 X_1 + \alpha_2 X_2,$$

where $\alpha_i = a_i/b \, (e^{bt} - 1)$, and $\beta = e^{bt}$.

To provide in part a test of the usefulness of this model, Sørensen and Hallinan estimate the parameters of equation (4.7) from two waves of panel data from the Project TALENT study. Of particular interest is the variability of the estimates of b over schools and the relations of the estimates of b for each school with measures of school resources. The latter quantity, given the process of learning postulated by the model, is a measure of the relation between resources and achievement.

S\o rensen and Hallinan estimate the parameters of equation (4.7) by a multiple regression of Y_2 on Y_1, X_1, and X_2 and use the relations $a_i = \alpha_i \log\beta/t(\beta - 1)$, $b = \log \beta/t$ to obtain estimates of the parameters of the dynamic change model. When school learning is represented by measures of mathematics achievement, the parameter estimates are consistent with the predictions of the model concerning the relations between opportunities for learning and school resources.

Equilibrium Assumptions and Cross-Sectional Studies

Dynamic change models also allow further comparisons of the properties of cross-sectional data and longtitudinal data. Coleman characterizes cross-sectional studies by an assumption of equilibrium:

> The cross-section analysis assumes, either implicitly or explicitly, that the causal processes have resulted in an equilibrium state. That is, the implicit assumption in regression analysis is that this is a stable relationship, which would give the same values for the regression coefficients in a later cross-section unless an exogenous factor disturbed the situation (1968:444)

In dynamic change models like equation (4.7), the assumption of equilibrium is simply that $dY(t)/dt = 0$; the system is assumed to be in a steady state.

S\o rensen and Hallinan (1977) obtain the equilibrium value in their model by letting t go to infinity in equation (4.7):

$$Y_e = -\frac{a_0}{b} - \frac{a_1}{b} X_1 - \frac{a_2}{b} X_2 .$$

In cross-sectional research, an equation of the above form is estimated. Although the ratio a_i/b can be estimated from cross-sectional data, the key parameter b cannot be estimated even when the equilibrium assumption is tenable. When the system is not in equilibrium, the parameters will diverge from this ratio. In discussing previous cross-sectional research on organizational size, Freeman and Hannan state that "repeated cross-sections from a panel of organizations which are out of equilibrium will ordinarily produce estimates varying considerably from cross-section to cross-section. Depending on which of them one takes, the results will be closer or farther from those estimated from a time-series" (1975:216).

The Luecke and McGinn (1975) paper can be considered a numerical investigation of the equilibium assumption. Using artificial data generated under alternative hypothetical causal structures (Figure 4-1), Luecke and McGinn asked whether the analysis strategies that they considered could recover the structure (i.e., the correlations or direct effects) induced at the time 1 cross-section using data from the time 5 cross-section. Discrepancies between the time 1 and time 5 correlations (or any other pair of time periods) indicate the extent of the violation of the assumption of equilibrium.

Alternative Formulations

In a commentary on the Sørensen and Hallinan analysis, Hauser asserts that "their reconceptualization of school effects is neither novel nor plausible" (1978:68). Much of Hauser's criticism stems from the equivalence of the solution of the dynamic change model with a lagged regression model of later achievement regressed on earlier achievement and background characteristics. Sørensen (1978) responds to Hauser's critique by emphasizing that the formulation of the dynamic change model and the interpretation of the basic parameters, not the mathematical form of the solution, are the distinguishing features of the Sørensen and Hallinan model. Other very different models may also yield similar regression equations, and Sørensen presents a geometrically declining distributed-lag model to demonstrate that estimates of relationships among the observed variables can lead to very different interpretations for different underlying models. The model and its substantive rationale, and not the means by which the model is fit to data, govern the interpretation of parameters and their estimates.

Models of change are novel, at least in educational research, because of their explicit investigation of the process of change. The design and analysis of longitudinal research in education would profit from an increased emphasis on the analysis of the process of change, as opposed to the traditional focus on the consequences of change.

INVESTIGATING CAUSAL FEEDBACK AND RECIPROCAL CAUSAL EFFECTS

Longitudinal data are considered crucial for the analysis of reciprocal causal effects. Typically, an assessment of reciprocal causal effects is preceded by a body of cross-sectional research studies that establish associations among the variables. Longitudinal data are then collected in an attempt to unravel the causal feedback. Examples of research on reciprocal causal effects are investigations of reciprocal influences between teacher expectation and student achievement (Humphreys and Stubbs, 1977; Crano and Mellon, 1978; West and Anderson, 1976), between self-concept and academic achievement (Purkey, 1970; Calsyn and Kenny, 1977), and between money and income (Sims, 1972). Empirical research on these and similar topics has resulted in the collection and analysis of large amounts of longitudinal panel data. However, most of the empirical research and methodological discussion has focused on the rather limited two-wave, two-variable (2W2V) panel design.

In this section a number of alternative analysis strategies for assessing reciprocal causal effects from longitudinal panel data are presented, along with empirical applications of the various procedures. The four methods to be considered are structural equation models, dynamic change models, multiple time-series models, and the method of cross-lagged correlation.

Structural Equation Models

Models for reciprocal causal effects in longitudinal panel data based on structural regression formulations were originally introduced in the path analysis literature (Duncan, 1969, 1972; Heise, 1970). In these models a causal effect is represented by the change increment to an outcome variable that results from an increment to an antecedent variable. For two variables, X and Y, the causal influences are represented by the regression parameters of the path from a prior X to a later Y and from a prior Y to a later X. This representation can be formulated for two wave or multiwave panel data. In structural regression models, X and Y may be latent variables having multiple indicators at each time point. The causal effects are represented by the regression parameters for the structural regression equations that relate the latent variables. An analysis based on a multiwave structural regression model with latent variables is presented later in this section.

Previous formulations of regression models for panel data with reciprocal causal effects have focused on models for 2W2V data (Duncan, 1969, 1972, 1975; Heise, 1970; Goldberger, 1971). For the simple 2W2V panel design the structural regression model is equivalent to a path analysis model. Figure 4–2 is a representation of a specific structural regression model for 2W2V data. This config-

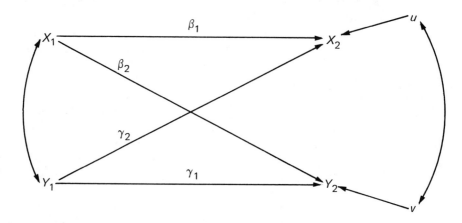

Figure 4-2. Representation of the Structural Model for Data from a 2W2V Longitudinal Panel.

uration can also be represented by the structural regression equations:

$$X_2 = \beta_0 + \beta_1 X_1 + \gamma_2 Y_1 + u;$$

$$Y_2 = \gamma_0 + \beta_2 X_1 + \gamma_1 Y_1 + v. \tag{4.8}$$

The parameters β_2 and γ_2 represented the lagged, reciprocal causal effects between X and Y and thus are of central importance in the investigation of reciprocal causal effects. The parameters β_1 and γ_1 represent the influence of a variable on itself over time. Equation (4.8) is identical to the system considered by Goldberger (1971) and by Heise (1970).

Some important restrictions on the nature of the causal influences between X and Y are built into Figure 4-2 and equation (4.8). Most important is the assumption that all causal influences are lagged; simultaneous causal influences between X_2 and Y_2 are not included. Also, assumptions of linearity and additivity of causal influences are built into this model. Duncan (1969, 1972) considers general forms of path analysis models for causal relationships in 2W2V data and also various restricted models such as Figure 4-2. One important outcome of Duncan's investigations is the illustration of the limitations of 2W2V designs. With 2W2V data, it is frequently not possible to distinguish between different underlying models. And with data that are consistent with widely differing models, the attribution of causal influences becomes very difficult.

As Duncan concludes: "No set of 2W2V data will answer a question about direction of causal influence or relative importance of causes except on some set of definite assumptions. If one wishes to avoid assumptions of the type illustrated here, the only recourse is to expand the study design beyond the limits of 2W2V" (1969:181).

Similar representations of reciprocal causal effects can be made in structural regression models for data from longitudinal panel designs far more complex than a 2W2V design. For example, multiple indicators of two latent variables (X^* and Y^*) may be available at each time point. In a 2W2V2I design, two indicators of each variable are available at both waves. In such a model, β_2 and γ_2 represent the reciprocal causal influences between the latent variables X^* and Y^*. A number of structural regression models for reciprocal causal effects in multiwave panel data with multiple indicators are constructed and discussed in Jöreskog and Sörbom (1977) and in Rogosa (1979a). These models follow the basic structure of the 2W2V models.

To illustrate the formulation of structural regression methods and their application in the study of reciprocal causal effects, an analysis of the Berkeley Growth data carried out by David Brandt, Michele Zimowski, and myself is reported. The motivation of this particular analysis is that of Crano (1977), who used the method of cross-lagged correlation (see below) to investigate reciprocal causal influences between infant behavior and infant intelligence. The data consist of four waves representing averages of the infant observations over the periods ten to twelve months, thirteen to fifteen months, eighteen to twenty-four months, and twenty-seven to thirty-six months. Observations were obtained for a mental ability measure and for seven measures of infant behavior. (The data for this analysis were kindly supplied by the Institute for Human Development, University of California, Berkeley.)

Crano found that "the factors underlying mental scores operated as causes of later behavior" (1977:147). With four waves of data, one intelligence measure, and six behavior measures (Crano discarded one of the behavior measures), thirty-six cross-lagged comparisons of behavior and intelligence were available. After adjusting these correlations for changes in reliability over time, thirty-one of these comparisons favored the conclusion that intelligence causes later behavior: seven of these thirty-one differences were statistically significant. (Most of the significant cross-lagged differences were found with speed and activity.) The serious shortcomings of the method of cross-lagged correlation are discussed in a later section. Also, Crano apparently used a within-sexes pooled correlation matrix instead of a correlation matrix for all cases in his analyses.

The structural regression analysis of the Berkeley Growth data to be described is based on the model shown in Figure 4-3. The lagged reciprocal influences between intelligence (I) and infant behavior (B) are represented by the parameters β_i and γ_i ($i = 1, \ldots 6$). Two indicators of behavior, speed (S) and activity (A), are used as indicators of the latent behavior variable in this analysis and are shown in the model. Autocorrelations of lag 1 among the unique parts of the activity measure are included in this model because these correlations were found to be important during the estimation of various structural regression models for these data. Many plausible structural models can be formulated for the data, and the model in Figure 4-3 incorporates important restrictions. The lagged causal influences are assumed to span only one time period—for example, no direct causal influences are postulated on behavior at time 3 by either intelligence at time 1 or behavior at time 1.

The strategy for investigating the reciprocal influences between intelligence and behavior consists of fitting a series of restricted models to the data and evaluating the effects of the restrictions built into these models on the ability of the model to fit the data. To investigate the reciprocal causal influences between intelligence and behavior, the fit of four models derived from the model in Figure 4-3 is considered: (1) a null model with all lagged causal paths between the variables set to zero, (2) a model with causal paths between intelligence and behavior set to zero, (3) a model with the causal paths between behavior and intelligence set to zero, and (4) a full model, the model in Figure 4-3.

Estimation of each of these models by the maximum likelihood methods of LISREL IV (Jöreskog and Sörbom, 1978) yields parameter estimates and associated statistics and an overall goodness of fit statistic for the fit of each model to the data. The goodness of fit statistics, which indicate lack of fit and thus decrease as the fit improves, are reported in Table 4-2.

Inspection of the numbers in Table 4-2 reveals that the data contain very little evidence for an influence of behavior on intelligence, since eliminating these paths from the full model produces negligible decrement in the fit of the model. A test statistic for an effect of behavior on intelligence would be the difference of the chi-square statistics for models 3 and 4 of 0.3, which would be compared with a critical value of the chi-square distribution with three degrees of freedom. The paths from intelligence to behavior appear far more important, as the decrement to the fit is significant

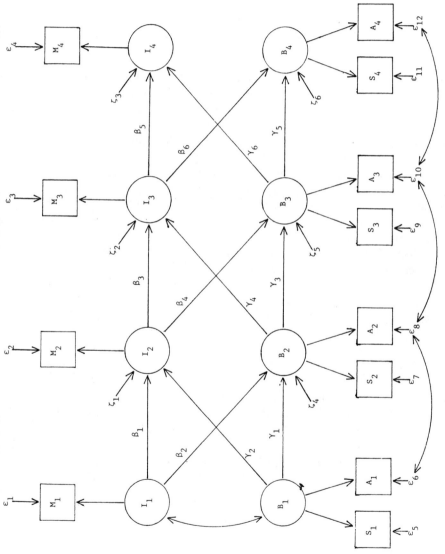

Figure 4-3. A Structural Regression Model Used in the Analysis of the Berkeley Growth Data.

Table 4–2. Estimation of Models for the Berkeley Growth Data.

Model	Chi-square Goodness of Fit Statistic
(1) null model	$\chi^2_{56} = 72.4$
(2) $B \to I$ paths only	$\chi^2_{53} = 72.1$
(3) $I \to B$ paths only	$\chi^2_{53} = 60.6$
(4) All lag 1 paths	$\chi^2_{50} = 60.3$

when these paths are constrained to be zero. Two of the three paths from I to B in Figure 4–3 are statistically significant, according to the estimated standard errors for these parameter estimates.

While this analysis illustrates a strategy for addressing some questions about reciprocal causal effects, for many of the most important questions no clear analysis procedures have been developed. Questions about the strength and duration of causal effects, stability and change in causal patterns over time, and appropriate causal lags in the design and analysis of longitudinal panel data cannot at present be comprehensively addressed by well-developed procedures. Additional discussion of the formulation and interpretation of these types of models for the investigation of reciprocal causal effects may be found in Rogosa (1979a).

Dynamic Change Models

Representation of reciprocal causal influences through models for rates of change is an alternative to the regression models for changes in levels discussed in the previous section. Representative empirical applications of models for rates of change to the study of reciprocal causal influences are the Freeman and Hannan (1975) analysis of organizational growth and decline in school districts and the Thomas and Martin (1976) analysis of mother-child interaction. (Models for change in a single variable were presented and illustrated in the previous section.)

A simple two variable dynamic change model that incorporates reciprocal influences between X and Y is:

$$\frac{dX(t)}{dt} = b_0 + b_1 X(t) + c_2 Y(t), \qquad (4.9)$$

$$\frac{dY(t)}{dt} = c_0 + c_1 Y(t) + b_2 X(t).$$

Equation (4.9) is a simple system of coupled differential equations. It stipulates that the rates of change of X and Y at any time depend linearly on the levels of X and Y. The parameters b_2 and c_2 represent the cross effects or couplings between X and Y. Note that equation (4.9) is deterministic; for our purposes this limitation is not crucial. Similar interpretations and analysis methods can be applied to models for change that include exogenous variables, stochastic components, and other generalizations. Of course, analyses based on these more general models will be more complex.

Rates of change are not directly observable. However, the solution of the system of differential equations in equation (4.9) yields equations in terms of the observable variables of the same form as equation (4.8). The cross-causal parameters β_2 and γ_2 are nonlinear functions of the time between waves and the parameters of the dynamic change model (Coleman, 1968; Kaufman, 1976). That the solution to the dynamic change model in equation (4.9) has the same form as the regression model for 2W2V data makes the two wave panel design less restrictive than it might appear. That is, the time between waves in the 2W2V design appears to limit the sensitivity and scope of the data, in that Figure 4–2 appears to presume that the interactive influences operate over discrete time intervals: indeed, if the time between observations does not correspond to the actual causal lag, it appears that this panel design may be insensitive to important causal interactions. However, the dynamic change model in equation (4.9) shows that the 2W2V data can be thought of as arising from a process in which X and Y adjust continuously to levels of X and Y during the period of observation. Thus, instead of corresponding only to the experimental lag, models for 2W2V data can be thought of as reflecting a more general process, that of causal influences and resulting adjustments that are continuous in time (Coleman, 1968; Hannan, 1978; Kaufman, 1976).

Organizational Growth and Decline.   Freeman and Hannan (1975) formulate dynamic change models for the sizes of the direct component (teachers) and the supportive component (staff) of school districts. This dynamic model of organizational demography is employed in a comparison of the effects of enrollments on organizational structures for periods of growth and decline: "It is our position that the relationship between enrollment and the direct component (teachers) should be symmetrical in growth and decline, but this should not be the case with the supportive component. Increases in enrollment should have greater effects than declines" (217).

The differential equation model for changes in the direct component (*T*) is based on the statement that "change in enrollments ought to have proportionate effects on change in number of teachers" (217):

$$\frac{dT}{dt} = a + bT + cE, \qquad (4.10)$$

where district enrollment is denoted by *E*. The rate of change of the size of the supportive component (*SUP*) is presumed to be a function of the size of the direct component and the supportive component:

$$\frac{dSUP}{dt} = d + eSUP + fT. \qquad (4.11)$$

The major hypothesis in the Freeman and Hannan study is that the parameters of equation (4.10) are the same for school districts that are growing (enrollment increasing) and for school districts that are declining (enrollment decreasing) and that the parameters of equation (4.11) differ for growers and decliners. If estimates of the parameters of equations (4.10) and (4.11) were obtained for subsamples of districts classified as growers and of districts classified as decliners, the tenability of this hypothesis could be evaluated. For technical reasons, instead of estimating the parameters of equations (4.10) and (4.11), Freeman and Hannan estimate the analogous parameters of the solution of this system of differential equations. The solution has the form of a system of lagged regression equations (Kaufman, 1976). Data from 805 California school districts were found by Freeman and Hannan to be consistent with their hypothesis.

Multiple Time-Series Models

In econometrics the detection of reciprocal causal effects from time-series data has attracted considerable interest. Sims's (1972) analysis of the reciprocal causal influences of money stock and income is the best known example of this work. Sims was primarily interested in establishing the validity of the practice of making causal interpretations from distributed lag regressions of income on money. These causal interpretations are invalid if a reciprocal causal influence of income to money exists, because the logic and statistical assumptions underlying the regression analysis depend on unidirectional influences of money to income.

The statistical procedures used by Sims were derived from the definitions of Granger (1969). These definitions of causality are based on predictability criteria. Loosely speaking, one time series, say $X(t)$, is said to cause another time series, $Y(t)$, if present Y can be predicted better using past values of X than by not using past values of X, other relevant information (including past values of Y) being used in both cases. This notion can be formalized by the following definitions. Let $[A_t]$ be the set of all relevant information ($t = 0, \pm 1 \ldots$), including at least the two time series $[(X_t, Y_t)]$. The set of all relevant information prior to time t is denoted by $\overline{A}_t = [A: s < t]$. The set of all relevant information prior to and including time t is denoted by $\overline{\overline{A}}_t = [A: s \leqslant t]$; $\overline{X}_t$, $\overline{\overline{X}}_t$, $\overline{Y}_t$, and $\overline{\overline{Y}}_t$ are defined in the same way. Also let $A_t - X_t$ be the set of elements in A_t without the element X_t.

Define $\sigma^2(Y|B)$ as the mean square error of the minimum square error prediction of Y_t, given the set of information in B. Then X causes Y if $\sigma^2(Y|A) < \sigma^2(Y|\overline{A} - \overline{X})$—that is, the prediction of Y using prior X is more accurate than the prediction without using X. Feedback is said to occur if $\sigma^2(Y|\overline{A}) < \sigma^2(Y|\overline{A} - \overline{X})$, and $\sigma^2(X|\overline{A}) < \sigma^2(X|\overline{A} - \overline{Y})$. Feedback is equivalent to what we term "lagged reciprocal causation." Also, X causes Y instantaneously if $\sigma^2(Y|\overline{A}, \overline{\overline{X}}) < \sigma^2(Y|\overline{A})$.

Pierce and Haugh (1977) classify 256 (2^8) possible patterns of causal influence that arise from eight forms of causal influences representing the presence or absence of X causes Y, Y causes X, and instantaneous causation. They present an array of data analysis procedures for detecting these events, all essentially based on the correlations of residuals across variables from the separately filtered time series.

In Sims's analysis the condition for unidirectional causality is expressed: "If and only if causality runs one way from current and past values of some list of exogenous variables to a given endogenous variable, then in a regression of the endogenous variable on past, current, and future values of the exogenous variables, the future values of the exogenous variables should have zero coefficients" (1972:541). That is, if we denote money at time t by Y_t and income by X_t, then the $\gamma_i = 0$ in the equation:

$$Y_t = \sum_{k=0} \beta_k X_{t-k} + \sum_{k=1} \gamma_k X_{t+k} + \epsilon_t,$$

where the summations are over the duration of the lag employed and the extent of the data, respectively. From this analysis no influence in the direction of income to money (income measured as GNP) was detected. Sims (1972) states and proves two theorems that relate his empirical procedure to Granger's conditions and employs a conventional F-test in distributed lag estimation for the statistical significance of the $\hat{\gamma}_i$ as the criterion for the determination of univariate causality. Hosoya (1977) proves that the causality conditions developed by Sims apply to more general bivariate processes.

Another example of the analysis of causal effects in multiple time-series data is Pierce's (1977) analysis of the relationship between money and interest rates—an analysis in which a surprising lack of relationship was found. In fact, the most striking result from a number of empirical analyses based on these methods for detecting causal effects in multiple time series is the apparent weakness of the causal effects. "In studies of cross relations among economic time series, once proper account is taken of serial correlation, many pairs of variables which one might have thought would show some relation are in fact not 'significantly' related according to hypothesis tests at standard significance levels" (Sims, 1977:23). Pierce (1977) attempts to reconcile this finding with the basic economic fact that the relationships examined do exist. He contends that the problem lies in the rather small variation, the relative insensitivity, and the likely fallibility of the available economic indicators:

> Our belief is that while most likely there are very strong economic relationships between these variables, they are perhaps inherently not verifiable, empirically, at least using recent-period data on the U.S. economy. Our description of the situation may be summed-up with the statement, "The economy is a miserable experimental design." (Pierce, 1977:20)

Educational researchers should feel some sympathy for the economists' troubles, as the educational system is a far from optimal experimental design. For example, researchers look for school effects even though it is estimated that over 75 percent of the variance is within schools and that school inputs for the individual students can be only crudely assessed at the level of schools and school districts. Upon application of these methods to data on educational outcomes, a forewarning of unspectacular results might be in order. Relationships found to be strong in cross-sectional or limited longitudinal designs may vanish under closer scrutiny and more elaborate analysis. Such a result might be more an indication of the inadequacy of the measures and design in these research studies than of an educational phenomenon (or lack thereof).

Because longitudinal panel data can be viewed as a collection of many short time series, the definitions and procedures for detecting causal effects in econometric time series have some potential for application in analyses of longitudinal panel data. At least four important differences between the econometric investigations and the "typical" longitudinal panel investigation of reciprocal causal effects in educational research are apparent. The first and most obvious difference is that of design; in the longitudinal panel design, the amount of temporal information gathered on any individual is not sufficient for the application of the econometric time-series methods. Second, the (acknowledged) presence of errors of measurement in psychological and sociological data and the concomitant emphasis on multiple measures of important variables serve to differentiate between the panel data commonly gathered in educational research and the econometric time-series data. Third, the substantive knowledge and certainty about the appropriate causal specification assumed in Granger's definitions (and plausible in some econometric settings) is lacking in most areas of educational research. Fourth, the goal of the analysis—for example, Sims's desire to establish unidirectional causality—will differ in different substantive settings; in many of the settings in which longitudinal panel data are gathered, questions of the duration, strength, and variability over time of the reciprocal causal influences are of primary interest.

With these differences in mind, some adaptations of the time-series definitions of causality to longitudinal panel data are worth noting. The conditions are particularly simple for 2W2V data. For example, the condition for X causes Y for the 2W2V model in equation (4.8) can be expressed as a relation between the population multiple correlations: $\overline{R}^2_{Y_2 \cdot Y_1, X_1} > \overline{R}^2_{Y_2 \cdot Y_1}$. This inequality is satisfied when $\rho^2_{Y_2(X_1 \cdot Y_1)} > 0$. That condition is satisfied if and only if $\beta_2 \neq 0$. Also, the condition for Y causes X is that $\gamma_2 \neq 0$. And the condition for feedback is that both β_2 and γ_2 are nonzero.

For models of multiwave panel data, these definitions of causal effects are satisfied whenever a nonzero causal path between the variables exists. Although much of the sophistication of the time-series formulation is lost when these definitions of causality are adapted to longitudinal panel data, it is useful to see that these definitions are consistent with the representations of reciprocal causal effects for longitudinal panel data developed in previous sections.

The Method of Cross-lagged Correlation
The method of cross-lagged correlzation is currently the most popular procedure in psychological and educational research for

making causal inferences from longitudinal panel data. Most often cross-lagged correlation is applied to determine a predominant causal influence—a causal "winner."

Users of the method of cross-lagged correlation often make enthusiastic claims. For example, Crano and Mellon assert: "With the introduction of the cross-lagged panel correlation method, causal inferences based on correlational data obtained in longitudinal panel studies can be made and enjoy the same logical status as those derived in the more standard experimental settings" (1978:41). Although technical deficiencies of cross-lagged correlation have been noted (Bohrnstedt, 1969; Duncan, 1969; Goldberger, 1971; Heise, 1970), its use is still widely recommended (Calsyn and Kenny, 1977; Crano, 1977; Humphreys and Stubbs, 1977; Kenny, 1975).

Nonetheless, the method of cross-lagged correlation is not a useful procedure for the analysis of longitudinal panel data. Rogosa (1979b) provides a detailed critique and an enumeration of the many logical and technical shortcomings of cross-lagged correlation. Rogosa (1979a) presents a number of empirical applications of cross-lagged correlation, and Rogosa (1979b) discusses additional problems with conventional applications of the method.

Figure 4-4 is the diagram that accompanies expositions of the method of cross-lagged correlation. The figure presents the population correlations among the variables in a 2W2V panel design. The population cross-lagged correlations are $\rho_{X_1 Y_2}$ and $\rho_{Y_1 X_2}$. The within-time period, between variable correlations $\rho_{X_1 Y_1}$ and $\rho_{X_2 Y_2}$, are called the synchronous correlations (e.g., Kenny, 1973). The between-time correlations of the same variable, $\rho_{X_1 X_2}$ and $\rho_{Y_1 Y_2}$, are called the stabilities of the variable.

The attribution of a predominant causal influence is based on the difference of the cross-lagged correlations, $\rho_{X_1 Y_2} - \rho_{Y_1 X_2}$. If the

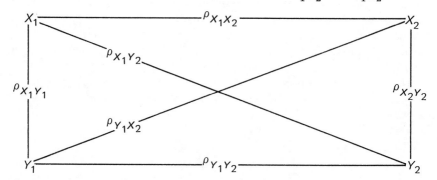

Figure 4-4. The array of population correlations in a 2W2V panel.

data indicate that $\rho_{X_1 Y_2} - \rho_{Y_1 X_2}$ is positive, the predominant causal influence is concluded to be in the direction of X causing Y. If the data indicate that $\rho_{X_1 Y_2} - \rho_{Y_1 X_2}$ is negative, the predominant causal influence is concluded to be in the direction of Y causing X. Usually, attributions of predominant causal influences are made only when the difference of the sample cross-lagged correlations is statistically significant.

When a statistically significant difference between the sample cross-lagged correlations is not obtained, the usual interpretation is that no direct causal influences exist between X and Y—either the two variables have no functional relationship or a common causal influence is responsible for the observed associations between them. Kenny (1975) emphasizes the latter interpretation, which he terms "a null hypothesis of spuriousness."

A major problem with the method of cross-lagged correlation is the lack of explicit definition of what a causal effect of one variable on another is presumed to be. Without a clearly defined quantity to be estimated, it is not surprising that serious confusions result when this method is applied to longitudinal panel data. Also, the logic of emphasizing the determination of a preponderant causal influence is questionable. This is simply not the right approach. The recognition that many social and developmental processes are reciprocal renders this sort of conclusion not of supreme importance. Measures of the strength and duration of the reciprocal relationship and the specific causal effects are far more informative.

The technical deficiencies of the method of cross-lagged correlation can be demonstrated by comparing the difference of the cross-lagged correlations with the definitions of reciprocal causal effects developed in the preceding sections. For 2W2V panels, the difference of the population cross-lagged correlations can be written:

$$\rho_{X_1 Y_2} - \rho_{Y_1 X_2} = \left(1 - \rho_{X_1 Y_1}^2 \right) \left\{ \beta_2 \left[\frac{\sigma_{X_1}}{\sigma_{Y_2}} \right] - \gamma_2 \left[\frac{\sigma_{Y_1}}{\sigma_{X_2}} \right] \right\} \quad (4.12)$$

$$+ \rho_{X_1 Y_1} \left(\rho_{Y_1 Y_2} - \rho_{X_1 X_2} \right).$$

In terms of standardized versions of the structural parameters (β^* and γ^*), equation (4.12) can also be written:

$$\rho_{X_1 Y_2} - \rho_{Y_1 X_2} = \left(1 - \rho_{X_1 Y_1}^2 \right) \left(\beta_2^* - \gamma_2^* \right) + \rho_{X_1 Y_1} \left(\rho_{Y_1 Y_2} - \rho_{X_1 X_2} \right)$$

$$= (\beta_2^* - \gamma_2^*) + \rho_{X_1 Y_1} (\gamma_1^* - \beta_1^*).$$

The difference of the cross-lagged correlations is a mixture of the difference of the parameters β_2 and γ_2 (representing lagged causal influences between X and Y) and the difference of the stabilities of X and Y, $\rho_{X_1 X_2}$ and $\rho_{Y_1 Y_2}$. An estimate of the difference of the cross-lagged correlations is not an estimate of a quantity that is directly interpretable. Consequently, the meaning of testing whether this estimate significantly differs from zero is far from clear.

Based on the relations above, Rogosa (1979b) presents numerical examples and detailed discussion of the problems with interpretation of the difference of the cross-lagged correlations. One way of summarizing these results is to say that when there are no reciprocal causal effects, the difference of the cross-lagged correlations may be small or may be large; and when there are considerable reciprocal causal effects (balanced or dominant), the difference of the cross-lagged correlations may be small or may be large. A zero difference of the cross-lagged correlations is consistent with large reciprocal causal influences (balanced or unbalanced) and with small or non-existent causal influences between the variables. Also, it is quite possible that the method of cross-lagged correlation will indicate a causal predominance opposite to that of the actual causal structure of the data. The method of cross-lagged correlation does not provide dependable information as to the causal structure underlying the data.

Methodological expositions of cross-lagged correlation sometimes discuss that equality of the synchronous correlations ($\rho_{X_1 Y_1} = \rho_{X_2 Y_2}$) is a necessary (but not sufficient) condition for the assumption of stationarity implicit in the factor analysis model underlying the method of cross-lagged correlation. We note that incorporating this condition into the analysis of equation (4.12) does not provide any additional justification for interpretation of the difference of the cross-lagged correlations as indicating a predominant causal influence.

It is important to point out that the assumption of equal synchronous correlations is an assumption of equilibrium, as discussed earlier. It seems counter-productive to collect longitudinal data and then make a major restrictive assumption that characterizes cross-sectional studies. Also, especially in developmental studies, this assumption is likely to be violated (e.g., Clarke-Stewart, 1973). In practice, the assumption is rarely examined.

The extension of the method of cross-lagged correlation to multiwave longitudinal panel data consists of the comparison of cross-lagged correlations from all possible two-wave combinations (see

Calsyn and Kenny, 1977; Crano, 1977). Multiple waves of data are considered replications of 2W2V patterns, and thus data with T waves of observations are analyzed as $\binom{T}{2}$ two-wave pieces. This strategy represents a rather short-sighted view of the value of temporal information. Using multiple waves to replicate two-wave patterns assumes a static pattern of causal influences over time. This thinking rules out investigation of patterns of change in causal influences and makes nearly impossible the discovery of many plausible patterns of causal influence that cannot be clearly detected from the series of two-wave snapshots.

The usual practice in multiwave, multivariable analyses is to tally the statistically significant differences between the cross-lagged correlations in both directions; the preponderant causal influence is awarded to the variable with the greater number of significant differences in the appropriate direction. Rogosa (1979b) demonstrates that over and above the problems with the interpretation of the difference of the cross-lagged correlations in 2W2V data, the strategy of replication of cross-lagged patterns through the use of additional waves is more likely to generate confusion than corroboration.

The Crano (1977) analysis of the Berkeley Growth data using the method of cross-lagged correlation was considered in the introduction to the structural regression analysis of those data. To illustrate the widespread use of cross-lagged correlation and, more important, the widespread interest in and importance of reciprocal causal effects for educational research, applications of cross-lagged correlation in three educational research settings are sketched below.

Teacher Expectancy. Two recent applications of the method of cross-lagged correlation have addressed the question, Do teacher expectations cause student achievement or does student achievement cause teacher expectations? Crano and Mellon (1978) analyze data from a four-wave longitudinal panel consisting of observations on 4,300 British elementary school children. They find that "teacher's expectations caused children's performance to an extent appreciably exceeding that to which performance influenced expectations" (47). Humphreys and Stubbs (1977) analyzed data from a three-wave longitudinal panel on approximately 6,000 Canadian high school students. The cross-lagged comparisons that they examined "show very strong evidence for grades causing expectations rather than the reverse effect" (269). These two analyses thus add a new dimension of confusion to this debate.

Self-concept and Achievement. A reanalysis of data from a five-wave longitudinal panel design that included measures of self-concept and academic achievement was reported by Calsyn and Kenny (1977). The original study included data collected on 556 adolescents over a five year span. Data from this five-wave panel were analyzed by the method of cross-lagged correlation in order to investigate the causal influences of academic achievement and self-concept. For the females in the sample, multiple comparisons of the cross-lagged correlations led Calsyn and Kenny to conclude that grade point average is causally predominant over self-concept of ability. This conclusion was not supported by the data on the males in the study.

An interesting complication in Calsyn and Kenny's analysis was their attempt to test the validity of the self-enhancement model, which predicts that perceived evaluation of others causes self-evaluation that in turn causes academic achievement. Measures of the perceived evaluations of teachers, parents, and friends were included in the original study. Using cross-lagged correlations, Calsyn and Kenny found little support for this model. More support was found for a skill-development model in which academic achievement causes both self-concept and perceived evaluation of others. Analyses of alternative causal models for these longitudinal data (see Rogosa, 1979a) incorporating the alternative causal orderings posited by the alternative theories may yet yield useful information about the relative validities of the self-enhancement and skill development models.

Influence on Cognitive Growth. Atkin, Bray, Davison, Herzberger, Humphreys, and Selzer (1977) presented a complex method for estimating cross-lagged correlations when there are many measures of each variable. They reanalyzed the ETS growth data (Hilton, 1969) and considered data from two waves, grades five and eleven, for the sixteen cognitive tests administered in the study. The featured result of their analysis was a comparison of the Listening test (an aural comprehension test) with an Intellectual Composite formed from the remaining fifteen measures. Because the correlation (0.73) between Listening at grade five and the Intellectual Composite at grade eleven was larger than the correlation (0.60) between Listening at grade eleven and the Intellectual Composite at grade five, Atkin et al. suggested that "individual differences on the measure of aural comprehension was causally related to later intellectual development" (1977:947).

The stabilities of the two variables differed considerably—0.86 for the Intellectual Composite and 0.62 for Listening. Thus the difference of the cross-lagged correlations may not accurately reflect the relative magnitudes of the underlying structural parameters. Unfortunately, Atkin et al. did not report the relevant variances, and thus only estimates of the standardized structural parameters β_2^* and γ_2^* can be calculated. This calculation yields a result in conflict with that of Atkin et al.—the estimates of β_2^* and γ_2^* are 0.20 and 0.28, respectively, when Listening is identified with X and the Intellectual Composite with Y in Figure 4-2. Thus if an attribution of preponderant causal effect must be made from these data, it should be opposite from that of Atkin et al. At the very least, this conflict in results renders equivocal their causal attributions.

SUMMARY AND DISCUSSION

A large number of important topics were not explicitly discussed in this chapter. Perhaps foremost among them is measurement error. A reasonable case could be made that measurement error overshadows many of the concerns here—that is, that the biases resulting from analyses of fallible data exceed distortions resulting from use of cross-sectional data as a proxy for longitudinal data or from inadequate analyses of longitudinal data. Coleman (1968) explicitly addresses fallible variables in the formulation and analysis of dynamic change models. Duncan (1975), Jöreskog and Sörbom (1977), Werts, Jöreskog, and Linn (1971), Wheaton et al (1977), Wiley and Hornik (1973), and Wiley and Wiley (1970) formulate measurement models and discuss likely effects of measurement error in analyses of longitudinal panel data. The structural regression methods that incorporate latent variables and their fallible indicators developed by Jöreskog and his associates provide useful estimation techniques (Jöreskog and Sörbom, 1977) that allow for prespecified patterns of measurement error.

Problems of measurement error in two-wave longitudinal data have been discussed extensively in the literature on the analysis of simple gain and change scores. The analysis of change (as summarized in Cronbach and Furby, 1970; and in Linn and Slinde 1977) is reviewed with an emphasis on the application of measures of change to multiwave panel data in Rogosa (1979d).

The interaction of biases from the analysis of fallible data and of biases from analysis of cross-sectional data is an interesting technical question. In the aggregation literature, aggregation is sometimes seen as a form of disattenuation (e.g., Aigner and Goldfeld, 1974). A resultant speculation is whether this notion is at all viable for temporal aggregation. Are longitudinal analyses more distorted by errors of measurement than are analyses of cross-sectional data?

Another topic that merits detailed treatment is the use of novel outcome measures in studies of educational systems. Brown and Saks (1975) employ within-group standard deviations as outcome measures for educational effects. The substantive arguments for the efficacy of such measures certainly warrant investigation of their analytic properties in cross-sectional and longitudinal data.

Throughout this chapter unsolved methodological problems have been given greater attention than procedures that are well developed and soundly applied. Several topics in analysis of variance with repeated measures fall in this category. Also, we have essentially ignored many potential applications of standard time-series methods (e.g., Fuller, 1976; Glass, Willson, and Gottman, 1975) by focusing attention on longitudinal panel designs. In panels, the number of waves is almost always insufficient for the usual time-series methods. Careful analysis of lag structures is also precluded by this lack of large numbers of repeated observations.

A better survey of data analysis practice would also be useful. In general, it seems that longitudinal data are often not analyzed much differently from cross-sectional data; regrettably, many of the important properties and opportunities that longitudinal panel data present for answering difficult questions in educational research are overlooked. This is not surprising, since much of the methodological advice offered to the educational research community has been far from comprehensive.

In his papers on longitudinal panel data, O.D. Duncan has stressed that the analysis of longitudinal panel data cannot be reduced to a mechanical procedure that produces trustworthy inferences about the causal structures that generate the data. A minimal requirement for success in this objective is the formulation of explicit (and often specialized) models for the causal processes in which careful attention is given to substantive considerations and peculiarities. This sentiment is echoed by Bielby and Hauser: "There are no stock or universal models for analyzing panel data" (1977:148). Unfortunately, in the educational research literature, methodological advice and demonstrations have been based on (often unsound) generalizations produced by limited numerical examples. Too little effort and too few resources have been allocated to careful problem formulation and the generation of trustworthy analytic results. This chapter represents an attempt at a formulation of some approaches to the analysis of longitudinal panel data with reference to what we know, what we want, what is known but has not been exploited, what we do not know, and what we may never know.

REFERENCES

Aigner, D.J., and S.M. Goldfeld. 1974. "Estimation and Prediction from Aggregate Data When Aggregates Are Measured More Accurately than Their Components." *Econometrica* 42:113-34.

Atkin, R.; R. Bray; M. Davison; S. Herzberger; L. Humphreys; and U. Selzer. 1977. "Cross-Lagged Panel Analysis of Sixteen Cognitive Measures at Four Grade Levels." *Child Development* 48:944-52.

Baltes, P.B. 1968. "Longitudinal and Cross-Sectional Sequences in the Study of Age and Generation Effects." *Human Development* 11:145-71.

Bidwell, C.E., and J.D. Kasarda. 1978. "Conceptualizing and Measuring the Effects of Schools and Schooling." University of Chicago. Unpublished.

Bielby, W.T., and Hauser, R.M. 1977. "Structural Equation Models." *Annual Review of Sociology* 3:137-61.

Bohrnstedt, G.W. 1969. "Observations on the Measurement of Change." In *Sociological Methodology 1969*, edited by E.F. Boratta, pp. 113-33. San Francisco: Jossey-Bass.

Brown, B.W., and D.H. Saks. 1975. "The Production and Distribution of Cognitive Skills within Schools." *Journal of Political Economy* 83:571-93.

Bryk, A.S., and H.I. Weisberg. 1977. "Use of the Nonequivalent Control Group Design When Subjects Are Growing." *Psychological Bulletin* 84:950-62.

California State Department of Education. 1977. *Technical Report of the California Assessment Program*. Sacramento: Department of Education.

Calsyn, R.J., and D.A. Kenny. 1977. "Self-Concept of Ability and Perceived Evaluation of Others: Cause or Effect of Academic Achievement?" *Journal of Educational Psychology* 69:136-45.

Campbell, D.T., and A. Erlebacher. 1970. "How Regression Artifacts in Quasi-Experimental Evaluations Can Mistakenly Make Compensatory Education Look Harmful." In *Compensatory Education: A National Debate*, vol. 3: *The Disadvantaged Child*, edited by J. Hellmuth, pp. 185-210. New York: Brunner/Mazel.

Clarke-Stewart, K.A. 1973. "Interactions Between Mothers and Their Young Children: Characteristics and Consequences." *Monographs of the Society for Research in Child Development* 38 (serial no. 153).

Coleman, J.S. 1968. "The Mathematical Study of Change." In *Methodology in Social Research*, edited by H.M. Blalock and A.B. Blalock, pp. 428-78. New York: McGraw-Hill.

Coleman, J.S.; E.Q. Campbell; C.J. Hobson; J. McPartland; A.M. Mood; F.D. Weinfield; and R.L. York. 1966. *Equality of Educational Opportunity*. Washington, D.C.: Government Printing Office.

Convey, J.J. 1977. "Determining School Effectiveness Following a Regression Analysis." *Journal of Educational Statistics* 2:27-39.

Crano, W.D. 1977. "What Do Infant Mental Tests Test? A Cross-Lagged Panel Analysis of Selected Data from the Berkeley Growth Study." *Child Development* 48:144-51.

Crano, W.D., and P.M. Mellon. 1978. "Causal Influence of Teachers' Expectations on Children's Academic Performance: A Cross-Lagged Panel Analysis." *Journal of Educational Psychology* 70:39-49.

Cronbach, L.J., and L. Furby. 1970. "How Should We Measure 'Change'— Or Should We?" *Psychological Bulletin* 74:68–80.

Cronbach, L.J., and N. Webb. 1975. "Between-Class and Within-Class Effects in a Reported Aptitude X Treatment Interaction: Reanalysis of a Study by G.L. Anderson." *Journal of Educational Psychology* 67:717–27.

Damon, A. 1965. "Discrepancies between Findings of Longitudinal and Cross-Sectional Studies in Adult Life: Physique and Physiology." *Human Development* 8:16–22.

Duncan, O.D. 1969. "Some Linear Models for Two-Wave, Two-Variable Panel Analysis." *Psychological Bulletin* 72:177–82.

———. 1972. "Unmeasured Variables in Linear Models for Panel Analysis." In *Sociological Methodology 1972*, edited by H.L. Costner, pp. 36–82. San Francisco: Jossey-Bass.

———. 1975. "Some Linear Models for Two-Wave, Two-Variable Panel Analysis with One-Way Causation and Measurement Error." In *Quantitative Sociology*, edited by H.M. Blalock et al., pp. 285–306. New York: Academic Press.

Dyer, H.S. 1972. "Some Thoughts About Future Studies." In *On Equality of Educational Opportunity*, edited by F. Mosteller and D.P. Moynihan, pp. 384–422. New York: Random House.

Dyer, H.S.; R.L. Linn; and M.J. Patton. 1969. "A Comparison of Four Methods of Obtaining Descrepancy Measures Based on Observed and Predicted School System Means on Achievement Tests." *American Educational Research Journal* 6:591–605.

Forsyth, R.A. 1973. "Some Empirical Results Related to the Stability of Performance Indicators in Dyer's Student Change Model of an Educational System." *Journal of Educational Measurement* 10:7–2.

Freeman, J., and M.T. Hannan. 1975. "Growth and Decline Processes in Organizations." *American Sociological Review* 40:215–28.

Fuller, W.A. 1976. *Introduction to Statistical Time Series.* New York: John Wiley and Sons.

Glass. G.V.; V.L. Willson; and J.M. Gottman. 1975. *Design and Analysis of Time-Series Experiments.* Boulder: Colorado Associate University Press.

Goldberger, A.S. 1971. "Econometrics and Psychometrics: A Survey of Communalities." *Psychometrika* 36:83–105.

Goulet, L.R. 1975. "Longitudinal and Time-Lag Designs in Educational Research: An Alternative Sampling Model." *Review of Educational Research* 45:505–23.

Granger, C.W.J. 1969. "Investigating Causal Relations by Econometric Models and Cross-Spectral Methods." *Econometrica* 37:424–38.

Griliches, Z. 1977. "Estimating the Returns to Schooling: Some Economic Problems." *Econometrica* 45:1–22.

Hannan, M.T. 1971. *Aggregation and Disaggregation in Sociology.* Lexington, Mass.: D.C. Heath.

———. 1978. "Issues in Panel Analysis of National Development: A Methodological Overview." In *National Development and the World System: Educational, Economic and Political Change, 1950-70*, edited by J.W. Meyer and M.T. Hannan, pp. 17–33. Chicago: University of Chicago Press.

Hannan, M.T., and L. Burstein. 1974. "Estimation from Grouped Observations." *American Sociological Review* 39:374-92.

Hannan, M.T., and A.A. Young. 1976. "On Certain Similarities in Estimation of Multi-Wave Panels and Multi-Level Cross-Sections." Paper presented at the Conference on Methodology for Aggregating Data in Educational Research, Stanford University, Obtober 23-24.

———. 1977. "Estimation in Panel Models: Results on Pooling Cross-Sections and Time Series." In *Sociological Methodology 1972*, edited by D.R. Heise, pp. 52-83. San Francisco: Jossey-Bass.

Hauser, R.M. 1978. "On 'A Reconceptualization of School Effects.' " *Sociology of Education* 51:68-72.

Heise, D.R. 1970. "Causal Inference from Panel Data." In *Sociological Methodology 1970*, edited by E.F. Borgatta and G.W. Bohrnstedt. San Francisco: Jossey-Bass.

Hibbs, D.A., Jr. 1977. "On Analyzing the Effects of Policy Interventions: Box-Jenkins and Box-Tiao vs. Structural Equation Models." In *Sociological Methodology 1977*, edited by D.R. Heise, pp. 137-79. San Francisco: Jossey-Bass.

Hilton, T.L. 1969. "Growth Study Annotated Bibliography." Progress Report 69-11. Princeton, N.J.: Educational Testing Service.

Hilton, T.L., and C. Patrick. 1970. "Cross-Sectional versus Longitudinal Data: An Empirical Comparison of Mean Differences in Academic Growth." *Journal of Educational Measurement* 7:15-24.

Hosoya, Y. 1977. "On the Granger Condition for Non-Causality." *Econometrica* 45:1735-36.

Hsiao, C. 1977. "Linear Regression Using Both Temporally Aggregated and Temporally Disaggregated Data." Technical Report no. 251, Economics Series, Institute for Mathematical Studies in the Social Sciences, Stanford University.

Humphreys, L.G., and J. Stubbs. 1977. "A Longitudinal Analysis of Teacher Expectation, Student Expectation, and Student Achievement." *Journal of Educational Measurement* 14:261-70.

Jencks, C., and M. Brown. 1975. "Effects of High Schools on Their Students." *Harvard Educational Review* 45:273-324.

Jöreskog, K.G., and D. Sörbom. 1977. "Some Models and Estimation Methods for Analysis of Longitudinal Data." In *Latent Variables in Socioeconomic Models*, edited by D.J. Aigner and A.S. Goldberger, ch. 16. Amsterdam: North Holland Publishing Company.

———. 1978. "LISREL: Estimation of Linear Structural Equation Systems by Maximum Likelihood Methods." Chicago: International Educational Services.

Kaufman, R.L. 1976. "The Solution and Interpretation of Differential Equation Models." *American Sociological Review* 41:746-47.

Kenny, D.A. 1973. "Cross-Lagged and Synchronous Common Factors in Panel Data." In *Structural Equation Models in the Social Sciences*, edited by A.S. Goldberger and O.D. Duncan, pp. 153-65. New York: Seminar Press.

———. 1975. "Cross-Lagged Panel Correlation: A Test for Spuriousness." *Psychological Bulletin* 72:887-903.

Klitgaard, R.E., and G.R. Hall. 1977. "A Statistical Search for Unusually Effective Schools." In *Statistics and Public Policy*, edited by W.B. Fairley and F.M. Mosteller, pp. 51–86. Reading, Mass.: Addison-Wesley.

Kuh, E. 1959. "The Validity of Cross-Sectionally Estimated Behavior Equations in Time-Series Applications." *Econometrica* 27:197–214.

Kuhlen, R.G. 1963. "Age and Intelligence: The Significance of Cultural Change in Longitudinal vs. Cross-Sectional Findings." *Vita Humana* 6:113–24.

Laub, P.M. 1972. "Some Aspects of the Aggregation Problem in the Dividend-Earnings Relationship." *Journal of the American Statistical Association* 67:552–59.

Linn, R.L., and J.A. Slinde. 1977. "The Determination of the Significance of Change between Pre- and Posttesting Periods." *Review of Educational Research* 47:121–50.

Luecke, D.F., and N.F. McGinn. 1975. "Regression Analyses and Education Production Functions: Can They Be Trusted?" *Harvard Educational Review* 45:325–50.

Maddala, G.S. 1971. "The Use of Variance Components Models in Pooling Cross-Section and Time-Series Data." *Econometrica* 39:341–58.

Marco, G.L. 1974. "A Comparison of Selected School Effectiveness Measures Based on Longitudinal Data." *Journal of Educational Measurement* 11:225–34.

Mayeske, G.W.; T. Okoda; A.E. Beaton, Jr.; W.M. Cohen; and C.E. Wisler. 1973. *A Study of the Achievement of Our Nation's Students.* Washington, D.C.: Department of Health, Education, and Welfare.

Nerlove, M. 1971a. "Further Evidence on the Estimation of Dynamic Economic Relations from a Time Series of Cross-Sections." *Econometrica* 39:359–82.

——. 1971b. "A Note on Error Components Models." *Econometrica* 39:383–96.

Nesselroade, J.R., and P.B. Baltes. 1974. "Adolescent Personality Development and Historical Change: 1970-1972." *Monographs of the Society for Research in Child Development* 39 (serial no. 154).

Pedhazur, E.J. 1975. "Analytic Methods in Studies of Educational Effects." In *Review of Research in Education, 3,* edited by F.N. Kerlinger, pp. 243–86. Itasca, Ill.: F.E. Peacock.

Pierce, D.A. 1977. "Relationships—and the Lack Thereof—between Economic Time Series, with Special Reference to Money and Interest Rates." *Journal of the American Statistical Association* 72:11–22.

Pierce, D.A., and L.D. Haugh. 1977. "Causality in Temporal Systems: Characterizations and a Survey." *Journal of Econometrics* 5:265–93.

Purkey, W.W. 1970. *Self Concept and School Achievement.* Englewood Cliffs, N.J.: Prentice-Hall.

Richards, J.M., Jr. 1975. "A Simulation Study of the Use of Change Measures to Compare Educational Programs." *American Educational Research Journal* 12:299–311.

Rogosa, D.R. 1979a. "Causal Models in Longitudinal Research: Retionale, Formulation, and Interpretation." In *Longitudinal Methodology in the Study of Behavior and Development,* edited by J.R. Nesselroade and P.B. Baltes, pp. 263-302. New York: Academic Press.

———. 1979b. "A Critique of Cross-Lagged Correlation." *Psychological Bulletin.* In press.

———. 1979c. "Mixing Levels of Analysis: An Example from Research on School Effects." Paper presented at the Annual Meetings of the American Educational Research Association, San Francisco, April 8-12.

———. 1979d. "Some Alternative Procedures for Analyzing Longitudinal Panel Data." *Journal of Economics and Business.* In press.

Schaie, K.W. 1965. "A General Model for the Study of Developmental Problems." *Psychological Bulletin* 64:92-107.

Sims, C.A. 1972. "Money, Income, and Causality." *American Economic Review* 62:540-52.

———. 1977. "Comment on Pierce." *Journal of the American Statistical Association* 72:23-24.

Sørensen, A.B. 1978. "Reconceptualizing School Effects: A Reply to Hauser." *Sociology of Education* 51:230-33.

Sørensen, A.B., and M.T. Hallinan. 1977. "A Reconceptualization of School Effects." *Sociology of Education* 50:273-89.

Thomas, E.A.C., and J.A. Martin. 1976. "Analyses of Parent-Child Interaction." *Psychological Review* 83:141-56.

Wallace, T.D., and A. Hussain. 1969. "The Use of Error Components Models in Combining Cross-Section with Time-Series Data." *Econometrica* 37:55-72.

Werts, C.E.; K.G. Jöreskog; and R.L. Linn. 1971. "Comment on 'The Estimation of Measurement Error in Panel Data.' " *American Sociological Review* 36:110-13.

West, C.K., and T.H. Anderson. 1976. "The Question of Preponderant Causation in Teacher Expectancy Research." *Review of Educational Research* 46:613-30.

Wheaton, B.; B. Muthén; D.F. Alwin; and G.F. Summers. 1977. "Assessing Reliability and Stability in Panel Models." In *Sociological Methodology 1977,* edited by D.R. Heise. San Francisco: Jossey-Bass.

Wiley, D.E., and R. Hornik. 1973. "Measurement Error and the Analysis of Panel Data." Studies of Educative Processes, no. 5. Chicago: CEMREL.

Wiley, D.E., and J.A. Wiley. 1970. "The Estimation of Measurement Error in Panel Data." *American Sociological Review* 35:112-17.

Woolson, R.F.; Leeper, J.D.; and Clarke, W.R. 1978. "Analysis of Incomplete Data from Longitudinal and Mixed Longitudinal Studies." *Journal of the Royal Statistical Society A* 141:242-52.

Chapter 5

Educational Production Theory and Teacher Inputs

Henry M. Levin
Stanford University

INTRODUCTION

The past decade or so has witnessed a proliferation of studies on educational production. Broadly speaking, these endeavors have sought to determine the relations between educational inputs and educational outcomes. The inputs that have been considered include the attributes of students as well as the amounts and characteristics of teachers, administrators, other personnel, facilities, and materials; the outcome measures have focused primarily on cognitive achievement.[1]

Both practical and intellectual concerns have stimulated these investigations. From the practical perspective, the costs of education have risen at a very rapid rate, and it has become more and more difficult for the states and their local educational agencies to provide the necessary revenues.[2] Further, the recent court challenges to the present methods of financing education have also stressed the need to understand how new methods of educational finance might more nearly equalize both schooling inputs and outcomes (Pincus, 1974b). Finally, the relative lack of effectiveness of compensatory educational expenditures to more nearly equalize the educational attainments of economically disadvantaged pupils

---

Helpful suggestions for revision were received from Dan Lortie, Ed Bridges, Jim Catterall, and Cuir Riak. I also wish to acknowledge the assistance of Sharon Carter in preparing this manuscript.

with those of other students has tended to emphasize the high priority that must be assigned to ascertaining how educational resources might be used more effectively (Carnoy, 1972).

The study of educational production relations has also appealed to a broad set of intellectual interests. Traditionally, only educational psychologists studied the various aspects of teacher and school effects on students. However, more recently, sociologists, economists, and anthropologists have also begun to explore these subjects, and the current literature on school effects reflects the efforts of several of the social sciences.[3]

The concept of an educational production function is associated primarily with the application to schools of the theory of production from economics. The education industry is considered to be composed of a number of firms or schools that are engaged in converting educational inputs into educational outputs. Accordingly, most work on educational production functions attempts to estimate a statistical equation that is similar to

$$Y = a + b_1 X_1 + b_2 X_2 + \ldots + b_n X_n + e.$$

In this linear equation, Y is the educational output, and the Xs represent the various inputs such as the characteristics and numbers of teachers and other personnel as well as instructional materials and facilities. The bs signify the regression or slope coefficients for each input, showing the estimated effect of a unit increase of each input on output. The intercept term or constant, a, refers to that level of educational output that is not dependent on the inputs, and the residual or variance in Y that is unexplained by the equation is symbolized by e.

This type of equation has been estimated for school districts, schools, classrooms, and individual students (Burstein [1979] refers to studies and conceptual issues at different levels of aggregation). The typical measure of educational output has been a standardized reading or mathematics test, although some studies have utilized student attitudes or test scores that reflect other cognitive domains.[4] Student-related inputs include measures of pupil socio-economic status, race, and sex. School inputs have included such measures as class size, teacher experience, education, and verbal score, library facilities, and other indicators of educational resources (see the summaries in Brown and Saks, 1979; and in Averch et al., 1974). In a few cases the student and school inputs have been analyzed for their interactive effects on educational outcomes—for example, the possibility that smaller classes might have different impacts on children drawn from different socio-economic origins (Summers and Wolfe, 1977; Tuckman, 1971).

But in spite of the relatively rapid development of this type of research, it is probably fair to conclude that the investigations have been more successful in demonstrating the inherent complexities of the phenomenon than in producing useful results. A number of surveys of educational production studies suggest little commonality among their conclusions (Averch et al., 1974). Further, few studies have provided results which would suggest that feasible policy differences in the magnitudes and types of educational resources would change appreciably the existing patterns of educational outcomes (Levin, 1977). Perhaps the only consensus one can find is that differences in student backgrounds are highly related to differences in student achievement and that the effects of specific school resources on student achievement will vary according to the social class and race of pupils (see Averch et al. [1974], as well as the works cited in n.1).

Many reasons have been given for the inconsistency of the findings and for their lack of relevance for educational policy. Among them have been the difficulties of measurement of both inputs and outputs (multicollinearity) that often prevent separating their unique effects on educational outcomes, incorrect specifications of the inputs and outputs of the schooling process and their functional relations, and a variety of other problems that run the gamut of econometric challenges in estimation (Levin, 1976a; Lau, 1979; Hanushek, 1979).

In this chapter I will suggest that a major deficiency in the research on educational production functions is far more basic. This shortcoming arises from the fact that empirical studies of the educational production function are based on the attempt to link statistically a list of inputs with a particular output, without the assistance of any underlying theory. While this problem has been mentioned in the analytical surveys of educational production functions, its implications have not been appreciated fully. Typically, educational production functions are constructed by specifying lists of educational inputs chosen on the basis of their prominence in the educational budget, their correlations with student achievement in previous studies, the ready availability of data, speculations on what might be important, and other ad hoc criteria. While many studies have been careful and imaginative in their specification, measurement, and estimation, the lack of a guiding theoretical framework has created the inevitable result that they have failed to move beyond a relatively crude empiricism. It is also likely that this handicap has been primarily responsible for the failure of the body of educational production research to contribute to a cumulative pattern of knowledge with reasonable consistency and predictive power.

Normally, when a situation of conceptual and theoretical ambiguity persists for so long in an active field of research, there is a compelling reason for that situation. That is, the lack of theoretical development is not likely to be an oversight on the part of researchers. Rather, it is likely to derive from the underlying complexity of the phenomena that are being explored or from other obstacles that prevent the type of simplification and reductionism necessary for the systematic construction of a conceptual framework. Certainly, an understanding of how students and educational institutions function to augment the learning process is an area that is fraught with complexities. Indeed, there are at least two types of theoretical requirements that must be developed and joined if we are to have an appropriate conceptual base for improving the estimation of educational production functions.

First, it is necessary to delineate a theory of schooling that will enable the specification of the relation of inputs to outputs. Second, it is necessary to construct a theory of organizational behavior for schools that will address the principles on which schools are organized for learning and on which resource decisions are made.[5] The first requirement attempts to address how differences in educational inputs and their organization create differences in educational outputs. The second seeks to ascertain how and why schools select, utilize, and organize inputs in the ways they do. The principal purpose of this chapter will be to begin to address these two questions in the hope that some progress can be made along the arduous path of developing the appropriate theoretical frameworks. Two conceptual strands will be introduced, and an attempt will be made to integrate them in the context of educational production. They will then be applied to the particular problem of attempting to specify teacher inputs for the educational production function. Both research and policy implications of the approach will be explored.

In the next section I will present the theory of schooling that will be employed, and in the following section I will propose an organizational approach that seems to have some useful properties. Next I will suggest the implications of these two theoretical insights for the estimation of educational production functions and, in particular, for the specification of teacher characteristics. Finally, I will set out some of the consequences of this presentation.

THEORIES OF SCHOOLING AND EDUCATIONAL PRODUCTION

Before proposing a specific theory of schooling that might be useful for studying educational production, it is important to specify what is meant by a theory in the production context. This is particularly important because there exist at least two major theoretical approaches to learning in psychology—those associated with behavioral psychology and those with developmental psychology (a presentation of these and other approaches to learning is found in Hilgard and Bower, 1975). Both represent broad paradigms for ordering and understanding the process of learning. However, an educational production function does not need a basic understanding of the learning process as much as it requires an understanding of the "technology" of that process. For example, studies of agricultural production do not specifically address the fields of plant biology or physiology. They do not necessitate an intricate knowledge of photosynthesis or of the biochemical processes by which nutrients are converted into plant growth. All that is required is an overall understanding of which nutrients and conditions must be present to stimulate growth. No explication of basic science is required for such an understanding, but the underlying scientific knowledge must be translated into a technical or engineering relationship (for a more complete discussion of these issues, see Salter, 1960).

Given this criterion, a most appropriate candidate for a useful learning theory in the educational production context is the model of school learning that has been proposed by John Carroll (1963) and further developed by Bloom (1976) and Block (1971, 1974). This particular approach has the desirable properties of simplicity, elegance, and utility. Consistent with the previous discussion, Carroll has noted:

> This model of school learning should not be confused with what is ordinarily called "learning theory," that is with the exact scientific analysis of the essential conditions of learning and the development of systematic theory about this process. Rather the model may be thought of as a description of the "economics" of the school learning process; it takes the fact of learning for granted. (1963:725)

Carroll's model has five components, three relating to the individual learner and two pertaining to the learning conditions. Individual factors include (1) student aptitude, which is defined as "the amount of time needed to learn the task under optimal instructional conditions" (1963:729); (2) student ability to understand instruction; and (3) student perseverance, which is "the amount of time the learner is willing to engage actively in learning" (729). Factors external to the student are (4) time allowed for learning and (5) quality of instruction, which is viewed as a measure of the degree to which instruction enables a student to master a task in the shortest time consonant with his or her aptitude. Carroll then relates these variables to the degree of learning of a student, which is determined by the time actually spent relative to the time needed.

In this exposition I wish to disregard individual learner characteristics and address the two external or school factors that can be used to construct the input requirements for educational production. More specifically, I wish to focus only on the specification of the teacher inputs. The reason for this restriction is to develop the conceptual framework within an initially tractable, but significant, part of the schooling process. If this initial foray seems useful, it will be possible to extend the analysis to student characteristics and behavior and to other school inputs.

Using the Carroll formulation, we can address the question, for a given group of students, which characteristics of teachers and instructional activities will determine learning outcomes? Carroll has identified the quality of instruction and the time that students are exposed to instruction as the crucial variables determining the amount that will be learned. Accordingly, we might address the specification of teacher inputs into the educational process by exploring the determinants of the quality of instruction and the allocation of teacher time to particular instructional tasks.

Capacity, Effort, and Time

There are three components of teaching input that, when taken together, determine the quality of instruction and the allocation of instructional time. These three components are the capacity, effort, and time allocation of the teacher, referred to by the acronym CET. Each dimension will be described, and the CET paradigm will be compared with the tacit assumptions underlying the usual specification of teacher inputs in educational production functions.

Capacity refers to the personal attributes of the teacher that can be used to provide instruction and to assist learners on any particular instructional task. Just as a student has an aptitude to learn in any specific area, a teacher has an aptitude to teach. Capacity to teach is determined by such factors as basic abilities, knowledge, creativity, and other personality traits, and it may be affected by the teacher's education, training, and experience. Precisely what capacities are necessary or beneficial for increasing the quality of instruction will obviously depend on the instructional task. That is, we are not assuming that there is a generalizable capacity for teaching that is equally applicable to all tasks. Just as the capacity to provide instructional services in mathematics may require very different skills than those needed for teaching literature, such narrower tasks as instruction in arithmetic operations may require considerably different capacities than does instruction in civics or creative writing. The important point is that capacity for instruction has meaning only when it is referenced to a particular instructional task. The difficulty of ascertaining what are the relevant capacities and for what instructional tasks besets the research literature on teaching effectiveness (Gage, 1978).

The quality of instruction depends not only on the capacity of the teacher, but also on the *effort* of the teacher to draw upon that capacity to provide instructional services. That is, capacity represents a set of traits possessed by the teacher that can be utilized in the instructional setting. The provision of instructional services requires that capacity be converted into teaching activity, a process that requires effort on the part of the teacher. Effort can be thought of as the level of energy used to convert capacity into instruction for each unit of instructional time. The greater the teaching effort, capacity being constant, the greater the quality of instructional services.[6] In this respect, teachers of great capacity who muster little effort may show poorer results than those with a lesser capacity and greater effort.

The final component of the CET complex is the amount of *time devoted* to a particular instructional task. This is obviously a crucial determinant in the Carroll model of how much will be learned, and it is sensible to assume that the amount of instruction provided by a teacher in any particular instructional area will have an effect on learning outcomes.[7] This relation is so straightforward that it needs little comment. It is also the strongest finding in one of the most extensive studies on teacher efforts: "Time allocated to instruction in a content area is positively associated with learning in that content area" (Fisher et al., 1978:11–17).

Integrating these three components into Carroll's conception of the external conditions that affect learning, we see a rather natural interface. Teacher capacity and effort taken together represent the determinants of the quality of instruction, while teacher time devoted to each instructional task signifies the opportunity to learn. It is these three basic dimensions of the teacher and the teaching activity that present a conceptual framework for specifying teacher input into the educational process.

It is useful to contrast these conceptual insights with the tacit underpinnings of the standard educational production function. The typical educational production function focuses only on those teacher variables that might represent proxies for the capacity dimension—measures of teacher experience, education, verbal score, attitudes, and other traits. They do not address themselves to either the effort or the time allocation that are necessary to transform capacity into instruction. Either the effort and time components are omitted because they are considered to be unimportant, or there is the tacit assumption that these factors are also reflected by the statistical indicators for teacher capacity. It is assumed that teachers with identical measures of capacity will provide identical measures of effort and time allocations with respect to each instructional area. Alternatively, it might be assumed that specifying teacher characteristics as inputs should preclude concern with teaching processes. But I have argued that the actual teaching input will depend on the complete CET complex rather than on teacher capacity alone.

Whatever the interpretation of the traditional specification of teacher inputs into production functions, the CET approach suggests that it is seriously flawed. But this assertion raises the difficult challenge of determining how schools are actually organized to manipulate each of the three components of the CET composite. That is, if differences in each of the dimensions of CET create differences in teacher performance and student learning, then a theory of school organization would need to take account of how schools select and train teachers with the appropriate capacities, motivate them to provide the level of effort necessary to convert those capacities into a high quality of instruction, and induce them to allocate their time appropriately to the different instructional foci. In the next section I will attempt to explore the nature of this problem and its solution.

SCHOOL ORGANIZATION AND
TEACHER PERFORMANCE

The issues raised by the CET approach can best be appreciated if we refer to a situation in which they are resolved with minimal institutional intervention. I will call this the autonomous professional paradigm.[8]

The Autonomous Professional Paradigm

Using a definition of professionalism that assumes almost complete autonomy on the part of teachers, the only requirement on the part of the school would be the selection and hiring of teachers to provide instruction in particular subjects. Once the teachers were hired, they would be given a group of students and a classroom or other facilities as well as a set of instructional priorities or subject areas that were considered important. In this way, teachers would be given a great deal of autonomy in recognition of their professional status and expertise (Bledstein, 1976: 87–88).

More specifically, teachers would be free to decide how to utilize their time, organize the instructional process, select instructional materials, assess and certify student progress, and so on. Presumably, the schools would hire teachers on the basis of their capacities. The actual organization and implementation of the instructional process would be carried out according to the professional judgments of the teacher. That is, teachers would have the autonomy and independence to allocate their time and effort in the manner that they saw fit. Organizational requirements from the perspective of the school would be minimal.

Obviously, teacher selection and budgetary allocation would be important, but school control over such matters as curriculum specification, administrative supervision, time allocation to specific subjects, selection of instructional materials, teaching methods, grading methods, and other organizational practices would be obviated by the autonomous professional model. Individual teachers would use their own professional training, experience, and judgments to make decisions on these matters, and teachers would largely control both the instructional process and the nature and outcome of their own work activity.

But while teachers are often referred to as professionals, it is hardly this definition of autonomous professionalism that is intended. Teachers are not autonomous craftsmen who are allocating their time and efforts according to their preferences and professional judgments. Instead, they are employed according to a wage contract by a complex, bureaucratic organization that defines to a large extent the nature of their work activity. The model of the school is not that of a professional anarchy, but of a highly organized bureaucracy in which the schooling process is set out in a clearly articulated fashion. Time allocations to particular subjects tend to be set according to institutional rules; instructional materials are selected according to centralized mandates; variations in teaching methods are circumscribed by mandatory confinement of students to orderly classrooms, supervisory evaluations, and organizational sanctions with respect to "unauthorized" subjects; and so on. On balance, standard operating procedures are far more important than professional judgments in describing the activities of teachers.[9]

Educational Professionals and Bureaucracy

Why does the bureaucratic model dominate the schools instead of the autonomous professional paradigm? According to the historical and analytical literature, there are many answers to this question. Some historians have argued that many leading educators, school administrators, and boards of governors were so heavily imbued with those principles of business organization that were sweeping America to the forefront of world production and commerce that they believed that these concepts would also create "efficient" schools.[10] In a more analytic mode, radical economists and revisionists historians have seen the centralization and bureaucratic control and organization of schools as a response to the forces of industrial capitalism and its need for the reproduction of appropriately socialized labor for the emerging corporate capitalism of the later nineteenth century.[11] They point out that changes in the organization of schools tended to correspond with similar changes taking place in business organization. Centralization of the educational bureaucracy, tracking according to ability, testing students for school allocation, and vocational specialization were all associated with prior changes in the organization of production that required new educational departures. Thus, these organizational features of the schools can only be understood by reviewing the needs of corporate capitalism for wage labor with the appropriate skills, attitudes, and individual values that would enable its domination and exploitation by the capitalist class.[12]

What is common to these explanations is that schools have an institutional agenda that is not left to chance. Rather, schools are organized to produce certain predictable learning outcomes, both cognitive and affective. In order to obtain these outcomes, schools have disdained the autonomous professional model and adopted a mode of bureaucratic organization with top-down control of the instructional process. Although there is no difficulty in obtaining instructional effort and time allocations from teachers when these conform with their own preferences and choices under the autonomous professional paradigm, there is great difficulty in obtaining their efforts and time when centralized control of the instructional process, relative uniformity of teaching activities, and predictability of results necessitate a different agenda. On these matters, the intrinsic needs of teachers and those reflected by the governing authorities and structures of schools might not be fully compatible. Thus, schools were faced historically with creating a mode of organization that would standardize the instructional process and teaching activities by taking control of them away from the vagaries of individual professional judgments.

Before reviewing how this was done, it is important to point out the parallel between this situation and the transformation of the labor process under industrial capitalism (see Marx, 1964a: pts. III and IV; and Braverman, 1974). While the autonomous professional paradigm refers to teachers as independent persons who control the process and product of their activities, the actual school setting utilizes teachers in ways that minimize their control over the instructional process. A similar loss of control by workers of the work process was an integral feature of the history of capitalism (Marx, 1964b; Ollman, 1971). Marx saw this as a necessary requirement of industrial capitalism, in which the needs of capital accumulation would create production activities that would alienate workers from each other as well as from the process and result of their work activities (Marx, 1964b). That is, the autonomy of workers would be subjugated to the needs of the owners of capital. This was accomplished through the establishment of a pyramidal hierarchy of control, in which most jobs would be transformed by the adoption of a minute division of labor into highly routinized and simple tasks that would be repeated endlessly (Braverman, 1974). Such an organization would minimize the skill requirements of work; simplify supervision of workers; increase discipline, as workers could be easily replaced in these unskilled and repetitious tasks; and divide the working class against itself as individual workers competed with each other for stable employment or promotion (Haber, 1964). In contrast with earlier forms of work and artisanship, work lost its intrinsic meaning, so that workers had to be motivated by a system of extrinsic rewards. That is, the boring and repetitious tasks could not create satisfaction in themselves, so workers became socialized to working for factors external to the work process such as the wages necessary for survival or for increased consumption.

Accordingly, Marx made a distinction between the hiring of labor power and the extraction of labor. The capitalist firm had to face two types of decisions. First, the firm had to hire workers for the lowest possible wage in order to acquire the labor power that was needed for production. But the hiring of labor power was not equivalent to obtaining labor. If jobs were not intrinsically satisfying, alienated workers would be loathe to put much effort into them. Thus the capitalist firm was faced with the second type of decision—how to create a form of organization of work that would extract a maximum of labor from labor power.

Under earlier conditions of slavery or possible starvation, the fear of losing employment was enough motivation for workers to put forth great effort. But as slavery and starvation became proscribed by society, the capitalist firm was pushed to adopt a method of organization that would extract labor in a standard and routinized manner. The evolving forms of organization of corporate capitalism are a response to the need to extract labor from alienated workers (Braverman, 1974; Noble, 1977; Marglin, 1974). Through a combination of bureaucratic and hierarchical work organization (based on the work of Max Weber), minute division of labor and wage incentives (based on the work of Frederick Taylor) at the level of the firm, and the disciplinary effect of a reserve army of unemployed on the work force and of recession on the level of the economy, monopoly capitalism was able to solve the problem of extraction of labor, a solution that has contributed historically to high rates of profit and capital accumulation.[13]

While schools are neither owned nor controlled directly by the capitalist class, they do face a similar organizational dilemma. As long as teachers are accorded professional status and autonomy, it is not difficult to extract labor from them. Their professional interests will generate those work efforts that will provide intrinsic satisfaction to them as professional teachers. But as the schools have been transformed historically along corporate and hierarchical lines, the teacher has lost much of this earlier autonomy. To an increasing degree, teaching has become highly routinized and controlled, in order to assure a continuous and uniform process that does not depend on individual preferences or differences among teachers. Indeed, a standard criterion discussed in curriculum construction is that of making the curriculum "teacher-proof."

As teacher preferences and judgments have become relatively inconsequential in terms of the organization of the instructional process, teachers have become alienated in the Marxian sense. That is, they have lost control over the process and product of their activity. This has meant that the schools must use a variety of devices to motivate or coerce teachers to devote effort and time to the overall organizational agenda, since many of these activities are not of intrinsic value to them. In this context it would hardly be surprising to find that the schools followed the corporate capitalist model for cementing control and created uniform teacher work roles and activities.[14]

The traditional educational production function utilizes only measures of teacher capacity in specifying teacher inputs. That is, it is assumed that capacity will be automatically transformed into the effort levels and time allocations that are consistent with the agenda of the school. On the contrary, success in converting the capacity of teachers (or labor power) into teacher effort and time allocation (or labor) will depend on how the school is organized to make this transformation. Teachers who are largely alienated from the instructional process in which they must participate must be manipulated by appropriate extrinsic rewards or forced by the structure of school organization and standard operating procedures to perform at the level of effort and in the manner that is consistent with the overall objectives of the institution. In the next section I will discuss some ways in which this is done and the consequences for educational production.

DETERMINANTS OF CET

I suggested above that a major deficiency of the present literature on education production functions is the lack of a conceptual framework underlying the work. Two specific needs were a theory of learning and an organizational framework that could explain the selection and utilization of teacher services. In response to the first requirement, I proposed the model of schooling that was developed by John Carroll (1963). On the basis of that model, I was able to suggest that there are three dimensions of the teaching function that contribute to learning: teacher capacity and effort represent the determinants of the quality of instruction, while teacher time devoted to each instructional task signifies the opportunity to learn.

But this poses a problem for the organization of teaching services and instruction if the instructional agenda differs substantially from the objectives and professional judgments of individual teachers. In some way the school organization is faced with providing a systematic program of instructional processes addressed to particular institutional objectives, but it must rely on individual teachers who are hired as professionals to provide the instruction. Under a professional autonomy model, teachers would be hired according to their capacity to teach and would be given control of the instructional process. From the institutional perspective, the consequences of professional autonomy are likely to differ from teacher to teacher. In order to provide greater uniformity of instruction and achievement of institutional goals, schools must utilize the three components of teacher capacity, effort, and time allocation to focus on the institutional mission.

This task of integrating teacher performance and institutional objectives is more difficult than it might seem at first glance. Even if all teachers who are hired have the capacity to carry out the standardized instructional processes and tasks expected of them, they might not agree with this version of teaching. To a large degree teachers view themselves as deserving some autonomy of judgment, and such tasks as keeping order and discipline or teaching certain subjects in the way that the school approves might not coincide with their values as professionals. These conflicts are clearly reflected in a summary of an extensive set of teacher interviews on the teaching role:

> Teachers seem to want conditions which favor more control over student involvement, more discretion to make decisions, and greater trust from principals and parents. Yet, one senses a reluctance to press the case to its logical extreme; it is as if these teachers half accept and half reject the limitation imposed by their status. Their status clearly does not grant them control over the conditions they believe are important and necessary; they are not permitted to arrange instruction in a driving, aggressive way. (Lortie, 1975:185-86)

Under such conditions, it is important to address the question of how educational institutions and the larger society that sponsors them are able to extract the appropriate amounts and types of work behaviors that provide a reasonably uniform and predictable set of learning outcomes for students. That is, we must focus on the manner in which schools are able to obtain teachers with the appropriate capacities for carrying out these tasks and to motivate them or to require them to put in the effort and time necessary to implement the tasks in a manner consistent with the instructional agenda of the institution. The success of the school organization in achieving these goals will determine the effectiveness of the teaching inputs into the educational production function. Accordingly, it is useful to review each component of CET and the methods that the school uses to manipulate them to achieve its objectives.

Capacity

Capacity was defined as that set of personal attributes the teacher brings to the instructional process that can be used to carry out the instructional task.[15] It is a measure of capability. Obviously, it must be judged with respect to the specific tasks that are thought to be a part of the instructional process. Such factors as competence in subject matter, ability to explain, speaking proficiency, imagination, and related traits might be used to assess capacity. Teacher selection would be based on these factors or on certain indicators that are thought to determine them, and in-service training and the socialization effects of experience might develop them further (teacher socialization is stressed in Lortie [1975: ch. 5]). What are the specific indicators of capacity? The most important ones are probably the individual's innate abilities and personality traits, educational characteristics with respect to the type and quality of training, and socialization such as work experience. Capacity might be measured by credentials, standardized tests, or interviews, or a combination of all of these.

As mentioned previously, teacher capacity variables represent the only measures of teacher characteristics that are normally included in educational production functions. It is presumed that the effort of the teacher and the time allocation pattern is either irrelevant or is reflected in the capacity measures. However, I have suggested that this tacit presumption is likely to be erroneous. This omission may represent the most salient reason that teacher capacity variables do not seem to have a powerful statistical effect on student achievement. That is, teacher efforts and time allocations to particular types of student achievement may vary in such a way that capacity is not transformed into a high level of instructional service.

Effort

Effort was defined as the level of energy used to convert capacity into instruction for each unit of instructional time.[16] A teacher with high capacity but no interest in the instructional task may provide only a lackluster effort, while one with lower capacity and greater interest could provide a higher level of effort. Clearly a high level of effort can compensate for low capacity and vice versa. There are at least two aspects of effort that require emphasis. First, the level of effort is likely to be related to the particular instructional task or process which the teacher is expected to address. Those tasks or processes that are consistent with the teacher's own values and sense of what is good teaching will likely induce higher levels of effort than those that are external to or that contradict the personal agenda of the teacher. This tenet suggests that, like capacity, effort must always be viewed in the context of a particular task or educational goal rather than as a general construct.

If we are concerned in our evaluations with the inculcation of certain attitudes in students or with a particular type of scholastic achievement, both capacity and effort must be assessed with respect to those particular outcomes.

Second, it is difficult to measure effort directly. While it is possible to assess the degree of teacher energy or enthusiasm or conscientiousness in some proximate way, there are probably no methods of judging effort outside of a direct assessment of teacher behavior in a particular instructional setting and situation (Gage, 1978). This means that a specification of effort in a school learning model probably must use approximate and indirect measurements or surrogates. Since it is difficult to measure effort directly, it is important to speculate on the functional determinants of the effort variable. This analysis will also throw light on school policies that are designed to obtain teaching services (labor) from teaching capacity (labor power) by attempting to maximize the level of effort put forth by the teacher.

There are at least four fairly distinct sets of determinants of teacher effort: (1) teacher preferences, (2) organizational incentives, (3) organizational climate, and (4) teacher training and retraining. Teacher preferences refer to those instructional situations which correspond with the professional judgments and personal views of the teacher in such a way that the teacher receives intrinsic satisfaction from the activities. To the degree that teachers are selected and assigned according to the consonance of their instructional tasks with their preferences, teacher motivation and resulting productivity are likely to be higher than when there is a poor match between preferences and teacher requirements. Thus, an overlap between the preferences of the teacher and the actual instructional situation with respect to subjects, types of students, characteristics of curriculum, and the nature of instructional materials is likely to contribute to greater teacher effort than a mismatch on these dimensions. Like other persons, teachers will devote more energy to those tasks that provide intrinsic satisfaction and that conform to their values and beliefs than to instructional tasks that are "forced" upon them.[17]

Teacher autonomy is closely related to the teacher preference determinant, and we would expect that the greater the degree of autonomy in controlling the instructional process, the greater the level of effort that would be devoted to that process. That is, when teachers are able to choose the methods by which they will accomplish tasks, they are likely to put more energy into their endeavors. Teacher autonomy can take many forms. For example, teachers as a group could participate in a democratic process that would set out goals and objectives as well as aspects of the instructional process such as time allocations, choice of instructional materials, and curriculum approaches.[18] In addition, greater tolerance or encouragement of individual teacher autonomy would work in the direction of greater motivation and enthusiasm for carrying out instruction.

The second category of organizational determinants of teacher effort is that of institutional incentives of an extrinsic nature. Every complex organization has both explicit and tacit rewards for appropriate work behavior. The most obvious of these are the structure of pay and opportunities for advancement. But in addition, the behavior required for retaining jobs, for obtaining better work or teaching assignments, and for attracting other scarce resources must also be considered. Probationary teachers must show a level of effort, motivation, and general behavior that conforms to institutional expectations for teacher performance. As mentioned previously, some teaching assignments are preferable to others. The allocation of these opportunities can be tied to the level of effort of a teacher in meeting instructional expectations of the institution.[19] Finally, such sanctions as accountability schemes based on observation of the teacher in the classroom setting or testing the students to ascertain teacher effectiveness can be used as institutional devices to get teachers to put appropriate levels of effort into their teaching.[20] In these cases the educational decisionmakers or administrators can manipulate teacher effort through a system of external rewards or sanctions.

The third category of policies and determinants of teacher effort include those that affect the organizational climate and working conditions. Any set of conditions that makes the teacher feel more a part of the decisionmaking apparatus or more appreciated or that provides better working conditions can contribute to the effort or productivity of the teacher (see Pencavel [1977a] for an analysis of the value of efforts at raising employee morale to increase work effort). Among these factors are such conditions as inspirational leadership, a feeling of teamwork and cooperation, an attractive physical environment, workable class size, and other factors that may contribute to teacher moral and esprit de corps.

Finally, teacher training and retraining might be used as a way of improving effort and productivity by altering the values and attitudes of teachers. For example, one strategy for attempting to improve the provision of instructional services for minority and educationally disadvantaged youngsters has been to provide in-service courses of training that would make teachers more familiar with the culture and the educational needs of such children. While these courses were designed to increase teacher capacity, they also were intended to create a greater willingness and desire to work with such students.

Time Allocation

While teacher capacity and effort determine the quality of instructional services in any particular area, the total amount of learning that will take place will also depend on the time devoted to the instructional task. Both common sense and research studies have emphasized the crucial role played by student exposure to instruction in explaining learning outcomes (Fisher et al., 1978). Under the professional autonomy model, teachers would decide how they would allocate their time to the different instructional activities that they chose. But school organizations attempt to make certain that there is at least a minimal allocation of time to each of the subjects and other activities that are considered to be important to the institution. Through organization of the curriculum into discrete areas and the day into discrete time periods, the school attempts to impose an allocative structure on the instructional process. Further, teachers are given other responsibilites such as taking attendance and various clerical chores that make particular time demands on their schedules. To a great extent—though not completely—the teaching day, week, and year are allocated to activities according to institutional design rather than according to the discretion of the teacher.

But even within this structure, different teachers may respond differently to time allocations. Some teachers may spend greater time on those subjects or activities that they feel are important while minimizing the time allocated to other activities. For example, at the elementary school level the transition from one subject to the next can be blurred. At the secondary level the teacher can emphasize some tasks, while minimizing others. External accountability devices such as evaluation of teaching by supervisors and testing programs can be used to get teachers to devote more time to those areas that are being evaluated òr tested. But there are still likely to be substantial differences among teachers in terms of the "true" time that is allocated to any particular instructional task, even though the ostensible or official time allocations are largely standardized by school practice.

In summary, the determinants of CET can affect the quality and amount of instructional services in a number of ways. Through selection and retraining of teachers, the capacity to provide instruction is determined. It is possible to affect the level of teacher effort or productivity in devoting energies in the institutional agenda through motivating teachers by matching them to experiences that they prefer; allocating extrinsic rewards such as pay, status, mobility, and job tenure according to institutional criteria; creating a supportive organizational climate; and providing additional training. Finally, the allocation of teacher time to activities is affected by curriculum structure and institutional demands as well as by accountability approaches that emphasize measuring particular outcomes. Such accountability schemes would also have the effect of increasing teacher effort in the areas that are evaluated. What implications do these theoretical insights yield for the specification of teacher inputs into the educational production function?

CONSEQUENCES FOR SPECIFICATION OF TEACHER INPUTS

This conceptual excursion has at least two major consequences for the specification of teacher inputs into educational production. The first is that the inclusion of teacher characteristics or capacity variables, by themselves, is inadequate because they do not reveal the degree to which such characteristics are converted into educational services. The second is that the organizational forms and content of schooling will determine to a great extent the effort and time allocations of teachers. Thus, a full model of educational production must take account of both effort and time allocation variables and their organizational determinants. Let us deal with each of these consequences in turn.

As I have emphasized previously, traditional approaches to the educational production function have utilized only measures of capacity of teachers, while ignoring effort and time allocations. Why is it that only the capacity measures have been specified? The answer is surely grounded in the general approach to estimating industry production functions in which only the characteristics of labor are used as inputs. That is, the distinction between the hiring of labor power and the extraction of labor is not normally considered in estimating industry production functions. The lack of a distinction between these two concepts in the neoclassical production function derives from the view that they are not different. The firm is viewed as hiring labor services, even though the wage contract hires merely the time of the worker. It is assumed that there is a uniform and consistent transformation of labor time into labor services, depending on the available technology and organization of production. Firms are considered to be operating in a competitive environment and seeking to maximize profits. Under such conditions, it is assumed that the extraction of labor services can be derived routinely from the quantity and quality of labor inputs or "human capital."

To a certain degree this assumption might be valid for a profit-maximizing firm. Both control of the production organization and the incentive to maximize extraction of labor might ultimately contribute to a standardization and uniformity of the transformation process between capacity of labor and extraction of labor services. Indeed, the attempt to routinize the work process into a large number of simplified and repetitive tasks represents a principal method by which a relatively predictable amount of labor could be extracted from relatively low wage and less skilled workers (Braverman, 1974). Historically, this process replaced the unpredictability and autonomy of activity of the more costly artisan or craftsman in the production process. Thus, the firm was able to cement greater control over the work process and to reduce the cost of output.

But when schools attempt to construct similar types of organizational devices, it is not clear that they yield the same results. Schools are not profit-maximizing firms, but organizations that must respond to a wide variety of political pressures with respect to educational content and process while preparing students for the realities of capitalist work. They represent the major vehicle for social mobility and opportunity, while reproducing the unequal hierarchy of skills and behaviors that are required for production under monopoly capitalism. To a certain extent these roles are incompatible, since the former suggests greater equality while the latter suggests the maintenance of inequality.[21] Further, teachers cannot be supervised as readily as can most blue and white collar workers, and the output of the teaching process cannot be readily measured since it is psychological in nature and inextricably linked to the nature of the student input. Thus, no matter how much schools attempt to routinize and regularize the instructional process, the actual effects are probably very diverse because of the lower level of control and internal contradictions in their operation. This means that the actual effort and time allocations of teachers devoted to the instructional process for any set of instructional tasks are likely to differ considerably (see Levin [1978] and Levin and Carnoy et al. [forthcoming] for a discussion of internal contradictions in the schooling process).

If the foregoing is correct, the omission of effort and time allocation variables in the existing educational production function research is a serious one. In contrast, recent emphasis on "time in learning" in the classroom setting does address the time dimension. However, while the time aspect of CET is specified in those studies, the effort and capacity variables are not (see Harnischfeger and Wiley, 1979; Thomas, 1977). Even in a time allocation study for a single classroom, the allotment of time to particular students or to specific subjects is not a sufficient measure of learning opportunity. To the degree that differences in effort are related to different subjects or to particular students and to the degree that teaching capacity differs according to subject, the full range of CET variation must be explicitly taken into account. Thus, research on specifying and measuring teacher inputs into educational production must focus on all three components.

One apparent issue that is not addressed here is the potential role of teacher collective bargaining in altering the institutional conditions that affect the CET complex. It is probably safe to speculate that those aspects of organizational behavior of schools that have an impact on teacher recruitment and utilization are not likely to change through the collective bargaining mechanism alone. First, most of the conditions that determine the work situation are probably difficult to alter, as they derive from state and federal laws, as well as from deeply accepted beliefs about the nature of schooling, parental pressures and expectations, and so on. Further, some issues are considered to be nonnegotiable by both parties, as the extension of collective bargaining in the public sector has reflected the sanctimony of property stewardship and its prerogatives in the use of labor in the private sector. The result is that bargaining takes place only within a fairly well-defined framework of issues such as salaries, fringe benefits, class size, and preparation time. That is, the bargaining arrangement tends to treat the basic parameters of school organization as sacrosanct, while negotiating employee benefits within that framework. Certainly, this has been the traditional role of trade unions in other industries, and it represents a historical limitation of trade unionism in obtaining structural changes in the capital-labor or employer-employee relation (Gorz, 1968; Aronowitz, 1973; Hyman, 1973).

Further, teachers do not see such basic challenges as promising success, and they are deeply aware of the risks in raising these types of issues. Lortie summarizes these feelings and the dilemma that they entail:

> There is a certain ambivalence, then, in the teacher's sentiments. He yearns for more independence, greater resources, and just possibly, more control over key resources. But he accepts the hegemony of the school system on which he is economically and functionally dependent. He cannot ensure that the imperatives of teaching, as he defines them, will be honored, but he chafes when they are not. He is poised between the impulse to control his work life and the necessity to accept its vagaries; perhaps he holds back partly because he is at heart uncertain that he can produce predictable results. (1975:186)

On the basis of his interviews, Lortie concludes that teachers accept the terms of control over students, space, supplies, and schedules that is set out for them by the organization: "For at the base of teacher status is the indisputable constaint that without access to a position in the schools the teacher cannot practice his craft" (185). Given the present situation of teacher oversupply (Freeman 1976; ch. 4) and falling enrollments because of changes in demography, it appears that this sanction has become even more dominant, despite the increase in collective bargaining.

There are a number of research challenges emanating from this analysis. First, if effort is such a key variable, its inclusion in the teacher specification of the production function is crucial. Yet there is no evidence that a useful metric for assessing effort is available. Further, it is not clear how one can even develop an approach to measuring what appears to be unmeasurable. This means that it may be necessary to assess effort indirectly by using various proxies or determinants of effort such as attitudes toward particular instructional tasks. Or alternatively, it may mean that the pursuit of the educational production function is a lost cause.

A second potential difficulty is separating those factors that are endogenous to the overall production model from those that are exogenous. That is, if the structure of educational institutions is determined by factors largely beyond the control of the educational manager, it will not be possible to think in terms of manipulating the various factors that determine the CET complex. Much of the historical analysis suggests that the particular organizational features of the schools reflect forces that emanated from the development of work organizations under a system of monopoly capitalism and state bureaucracy. From a different perspective, John Meyer (chapter 1 in this volume) has argued that educational institutions are embedded in a larger organizational framework that is often overlooked and may dominate institutional behavior. Certainly, a plethora of external influences tends to limit the options of educational administrators. The impact of state education codes just by themselves represents formidable constraints on managerial prerogatives with respect to curricular content, teacher licensing, selection of instructional materials, conditions of work, school facilities, and other matters. When one adds to these the values and beliefs held by teachers, students, parents, administrators, and the general public that also support the status quo, it is difficult to argue that the determinants of CET are endogenous to a particular school setting.

However, it is worth investigating the degree to which individual schools or school systems have discretion over the CET dimensions. To what degree do school administrators exercise managerial control over the selection of particular teacher capacities, and to what degree are they able to use various organizational devices for encouraging or discouraging the levels of effort and time allocations with respect to different instructional processes and tasks? Alternatively, to what degree do these practices reflect a social equilibrium among the political demands and social values created by other social, economic, and political institutions that are essentially external to the school?

This chapter has attempted to depart from the usual framework that is assumed in generating the statistical estimation of educational production functions. It has carried out this task by broaching a conceptual framework for understanding how teacher inputs are used in educational production to affect student learning. To some researchers it may provide a basis for improving the estimation of educational production functions, while to others it will document the futility of going further in that direction. At the very least, I hope that it provides an impetus for further discussion and refinement of the organizational functioning of schools.

NOTES

1. The most recent summaries of this literature are Hanushek (1979), Lau (1979), Thomas (1977) and Bridge, Judd, and Moock (1979). Examples of specific studies are Summers and Wolfe (1977), Brown and Saks (1975), Murnane (1975), and Hanushek (1972).

2. For example, between 1930 and 1977, current expenditures per student in average daily attendance in U.S. elementary and secondary schools increased from $298 to $1,578 in constant 1976-1977 dollars. Between 1960 and 1972, the expenditure levels rose from $749 to $1,412, with little change since 1974 (Golladay and Noell, 1978:72).

3. Witness the diverse efforts represented among the papers in these two volumes. See especially the studies discussed and cited by Brown and Saks (1979) and by Burstein (1979).

4. For example, student attitudes are incorporated into a model of the educational production function in Levin (1976b), and cognitive test scores and their variance among students are addressed in Brown and Saks (1975).

5. An interesting distinction between the school as an institution and the school as an organization is developed in Meyer chapter 1 in this volume.

6. It is assumed that the effect of effort on instructional services is positive within the normal ranges of effort that are relevant to the teaching process. However, this does not mean that the relation need be monotonic. There may be a level of "overeffort" at which the teacher is trying too hard so that instructional services deteriorate. For some evidence of this among students who were "overly motivated," see Atkinson, Lens, and O'Malley (1976).

7. The crucial effect of instructional time and exposure to instruction on student learning is emphasized in the research findings of Wiley (1976). An attempt by Karweit (1976) to replicate the Wiley results using similar data sets for other populations are unsuccessful. The time variable represents the crucial determinant of learning outcomes in the mastery learning paradigm (Bloom, 1976), and it is an important target of investigation in many recent analyses of learning at the classroom level. See, for example, Thomas (1977), Fisher et al. (1978), and Harnischfeger and Wiley (1979).

8. The meaning that I am imparting is close to that of autonomous artisan or craftsperson. However, since these terms are not likely to be used in conjunction with teachers, I have used the term "autonomous professional." The traditional concept of the professional was very much an autonomous individual who "defined the unique quality of a subject, its special basis in an exclusive and independent circle of natural experiences" (Bledstein, 1976:88).

9. Teachers are hardly unaware of the tension created by the constraints of the organization of their desires for greater autonomy in the instructional process (see Lortie, 1975:175-86).

10. Insights can be found in Tyack (1974). Callahan (1962) is more specific about the particular aspects of scientific management that were adopted by the schools. Wirth (1977) reviews the social efficiency mentality that contributed to the formation of the present educational approach.

11. Details on the evidence and processes are found in Bowles and Gintis (1976), Katz (1968, 1971), Cohen and Lazerson (1972), Feinberg and Rosemont (1975), and Levin (1978). Insights on the relations between school and workplace are found in Dreeben (1968).

12. Works that focus on changes in the work process and their determinants include Braverman (1974), Gutman (1977), Noble (1977), and Marglin (1974). The analysis of the organizational aspects of schools within this context is found in Bowles and Gintis (1976) as well as in the works cited in note 10.

13. See Weber (1946) for his well-known essay which explicated the advantages of bureaucracy for the emerging corporate capitalist order of the late nineteenth century. A representative work of Taylor's is *The Principles of Scientific Management* (1911), which summarizes his earlier publications. Taylor's major impact in the early twentieth century was to "streamline" the established corporate bureaucracies by making them more "efficient." The role of the emerging professional engineers and scientists in molding

technology to fit these social forms of production is found in Noble (1977; also see Baran and Sweezy, 1966).

14. It is interesting to cite Weber on the advantages of bureaucracy with respect to this transformation: "Bureaucratization offers above all the optimum possibility for carrying through the principle of specializing administrative functions according to purely objective considerations. Individual performances are allocated to functionaries who have specialized training and who by constant practice learn more and more. The 'objective' discharge of business primarily means a discharge of business according to *calculable rules* and 'without regard for persons'" (1946:215).

15. Related literature refers to many of the capacity variables as abilities rather than capacities. I have preferred to use the word "capacity" for two reasons. First, the word "ability" often connotes cognitive capacities, while I would argue that physical and emotional or affective capacities are also part of the overall construct of teaching capability. Second, ability connotes innate and fixed human traits, while I have asserted that capacity can be altered through experience, training, and other modes of socialization. See the use of the term ability in studies of work performance in Vroom (1964), Porter and Lawler (1968), and Heneman and Schwab (1972). These studies also utilize constructs of effort in conjunction with ability to explain employee performance. An ability-motivation approach to explaining intellectual performance is used by Atkinson, Lens, and O'Malley (1976).

16. Effort is considered to be a derivative of motivation in the work performance literature. See Vroom (1964) and Porter and Lawler (1968).

17. Of course, to a certain degree persons who offer their services into teaching are likely to be self-selecting or different from the general population with college degrees. That is, persons who feel that they are able to tolerate or even prefer the existing definition of the teacher role are more likely to become teachers than those who cannot accept the conditions of the job. While Lortie (1975:ch. 3) examines teacher recruitment, he does not review systemmatically many of the potential intellectual and personality differences between teachers and nonteachers. However, he concludes that teaching tends to attract females and rather conservative persons who are "favorably disposed toward the existing system of schools" (Lortie, 1975:54).

18. The concept of autonomy through workplace democracy is not a common one, but it is becoming increasingly salient as an approach to organizing work. The political theory underlying workplace democracy is found in Pateman (1970). Various applications are presented in Jenkins (1974). The educational implications are developed in Levin (1978).

19. Lortie (1975:ch. 4) does an excellent job of reviewing the reward structures. Teachers indicated that the psychic rewards of teaching—such as feeling that they had "reached" their students—gave them the greatest amount of satisfaction. How often this occurred, under what conditions, and the degree to which there are obstacles to "reaching" students are not explored by Lortie. However, inferences can be drawn from what appear to be relatively low proportions of respondents who would definitely choose teaching again (only about half) that these sources of satisfaction do not appear to compensate

many teachers for the negative conditions of their situation (see the data cited by Lortie, 1975:91); further insights into the frustrations of the teaching role are found in his chs. 7, 8, and 9. Pencaval (1977b) reviews the general problem of using systems of remuneration to increase effort and productivity, particularly under conditions where productivity cannot be easily assessed. Pincus (1974a) has reviewed more generally the system of external incentives in education.

20. At least thirty states have implemented or are in the process of implementing student testing programs for assessing and certifying that students have attained minimal competency levels. The organizational implications are explored in Mitchell and Spady (1978).

21. In my view, the independent dynamic of the school (such as its emphasis on equality while reproducing inequality) is a significant source of change that has been ignored in much of the radical literature, which has emphasized the correspondence of the school with the needs of capitalist production rather than its divergence from them. Compare the relatively functionalist approach of Bowles and Gintis (1976) and Carnoy and Levin (1976) with the emerging dialectical analysis in Levin (1978) and Levin, Carnoy et al. (forthcoming).

REFERENCES

Aronowitz, Stanley. 1973. *False Promises*. New York: McGraw-Hill.

Atkinson, John W.; Willy Lens; and P.M. O'Malley. 1976. "Motivation and Ability: Interactive Psychological Determinants of Intellectual Performance, Educational Achievement, and Each Other." In *Schooling and Achievement in American Society*, edited by W.H. Sewell, R.M. Hauser, and D.L. Featherman, pp. 29-60. New York: Academic Press.

Averch, Harvey A.; Stephen J. Carroll; Theodore S. Donaldson; Herbert J. Kiesling; and John Pincus. 1974. *How Effective Is Schooling?* Englewood Cliffs, N.J.: Educational Technology Publications.

Baran, Paul, and Paul Sweezy. 1966. *Monopoly Capital.* New York: Monthly Review Press.

Bledstein, Burton. 1976. *The Culture of Professionalism.* New York: W.W. Norton.

Block, James H. 1971. *Mastery Learning.* New York: Holt, Rinehart & Winston.

———., ed. 1974. *Schools, Society, and Mastery Learning.* New York: Holt, Rinehart & Winston.

Bloom, Benjamin S. 1976. *Human Characteristics and School Learning.* New York: McGraw-Hill.

Bowles, Samuel, and Herb Gintis. 1976. *Schooling in Capitalist America.* New York: Basic Books.

Braverman, Harry. 1974. *Labor and Monopoly Capital.* New York: Monthly Review Press.

Bridge, R. Gary; Charles M. Judd; and Peter R. Moock. 1979. *The Determinants of Educational Outcomes.* Cambridge, Mass.: Ballinger Publishing Company.

Brown, Byron W., and Daniel H. Saks. 1975. "The Production and Distribution of Cognitive Skills within Schools." *Journal of Political Economy* 83, no. 3 (May-June): 571-93.

―――. 1979. "Production Technologies and Resource Allocations within Classrooms and Schools: Theory and Measurement." In *The Analysis of Educational Productivity: Issues in Microanalysis*, edited by Robert Dreeben and J. Alan Thomas, pp. 000-00. Cambridge, Mass.: Ballinger Publishing Company.

Burstein, Leigh. 1979. "The Role of Levels of Analysis in the Specification of Education Effects." In *The Analysis of Educational Productivity: Issues in Microanalysis*, edited by Robert Dreeben and J. Alan Thomas, pp. 000-00. Cambridge, Mass.: Ballinger Publishing Company.

Callahan, Raymond. 1962. *Education and the Cult of Efficiency.* Chicago: University of Chicago Press.

Carnoy, Martin. 1972. "Is Compensatory Education Possible?" In *Schooling in a Corporate Society*, edited by Martin Carnoy, pp. 175-92. New York: David McKay.

Carnoy, Martin, and Henry M. Levin. 1976. *The Limits of Educational Reform.* New York: David McKay.

Carroll, J.B. 1963. "A Model of School Learning." *Teachers College Record* 64:723-33.

Cohen, David L., and Marvin Lazerson. 1972. "Education and the Corporate Order." *Socialist Revolution* 2 (March): 47-72.

Dreeben, Robert. 1968. *On What Is Learned in School.* Reading, Mass.: Addison-Wesley.

Feinberg, Walter, and Henry Rosemont, eds. 1975. *Work, Technology, and Education.* Urbana: University of Illinois Press.

Fisher, Charles W.; N.N. Filby; R.S. Marliave; L.S. Cahen; M.M. Dishaw; J.E. Moore; and D.C. Berliner. 1978. *Teaching Behaviors, Academic Learning Time and Student Achievement: Final Report of Phase III-B.* Technical Report V-1, Beginning Teacher Evaluation Study. San Francisco: Far West Laboratory for Educational Research and Development, June.

Freeman, Richard B. 1976. *The Overeducated American.* New York: Academic Press.

Gage, N.L. 1978. *The Scientific Basis of the Art of Teaching.* New York: Teachers College Press.

Golladay, Mary A., and Jay Noell, eds. 1978. *The Condition of Education, 1978 Edition.* National Center for Education Statistics. Washington, D.C.: Department of Health, Education, and Welfare.

Gorz, André. 1968. *Strategy for Labor.* Boston: Beacon Press.

Gutman, Herbert. 1977. *Work, Culture, and Society in Industrializing America.* New York: Vintage Books.

Haber, Samuel. 1964. *Efficiency and Uplift: Scientific Management in the Progressive Era 1890-1920.* Chicago: University of Chicago Press.

Hanushek, Eric. 1972. *Education and Race.* Lexington, Mass.: D.C. Heath.

―――. 1979. "Conceptual and Empirical Issues in the Estimation of Educational Production Functions." *The Journal of Human Resouces* 14, no. 3 (Summer): 351-88.

Harnischfeger, Annegret, and David E. Wiley. 1979. "Determinants of Pupil Opportunity." In *The Analysis of Educational Productivity: Issues in Microanalysis*, edited by Robert Dreeben and J. Alan Thomas, pp. 000-00. Cambridge, Mass.: Ballinger Publishing Company.

Heneman, Herbert G., III, and Donald P. Schwab. 1972. "Evaluation of Research and Expectancy Theory Predictions of Employee Performance." *Psychological Bulletin* 78, no. 1 (July): 1-9.

Hilgard, E.R., and G.H. Bower. 1975. *Theories of Learning.* 4th ed. Englewood Cliffs, N.J.: Prentice-Hall.

Hyman, Richard. 1973. "Industrial Conflicts and the Political Economy: Trends of the 60's and Prospects for the 70's." In *The Socialist Register, 1973*, edited by Ralph Milibrand, pp. 101-53. London: Merlin Press.

Jenkins, David. 1974. *Job Power.* Baltimore: Penguin Books.

Karweit, N. 1976. "A Reanalysis of the Effect of Quality of Schooling on Achievement." *Sociology of Education* 49:236-46.

Katz, Michael B. 1968. *The Irony of Early School Reform.* Boston: Beacon Press.

———. 1971. *Class, Bureaucracy and Schools: The Illusion of Educational Change in America.* New York: Praeger.

Lau, Lawrence J. 1979. "Educational Production Functions." In *Economic Dimensions of Education*, edited by Douglas Windham, pp. 33-70. Washington, D.C.: National Academy of Education.

Levin, Henry M. 1976a. "Concepts of Economic Efficiency and Educational Production." In *Education as an Industry*, edited by D. Jamison, J. Froomkin, and R. Radner, pp. 149-90. New York: National Bureau of Economic Research.

———. 1976b. "A New Model of School Effectiveness." In *Schooling and Achievement in American Society*, edited by W.H. Sewell, R.M. Hauser, and D.L. Featherman, pp. 267-89. New York: Academic Press.

———. 1977. "A Decade of Policy Development in Improving Education and Training of Low Income Populations." In *A Decade of Federal Antipoverty Programs: Achievements, Failures, and Lessons*, edited by R. Haverman, ch. 4. New York: Academic Press.

———. 1978. *Workplace Democracy and Educational Planning.* Paris: International Institute for Educational Planning of UNESCO.

Levin, Henry M.; Martin Carnoy; et al. Forthcoming. *The Dialectic of Education and Work.* Palo Alto, Calif: Stanford University Press.

Lortie, Dan C. 1975. *Schoolteacher: A Sociological Study.* Chicago: University of Chicago Press.

Marglin, Steve. 1974. "What Do Bosses Do?" *Review of Radical Political Economy* 6 (Summer): 60-112.

Marx, Karl. 1964a. *Capital.* Vol. 1. Edited by F. Engels. New York: International Publishers.

———. 1964b. *The Economic and Philosophic Manuscripts of 1844.* Edited with an introduction by Dirk Struik. New York: International Publishers.

Mitchell, Douglas E., and William G. Spady. 1978. "Organizational Contexts for Implementing Outcome Based Education." *Educational Researcher* 7, no. 7 (July-August): 9-17.

Murnane, Richard. 1975. *The Impact of School Resources on the Learning of Inner City Children.* Cambridge, Mass.: Ballinger Publishing Company.

Noble, David F. 1977. *America By Design.* New York: Alfred A. Knopf.

Ollman, Bertell. 1971. *Alienation: Marx's Conception of Man in Capitalist Society.* New York: Cambridge University Press.

Pateman, Carole. 1970. *Participation and Democratic Theory.* New York: Cambridge University Press.

Pencavel, John. 1977a. "Industrial Morale." In *Essays in Labor Market Analysis and Population in Honor of Peter Comay,* edited by O. Ashenfelter and W. Oates, pp. 129-46. New York: John Wiley and Sons.

———. 1977b. "Work Effort, On-The-Job Screening, and Alternative Methods of Remuneration." In *Research in Labor Economics,* edited by R.G. Ehrenberg, vol. 1, pp. 225-59. Greenwich, Conn.: JAI Press.

Pincus, John. 1974a. "Incentives for Innovation in the Public Schools." *Review of Educational Research* 44, no. 1 (Winter): 113-44.

———., ed. 1974b. *School Finance in Transition.* Cambridge, Mass.: Ballinger Publishing Company.

Porter, L.W., and E.E. Lawler. 1968. *Managerial Attitudes and Performance.* Homewood, Ill.: Irwin-Dorsey.

Salter, W.E.G. 1960. *Productivity and Technical Change.* New York: Cambridge University Press.

Summers, Anita A., and Barbara L. Wolfe. 1977. "Do Schools Make a Difference?" *American Economic Review* 67, no. 4 (September): 639-52.

Taylor, Frederick W. 1911. *The Principles of Scientific Management.* New York: Harper.

Thomas, J. Alan. 1977. *Resource Allocation in Classrooms.* Chicago: Educational Finance and Productivity Center, University of Chicago.

Tuckman, Howard P. 1971. "High School Inputs and Their Contribution to School Performance." *Journal of Human Resources* 6 (Fall): 490-509.

Tyack, David B. 1974. *The One Best System.* Cambridge, Mass.: Harvard University Press.

Vroom, V.H. 1964. *Work and Motivation.* New York: John Wiley and Sons.

Weber, Max. 1946. "Bureaucracy." In *From Max Weber: Essays in Sociology,* edited by H.H. Gerth and C.W. Mills, pp. 196-244. New York: Oxford University Press.

Wiley, David E. 1976. "Another Hour, Another Day: Quantity of Schooling, a Potent Path for Policy." In *Schooling and Achievement in American Society,* edited by W.H. Sewell, R.M. Hauser, and D.L. Featherman, pp. 225-65. New York: Academic Press.

Wirth, Arthur. 1977. "Issues Affecting Education and Work in the Eighties: Efficiency versus Industrial Democracy, A Historical Perspective." *Teachers College Record* 79, no. 1 (September): 58-68.

✳ *Chapter 6*

Choice in Education

James S. Coleman
University of Chicago

In this chapter I want to examine in detail an issue in education that has increasingly come under discussion—namely, the issue of parental and child choice in education. The principal aim will be an informative one: to exposit, as clearly as I can, both the variations in kinds and degrees of educational choice and the numerous issues that animate the discussions about it. In addition, I will discuss proposals that have been made to use systems of choice to accomplish certain extraeducational goals, such as school integration. Finally, I will offer some conjectures about the future role of choice in education.

Underlying the whole discussion is a fundamental issue of political philosophy: To what degree does the parent have, and to what degree does the state have, rights of control over the child?[1] Although this essay is commissioned by an agency of the state, I will attempt not to act as an agent of the state's interests in examining this question, but to view the question from the points of view of both the state and the parents.

THE DIVISION OF CONTROL OVER THE CHILD

When the community or the state began to provide public education, this generated a set of potential issues concerning control of the child. Before that time, control of the child, until he or she became independent or was apprenticed to another household, was in the hands of the family. Even when the family decided to send the child to one of the (private) schools that could be found

in the area, the family retained control of what school the child
would attend and how long the child would attend that school.

As public schools came into existence and became widespread,
there also came laws that transferred some of this control to the
state. Principal among them were school attendance laws, which
dictated that the child should be in school (except for cause) during
the school year, between certain ages, such as six to sixteen (differing
slightly in different states). In addition, there were laws that specified the school administration's right, if the child was to attend
a public school, to determine which school the child would attend
and what activities the child would carry out while in school. The
laws did not make private schools illegal, although in many states
they did make it illegal for parents to withhold the child from
school for home instruction.

There are many specific issues concerning the state's control
of the child's activities in the school—the child's right to refuse
to pledge allegiance to the flag, the child's right to due process
before suspension from school, the state's right to have prayers
during school, the state's right to determine the child's dress in
school, and others. These are continuing issues at the border line
between the state's and the parent's rights over the child.

One of the rights that the state has taken to itself (but often
delegated to the local school district) is the right to determine
which school the child will attend and which classroom the child
will be placed in. This right has been exercised in a wide variety
of ways, the most exotic variation being the prohibition in southern
states until recent years of attendance at the same schools by blacks
and whites. A somewhat less exotic variation has been the maintenance of single sex high schools in some cities in the East and
Midwest. Apart from this, the state's right of pupil assignment
to schools has ordinarily been exercised in one of two ways: (1) all
children living within a particular set of geographic boundaries
(the school's "attendance zone") are assigned to a school within
those boundaries, ordinarily a school somewhere near the center
of its attendance zone; (2) all children living within a given school
taxation district may choose a school within that district, sometimes subject to entrance examinations in the case of certain high
schools. The first of these two methods of assignment is by far
the more frequent and until recently has been nearly universal
at the elementary school level. The second method has been used
primarily at the high school level and primarily for certain specialized high schools within a city school district. This pattern has
been more characteristic of older cities and older school systems,

in which high schools were established before the model of the "comprehensive high school" was widespread. Thus the residues of that pattern of assignment, involving choice among specialized high schools, are found mostly in eastern cities and most prominently in New York.

Although the right of school assignment has been held by the state, there are certain related rights implicitly or explicitly held by the parents. Implicit in the school's exercise of school assignment rights has been the right of parents to choose a school by choosing their residence and to change their child's school by changing residence. Explicit is the right of parents to withdraw the child from public school and to place the child in a private school recognized by the state.

Thus there has been a subtle division of rights between state and parent over the child's school attendance, with each holding certain rights that, as they are jointly exercised, determine the distribution of children among schools.

In recent years, the state has changed radically its exercise of rights of student assignment. The most prominent changes have concerned assignment by race. This has come roughly in two stages. The first of these (although its completion required over sixteen years after the 1954 *Brown* decision) was elimination of what I described above as "the most exotic variation" in the state's assignment policies—that is, the assignment in the South of blacks and whites living in proximity to different schools, rather than to a single school serving that geographic area. The second stage, which blended with the first but at the extreme is clearly distinguishable from it, is assignment of children to schools at some distance from their homes, rather than to a school near their residence, in order to overcome the racial separation that exists by reason of residential segregation. The negative reactions of most white parents and many black parents to "busing" is a reaction to this exercise of the right of school assignment by the state, and the reaction has taken a predictable form: the parents' exercise of their part of this subtle division of rights by moving their residence to a location without busing or by enrolling their children in private schools.

A different kind of change in the state's exercise of its rights of student assignment came in the 1960s, partly as the student revolt against authority moved into secondary and elementary education and partly as city schools became increasingly unable to cope with their expanding lower-class black populations. This change was the relaxation of school attendance laws, and as I have indicated, it was in response to both middle-class and lower-class pressures. Authorities of the state in many cities acquiesced in children's attendance at the many "free" or "experimental" schools that grew up in the 1960s without requiring these schools to meet state standards. According to state laws, such children were truants, but the laws were not enforced. And in a similar fashion, the usual form of truancy, simple absence from the public school, which has become widespread in some schools in some cities, was overlooked. In short, the state stopped enforcing its attendance laws in some areas.

These recent changes in the state's exercise of its rights of assigning children to schools and requiring their attendance indicate that the whole question of how the state exercises its rights of control over the child is in some confusion and turmoil. This confusion raises once again the fundamental issue that was decided in one way when public school systems developed: What shall be the division of control over the child between the parent and the state? It is clear that a return to the past parental control is not desired by either party. But it is equally clear that the present allocation of rights is in some difficulty, as parents and state attempt to thwart one another's exercise of their portion of rights and as some parents and some state authorities abandon their responsibilites and leave some children unschooled or only intermittently schooled. There is a danger that there will be a wholesale withdrawal from the public school system in metropolitan areas by those parents with sufficient money to choose private schools or with sufficient mobility to avoid cities or even metropolitan areas. And there is a danger that there will be further erosion of responsibility for children's schooling on the part of both state and parent as both parties find that responsibility more difficult to exercise.

It is in this context that ideas about different kinds of division of rights of control over the child arise and become of more than incidental interest. Not only have such ideas arisen; some have been implemented. In the next section, I will describe a number of variations in rights of control, all of which have one element in common: the parent has a greater degree of choice concerning the child's schooling, choice that can be exercised without moving residence or without paying fees for private school attendance.

All the forms of choice that I shall discuss may be characterized as an increase of parental control through individual choice and as such are to be distinguished from a different form of increase of parental control through collective choice. In the late 1960s a number of instances of collective parental control under the rubric of "community control" were instituted. This arose particularly in cases where, as in New York City (where the initiation of community control provoked the greatest uproar), a black or hispanic minority demanded that control of the schools in its area be placed in the hands of local community members.

Such patterns of collective parental control are not different, in fundamental form, from the pattern of control that has long existed in smaller towns, where local school boards preside over the few schools in an ethnically homogeneous community. And the position of average parents is little different from their position in the city system before community control. In New York City, for example, parents continue to be required to send their child to an assigned school with a fixed program. The only difference is that staff and some aspects of the program are selected by a board representing about 30,000 children rather than by one representing a million. The minuscule change in the average parent's role produced by this shift in community control and its indistinguishability from traditional control in smaller communities do not warrant its being considered as a distinct form of parental choice.

FORMS AND DEGREES OF CHOICE IN EDUCATION

Choice Within Schools

In Alum Rock School District in San Jose, California, there are remnants of what was once intended to be a full-scale "voucher" experiment. I will return later to school vouchers, but focusing attention on Alum Rock will indicate a form of choice that is unusual but not to be overlooked. The experiment in Alum Rock was carried out in elementary schools. In principle, the experiment made it possible for families to choose to send their child to a public elementary school other than their neighborhood school, but in practice this choice was not strongly encouraged and not often exercised. Instead, what developed was a system of choice within each school: groups of teachers were free to set up "minischools" having different philosophies of educational instruction and, in some cases, emphases on different contents.

In the first year of the Alum Rock experiment, for example, there were twenty-two minischools set up in the six "voucher" schools. They could be characterized as follows in terms of their emphases:

General basic academic skills	11
Reading skills concentration	2
Math-science skills concentration	1
Fine arts concentration	2
Differing cultures	2
Activity centers or open classrooms	4

Parents were informed of the minischools within their local school to which they could choose to send their child. The child could transfer from one minischool to another without extensive complications, although each minischool was designed to carry the child through the whole set of years in that school. It is clear that this form evolved in Alum Rock when the district, under the necessity of carrying out an experiment involving parental choice, found that teachers were uneasy about competing with other schools for students and that most parents were content to leave their children in the closest school. What is not clear is whether such a form might evolve in the absence of a district's necessity to fulfill the requirements of a federally funded experiment. However, the fact that the form of choice it provided is one that is compatible with most parents' desire to send their early elementary children to a nearby school suggests that, despite its emergence in a some-what artificial situation, this form of choice could develop else-where and survive in the absence of federal funding.

Minischools as found in Alum Rock are only one form that within school choice can take. There is, of course, the very common form that arises increasingly as the child moves from elementary school to high school—the choice of courses. There are few high schools in the United States in which some freedom of choice among courses does not exist, and in most high schools the larger part of the curriculum is open to choice in the last two years.

The choice among courses, however, is on a different dimension than is the choice among programs in an arrangement like that in Alum Rock. The choice among courses is principally a choice among different contents to be learned, while the minischools in Alum Rock differ primarily in their methods of teaching and only secon-darily in content. This suggests a difference that is likely to arise more generally between systems of choice designed for elementary schools and those designed for secondary schools: at the elemen-tary level, choice is principally among different methods, while at the secondary level, choice is principally among different contents.

This is not to say that both types will not exist at both levels, for as will be evident in the discussion of choice among schools, both can already be found at both levels. This became particularly true at the high school level with the growth of alternative schools, in which learning takes place largely through practice and performance outside the classroom.

There is another form of parental choice within school that I will mention briefly. A problem often arises in school that a child does not like a particular teacher. Sometimes, if the child's disaccord with the teacher is sufficiently great, if the parent is particularly persistent, and if the principal is flexible, the child may be transferred to another classroom. The practice is discouraged, however, and since some teachers generate more dissatisfaction than others, it is difficult to imagine full freedom to choose among teachers if all teachers are to be supplied with about the same numbers of children in their classes. Thus is appears unlikely that this form of within school choice will ever be widely adopted by schools.[2]

Choice Among Public Schools Within a District

During the period of school desegregation in the South, many districts introduced a plan, designed to minimize the impact of desegregation, called "freedom of choice." This plan, in principle, allowed children to transfer from the neightborhood school that they had previously attended and to which they were assigned (a school that had previously been all the same race) to another school, ordinarily a school that had been reserved for the other race. As a means of bringing about full elimination of a dual school system, these plans were deficient—all in one way and some in two. All were deficient in that the preexisting state was one of total segregation, so that unless requests for transfers were actively exercised by parents, segregation would remain. Some were deficient as well in that barriers were placed in the way of transfers of black children into previously all white schools (there were few requests on the part of white parents to transfer their children to previously all black schools).

In circumstances where neither of these conditions exist—that is, where a dual school system has never existed or has been eliminated—choice among schools within a district is a potentially viable form of parental choice. It is, of course, not only potential; it exists in one or another form in a number of school districts. The forms can be roughly classified as two—open choice and restricted choice. Open choice in its most extreme form is parental choice unconstrained by capacity limitations of the school. Such a plan was in existence in Baltimore at the junior high school level in the 1960s. Parents chose, when their child was in sixth grade, three junior high schools in order of preference. The school board, wary of parental reaction to not receiving first choice, gave all children the schools first on their list.[3]

The result of this plan was widespread choice by blacks of schools in predominantly white neighborhoods that had previously been predominantly white and almost no choice by whites of schools that had previously been all, or nearly all, black. All previously white junior high schools were fully integrated, with a large minority, or in some cases a majority, of black students. There was overcrowding of the integrated schools, some of which went on split shifts or added temporary classrooms, and underutilization of some all black shools. The choice occurred during a period of general school overcrowding, so that the overcrowding was more severe than it would otherwise have been.

Such imbalances of distribution can be expected in a wholly unlimited system of choice such as that used in Baltimore. However, the use of temporary classrooms can alleviate all but major imbalances, and major imbalances (such as a doubled school population) do not seem to occur, partly because closeness to home is important to many parents and partly because very large schools are seen as undesirable by many parents. Thus it would seem that unlimited choice among public schools in a district is feasible if steps are taken to compensate for enrollment imbalances.

At the same time, a system of choice that includes restrictions but closely approximates this one in the range of choice it provides parents is choice without prior assignment but with capacity constraints on each school's enrollment. This would mean that enrollment in an oversubscribed school would be determined by lot among those who ranked it first, or by time of application, or by some other criterion of equity. Ordinarily in such a system, once children attended a given school, they would have the right to attend it in succeeding years; the right of open choice would be exercised in the initial year, and choice in succeeding years would be subject to the constraints and conditions that are ordinarily imposed on transfers. Chief among these constaints is the principle that the transferring child's rights of attendance are subordinate to the rights of those already attending the school. In such a system of choice there is no presumption that nearness of residence to a school gives first rights of attendance. The system is like a nonconstituency city council, in which all candidates run at large, each voter making a choice (or choices) from among the same set. Here, all schools are "at large," all parents choosing from among the total set.

Schools with Differing Educational Content. A system of choice between schools with different educational programs has been found most often at the secondary level, in cities with specialized high schools. A number of cities, particularly in the East, have had two sets of high schools—comprehensive schools with attendance zones and specialized citywide schools with no attendance zones. A child entering high school can choose to attend either the school in whose zone he or she lives or one of the citywide schools. Some of these schools have entrance examinations (or did have, before integration orders in some cases forced their abandonment); some have not. The former include the academic elite high schools, such as Boston Latin, Bronx High School of Science, Walnut Hills High School in Cincinnati, and others. The latter include some technical schools and most vocational schools.

This dual pattern of high schools in a city is less frequent than it was in the past. The pattern first retreated in the face of the comprehensive high school movement, together with the move of many high-achieving students out of the city system into the comprehensive high schools of the suburbs. It retreated still further in the face of desegregation orders, which have in some cases imposed state assignment of students to achieve racial balance and in other cases (as in Boston Latin) imposed racial quotas that take priority over entrance examination results and parental choice. However, vocational schools in a number of cities have maintained their status as citywide schools of choice.[4] This is very likely due to the specialized training they provide and the impossibility of providing a range of choice within each comprehensive high school that would include this specialized training.

As this account of citywide high schools of choice indicates, there has been a decline over time in the extent of parental choice available in many cities, even apart from and prior to the desegregation movement. This decline can be traced principally to a set of changes that, taken together, can be termed a movement of educational policy toward egalitarian homogeneity among schools (manifested primarily in the shift to comprehensive schools and in the shift away from single sex high schools), combined with a counteracting tendency on the part of parents to create residentially based differentiation in school quality in suburban communities. Both the public policies toward egalitarian homogeneity and the private actions toward differentiation acted to reduce the possibilities of choice among different kinds of high schools (except, of course, through choice of residence, which provided mainly differentiation in quality rather than in kind of training).

In view of all this, any move to expand the opportunities for choice in education in the high school level should attempt to achieve compatibility with both the general egalitarian direction that public policy has taken and the residential flexibility that some families have.

Returning to the broader consideration of both elementary and secondary levels, the most frequent pattern of choice among schools (not the most frequent pattern of school assignment, which is one that allows no choice among schools, except transfer under hardship conditions) is that in which there is initial assignment to a school on the basis of residence, and transfer to another school may be requested by parents and granted by the district. The granting of such transfers is constrained by capacity limitations at the receiving school and, in racially mixed districts, by a "majority-to-minority" transfer restriction. The latter restriction exhibits minor variations, but its main aim is to prohibit transfers that reduce racial integration and to encourage those that increase it. The usual restriction can be stated in this way: a transfer is allowed from a school in which the child's race is in the majority to a school in which the child's race is in the minority. A white child can transfer from a majority white school to a majority black school and a black child from a majority black school to a majority white school. Such transfer options exist in a number of city school districts as a part of the district's integration program. The options have been exercised primarily by blacks choosing to attend majority white schools, seldom by whites choosing to attend majority black schools.

One difference between choice exercised through a transfer request and choice exercised without a prior assignment is that with the former, choice occurs only if initiated by the parent, while with the latter, all parents must make a choice. This means that the transfer choice is likely to produce considerably less movement away from the neighborhood school to which the child would ordinarily be assigned. However, I know of no research comparing the rates of choice of nonneighborhood schools under the two different conditions.

Schools with Differing Educational Methods. A new kind of educational choice within the public school system has arisen in the past ten or twelve years—a choice among schools with sharply differing methods. At the elementary level, a number of variations can be found, but there are at least three distinct types. One is the "open school," with much greater freedom of activity for children, greater flexibility of scheduling, and greater variability in classroom organization. The second variation, which may be termed "basic education," deviates from the norm in the opposite direction—a tightening up of standards in the basic skills, a return to traditional methods, and a concentration on the three R's. The third is the Montessori school, which has found a niche in a few public school systems.

The demand for these schools that deviate from the standard arose from a general breakdown in the 1960s of consensus concerning education. There were parents who asked for greater flexibility and openness in education (in part a revivification of some of the ideas of progressive education), and there were parents who asked for greater emphasis on discipline, on basic skills, and on maintenance of standards.

The creation of programs by school systems to respond to these demands had several motivations. One was an attempt to compete with the free school movement, which had drawn some children out of the public schools. Another was to provide some degree of parental choice, and thus greater parental satisfaction, in a system in which some form of compulsory racial balance had been ordered. Pasadena, for example, under a court order to maintain racial balance, established both a "basic education" elementary school and an "open" elementary school, both of which operated as city-wide schools to which parents could apply rather than send their child to the assigned school.

Elementary schools that differ in teaching methods (and to some degree in content) and that are available for the exercise of parental choice, are not numerous. However, their existence in a few school districts suggests a form of educational option within the public school system that could become more widespread. In many other systems involving parental choice, there are few major content and method variations, so that parental choice tends to be based on location or on school reputation (which is often coincident with the level of economic background or with the race of the student body). Experience with schools having sharply different methods indicates both that many parents are less willing than before to let professional educators decide their child's education and that many parents will, even for elementary school, send their child some distance (and in some cases to an integrated school, which they might otherwise avoid) to receive an educational program that is distinctly different in method and educational philosophy.

The elementary schools described above are often termed "alternative schools." A form of alternative high school that deviates only in a single direction from the standard school has also developed. These schools, the first of which was the Parkway School in Philadelphia, involve little classroom work and a large amount of experiential education in a work setting. They are sometimes referred to as "schools without walls," because, following Parkway's example, they carry out most of their educational activities outside any school building, often in apprentice type relations to craftsmen or other skilled workers. Although their emphasis is usually on manual skills, the population of students that they draw includes middle-class children disaffected by classroom learning.

These alternative high schools exist in a number of cities and, like the East's elite academic schools, are citywide, attended by choice. Like the basic education, open school, and Montessori elementary schools, they attract a particular segment of the student population and do not have a general reputation within a status hierarchy of schools. Their considerable success in attracting students to an integrated school, without many physical facilities, without athletic tems and other extracurricular activities, and without a long tradition again indicates that some parents and students will undergo a number of inconveniences if the school offers a distinctively different program in a direction they prefer.

Magnet Schools. An element of choice has been injected into a number of school desegregation plans, some of which otherwise involve compulsory assignment to designated schools. This has taken place through the creation of "magnet" high schools. (The term "magnet school" has sometimes been used for any school of choice in a desegregation program otherwise using only compulsory assignment. Consequently, some of the schools described in the preceding section have been called magnet schools.) The term "magnet," unlike the previous terms, which were somewhat descriptive of the content or method specialization of the school, refers to the hope that the school will act as a magnet to attract both black and white students. Consequently, magnet schools of many varieties may be found, including schools that have little that is distinctive about them. Not much can be said in general about these schools, except that some have succeeded in attracting an integrated student body, while others have not. The general principle of choice is like that of the old elite citywide schools and the alternative high schools discussed above: magnet schools are citywide, offering an alternative to the school to which a child would otherwise be assigned. It is likely that the failure of some magnet schools to attract students stems in part from the starting point—the idea of attracting both blacks and whites, rather than a plan for a distinctive type of educational method or content. The term "magnet" would be better applied after the fact, when a distinctive school of choice in a city has proved itself able to attract both blacks and whites.

Interdistrict Choice

Two kinds of choice systems that extend beyond the public schools in a single district have been proposed: one involves choice among public schools in different districts, and one involves choice among private schools as well as public schools. I will treat the first in this section and the second in the next.

Interdistrict choice has long been in use on a small scale in many localities. It has been established primarily in response to parents' desires for their child to attend a specialized school in a different district (ordinarily suburban parents desiring to send their child to a specialized school within the city). Other reasons have included greater convenience of a school in another district or a child's ability to finish in a school attended before a residential move outside the district. In such cases, school districts have established tuition charges, and out-of-district parents have been charged for the child's enrollment.

Many districts have not allowed out-of-district children to transfer in, sometimes to prevent lower-class or black children from attending the district's schools, sometimes to prevent white children from using the district's schools as a haven from desegregation in a nearby district. However, voluntary groups in a few cities have developed programs (perhaps the best known of which is Metco in the Boston area) in which they obtain agreement from suburban districts to accept some number of black central city students. Students or their families volunteer to make the transfer, and the organizing group arranges transportation. Each plan, however, involves only a few children, and the total number involved is very small.

However, as many central city school districts have become predominantly black, interdistrict choice on a much broader scale has been proposed as a method of reducing the city-suburb separation of blacks and whites. Payment to the receiving district, including transportation costs, would come from the state rather than from the parents.

Roughly three degrees of choice are possible for such transfers—completely open choice, independent of locus of residence and not subject to rejection by the receiving school; choice in which the receiving school must accept a child under certain conditions, but has the right of refusal if those conditions are not met; and choice subject to full right of refusal by the receiving school.

The second of these two possibilities has been most fully discussed, with the two criteria most often suggested for permitting a school to reject an out-of-district student being (1) capacity limitations and (2) a proportion of the student's race already in the school equal to or above the proportion of that race in the metropolitan area. Under this system of choice, a school would have the right to refuse admission to an out-of-district student only if one of the two conditions was met. Other criteria are possible as well. In the case of specialized schools, entrance examinations, as have been used in citywide schools, might be used for metropolitanwide schools with a specialized curriculum.

One plan to make interdistrict transfers on a large scale possible has recently been initiated in Wisconsin, where the legislature has passed legislation enabling such exchanges. The Wisconsin legislation, to overcome the resistance of suburban districts (and in passage of the bill, suburban legislators), pays a bonus to the suburban district that receives the child transferring from the city. Similar legislation has been designed for Ohio and perhaps for other states as well.

While the legislation provides for voluntary transfers in both directions, its utilization in Wisconsin has been primarily by blacks in Milwaukee to attend suburban schools.[5] However, the transfers that took place earlier from suburb to city, accompanied by tuition payment, suggest that in the intermediate or long run, transfers to specialized city schools by suburban white children could very well develop. The fear of the city among suburban whites, particularly fear of the blacks within it, and the turbulence and conflict of school desegregation have made such a possibility unlikely in the immediate future in most large cities. Yet the locus of the city as the geographic center and most widely accessible part of the metropolitan area suggests it as a natural place, as these immediate problems dissipate, for schools with specialized content or distinctive methods that would attract students from the whole metropolitan area. Whether the leadership of central city systems, inexperienced in establishing specialized schools, beset by financial problems, and burdened by the difficulties of maintaining minimal standards in a large system populated by lower-class students, can initiate such distinctive and attractive schools is not at all certain; however, under the full voucher system of choice to be discussed next, this becomes a less important question.

Vouchers for Public and Private Schools

I will now turn to an examination of a full voucher system, the most frequently discussed and most controversial system of parental choice. Advocacy of voucher plans cuts across ideological differences, as does opposition to the plans. Milton Friedman, as an outspoken proponent of laissez-faire, has long advocated vouchers; Christopher Jencks, on the left, has advocated them as well and designed a full-scale voucher plan for what finally became Alum Rock's minischools; John Coons, who wrote the brief for the plaintiffs in the Serrano equal finance case, has published a book (Coons and Sugarman, 1978) advocating vouchers and has designed a voucher plan that is likely to be voted on in referendum in fall 1980, in California; and Mario Fantini, the designer of the Ocean Hill-Brownsville community control experiment that initiated extreme conflict in New York City, has now published a book, (Fantini, 1973) advocating a similar policy.

In the last section, I will try to capture the sources of advocacy of and opposition to vouchers and the intensity with which these positions are held. At this point, however, I will merely outline the characteristics of voucher systems.[6]

The simplest voucher systems provide each child with an educational entitlement. Much like a college scholarship, this entitlement may be used at any approved school, public or private, and the school redeems the voucher from the state at its face value to obtain finances to operate the school. With educational vouchers, the state becomes only one of the providers of publicly supported education. Its role shifts from providing services to a captive clientele to providing resources directly to the clientele who purchase services either from the state or from private providers.

The change is a simple one, but its implications are very great. It would involve a shift from local financing of education (using the property tax) supplemented by state funds to state financing (which would probably be partially supplied through use of a state-equalized property tax).[7] There exist variations in methods of financing (one of which is discussed in detail in Coons and Sugarman [1978]), in some cases allowing for local variations in the value of the voucher corresponding to variations in the local property tax rate.

One might expect that if there were a full shift from local property tax financing of education to state financing in order to provide equal value vouchers for all children, there would be a shift in control of educational content and methods from the community to the state. However, under a full voucher system, control passes not to the state, which neither assigns children to schools nor has a monopoly on the content and methods of schooling, but to parents and children, who exercise their control through choice of a school. Consequently, as the problems of local financing increase and as methods of state financing are proposed, it is likely that systems of full public-private vouchers will be increasingly discussed. This is one of the few means of statewide financing by which control of education would not move upward to the state.

In fact, the existence of vouchers—to be used in public or private schools and independent of residence (so long as it is within the state)—would constitute a greater shift of control of education from state to parent than would any change yet discussed. The qualitative difference lies in the fact that the parent not only may choose among schools, as in most of the types of choice discussed earlier, but may also choose a school not subject to the direct authority of the public educational system. It is this qualitative difference that induces much of the intense opposition to vouchers, as well as much of the support.

There are four principal dimensions of variation among the voucher systems that have been proposed. One is the variation between a restricted voucher and an unrestricted voucher that may be supplemented by additional money if the school chosen costs more than the voucher—like a scholarship of a fixed amount that only partially covers tuition. The rationale for restricting the voucher by not permitting supplementation is an equal opportunity one: the supplementation will put some schools beyond the ability of some parents to pay the supplement.[8] The rationale for unrestricted vouchers is that such supplementation would be within the reach of nearly everyone and that its prohibition would invite abuses and dodges of the sort that often arise when market forces are constrained.[9]

A second variation is that between vouchers with fixed values and those with variable value, depending, for example, on the educational disadvantage of the child. Vouchers with differential redemption value can be used to accomplish a variety of social purposes: to provide compensatory education (if the voucher is of higher value for disadvantaged children), to encourage school integration (if the vouchers for children whose race is in the minority in a school have greater redemption value), to encourage high learning rates (if the redemption value of the voucher depends on the achievement increment of the child), or still other purposes. The differential value can act as an incentive to the school to enroll certain students

or to achieve certain results with them. The rationale for opposition to differential value for vouchers is that there are many competing social values that might be encouraged, and the voucher's
use for one of these values rather than another cannot be justified.
This argument, however, would appear weak, for such decisions
between competing social values are exactly those for which legis-
latures are designed.

Another variation in the voucher systems that have been proposed stems from concerns about racial distribution in schools if
vouchers are used. The proposal is a constraint on use of a voucher
in a school that has more than a certain proportion of one race.
This is in fact a constraint on the school: it would be limited to
accepting vouchers only so long as it remained within certain racial
limits (or "quotas"). Such a restriction is of course only one of a
general class of restrictions that are possible concerning the conditions under which vouchers may be used. It is, however, the one
most frequently discussed, because of the current concern about
racial integration in the schools.

The last dimension of variation in vouchers that I will discuss
(although this does not exhaust the possibilities) is in the latitude
that schools have in selecting from among applicants. At one extreme is complete freedom on the part of the school principal
in selecting from applicants if the school is oversubscribed. This
would compare with the freedom of private colleges and universities
in selecting among applicants (although some state universities
are required by state law to accept any student who has graduated
from a high school in the state or has graduated in the upper half
of the class; this practice is like that in some European countries,
where a secondary school diploma [or baccalaureate] automatically
entitles its holder to attend a university). At the other extreme
admission is taken completely out of the hands of the principal
and is decided either by lot or by order of application. The voucher
design developed by Jencks and others for an Office of Economic
Opportunity (OEO) voucher experiment (which ultimately became
the Alum Rock experiment) allowed the principal full control
over a fraction of those admitted, while another fraction were
to be selected by lot. In the Coons California proposal, admissions
are determined by lot, with a grandfather clause for current students
and their siblings.

Although there are mechanisms somewhat like vouchers in use
in England and other European countries (a situation that has
arisen in the shift from a two-tiered secondary school system to
something closer to a comprehensive school), nothing approximating

vouchers has been introduced in the United States. There have been several moves in this direction, such as a near decision in New Hampshire to initiate vouchers experimentally but on a broad scale and a near decision by some cities (Seattle being the largest) to carry out OEO's proposed voucher experiment. But none of these have taken place, so there is no knowledge about how a voucher system would work in practice. In California, a voucher referendum may be on the ballot in the 1980 election, and if it passes, a full-scale voucher plan will be initiated.

In the absence of knowledge about what actual voucher programs do, there have been numerous arguments, pro and con, about their alleged benefits or harm. It is to these arguments that I now turn.

ISSUES SURROUNDING CHOICE
IN EDUCATION

I have discussed the various forms that parental choice in education has taken in the past and might take in the future, but except for brief allusions, I have not discussed the major issues that arise over parental choice and the arguments of those who favor or oppose particular forms of increased parental choice. Some of these arguments played a part in the first section, which examined the division of control over the child between parent and state. But it is useful to turn more directly to these issues and arguments, for they indicate some of the major forces that will shape the degree and form of parental control in the future.

I will present the issues and arguments that surround the most extreme degree of parental choice—the full voucher valid for use in public or private schools. This extreme case contains nearly all the issues that arise in lesser degrees of choice and thus provides for an exposition of them.

A central issue in the rise of vouchers is that of diversity versus unity. This issue takes many forms, depending on what dimension of potential cleavage is taken as the focus. The issue is ordinarily raised as an objection to vouchers and the forms that this objection takes include:

1. Potential religious cleavage, with Catholics attending one set of schools and Protestants another;[10]
2. Potential racial cleavage, with blacks attending one set of schools and whites another;
3. The establishment of schools by a radical left, which would be free to teach its message of subversion with the use of state funds;

4. Linguistic cleavage, with hispanics choosing to attend schools in which Spanish was the language of instruction, thus perpetuating and enlarging a linguistically based cleavage in the United States;
5. Economic cleavage, with children from upper economic backgrounds attending one set of schools and children from lower economic backgrounds another.

Proponents of vouchers counter this argument in several ways. One reponse is that voucher opponents are comparing possible voucher outcomes with an idealization of current school systems, rather than with reality—that the opponents are wholly out of touch with the degree of racial and class separation current in American schools, with enrollment based on residence and, in the case of private schools, on ability to pay. Voucher proponents argue that elimination of these two barriers to race and class integration will provide greater, rather than less, racial and economic integration, even if vouchers are wholly unrestricted, with principals having complete right of selection among applicants. (The proponents point to the application to Catholic schools by large numbers of non-Catholic blacks in many large cities and the acceptance of these children by the Catholics schools, even though their tuition covers only a fraction of the cost and the white Catholic parish ends up subsidizing the schooling of non-Catholic blacks).

A second response, made by other voucher proponents, is that vouchers are flexible and that the state can, by creating different voucher redemption values for different school compositions, provide sufficient incentives for attaining whatever distribution of students among schools is desired—something it has been unable to do with state-imposed assignment to schools, no matter how heavy handed. In addition to such inducements, the principal can be prevented from exercising choice in selection through use of a lottery for selecting among those who apply.

The issue that is most often raised by the proponents of vouchers is their role in bringing about equality of educational opportunity. Given constraints on schools imposed by geographic location and consequent differences in expenditure and given the opportunity for those with money to leave the public school for private schools, proponents argue that vouchers are the best, if not the only, way to eliminate these sources of inequality. Some of those (such as Coons and Sugarman) who have worked hardest to bring about equal financing of education through other means have turned to vouchers as the optimal means of doing so.

Opponents argue that the vouchers will bring about greater inequality because of self-selection into homogeneous schools, combined with the fact that inequality in schools is produced not only (or maybe not even primarily) by school expenditures, but by differences in student bodies. In addition, if the voucher system allows supplementation, the tendency for those with greater financial resources to congregate in the same schools will increase. To proponents, these arguments are again based on idealization of current school systems, rather than on their reality.

An issue that is frequently raised by opponents, related to the one above, is the greater ability of parents of advantaged children to make sophisticated choices. The result will be, it is argued, a greater advantage to those already advantaged, because of their greater skill in using the additional resources of choice. Thus, even if all become better off, those already best off will benefit most.

Proponents of vouchers respond in two ways: First, any voucher system must be accompanied by a requirement for disclosure by the school of certain information relevant to parental choice—information about achievement levels and achievement gains and information about staff and curriculum. (Some proponents argue that market forces will themselves induce schools to provide greater information about themselves; but most agree that without some disclosure rule, the information provided by schools would be, like college catalogs, noncomparable and self-serving.) Second, such disclosure will reduce the present differences in ability to locate a good school, an ability that depends on the capacity to infer school quality from subtle indicators. The greater information available from competing schools operating under a disclosure requirement will equalize the ability to choose a good school.

Finally, an issue raised by proponents of vouchers is that of market efficiency induced by the greater control exercised by those interested in its outcome—parents and students. Proponents of vouchers argue that school content and method are now controlled by educational administrators who have little interest in the outcomes of education and that vouchers, by changing the locus of control, would insure that greater attention was paid to educational outcomes for children. They further argue that the control exercised by parents and children gives them a greater stake in the education of the child and encourages greater effort toward making it successful. Opponents of vouchers do not have confidence in a market and point instead to the inefficiencies and distributional inequalities that exist in markets.

As I indicated earlier, these arguments surrounding extreme forms of parental choice in education, such as vouchers, take place in a vacuum, since there is no experience that can inform the discussion. However, it appears likely that, given the various problems of educational finances and of reaching consensus in education that have arisen in recent years, together with some of the new forms of choice (such as alternative schools at elementary and secondary levels), some experimentation with this extreme degree of parental choice will take place. Even if it does not, there already exist a variety of forms and degrees of parental choice as exercised in one place or another in American education, as described earlier. If state decisions in education are to be made wisely, they should be made in the presence of knowledge about how parents and children exercise educational choice under various conditions.

NOTES

1. Sometimes, where I use the word "state," the term "community" could be used just as well. However, in the case of most laws regarding education, the meaning is more specific. I mean by state sometimes the community and sometimes the nation state, but most often one of the fifty states within the United States. The reason is that education is a constitutional responsibility of the fifty states, and thus laws concerning school attendance are made by the states. However, this is modified in two ways. First, all states have delegated a portion of their constitutional responsibility for education to the local community. Second, since court decisions involving desegregation, beginning in 1954, there has been a significant element of national control of the child, through pupil assignment to schools by federal courts and through plans imposed by the Department of Health, Education, and Welfare.

2. This form of choice apparently does exist in at least one district. In Marin County, California, a cosmopolitan exurban county north of San Francisco, parents choose their child's teacher. The final assignments do not allow all parents to receive their choice, because of excess or deficient demand for particular teachers. This does, however, constitute a major increase in parental rights of choice.

3. The source of the difficulty can be seen as follows. Nearly all the choices of a school other than a nearby school were all blacks. If the school board failed to give a black child his or her first choice of a predominantly white school, while whites near the school received their first choice, discrimination could be charged. If the school board failed to give a white child his or her first choice of a school nearby, while black children from a distance received their first choice of this school, white parents would react against their child's not being allowed to attend the neighborhood school, a reaction that has fueled the busing controversies in other cities.

4. One generalization that can be suggested on the basis of experience in two cities (Louisville and Baltimore) is that academic elite schools have been less successful in holding their attraction in the face of comprehensive schools in the city neighborhoods and in the suburbs than have technical schools. (I distinguish technical schools from vocational schools, as they are distinguished in a number of cities, in that technical schools contain a college preparatory program oriented toward engineering and science and that vocational training is not as directly linked to particular trades and provides a broader training in manual skills with less intensive training in any one.) In Baltimore, Baltimore Polytechnic High School has remained racially integrated, while Baltimore City College High School, its academic elite twin (and with a somewhat more extensive elite tradition), rapidly turned from mostly white to nearly all black in the space of a few years in the 1960s. Similarly, Manual High School in Louisville, that city's counterpart to Baltimore Polytechnic, retained a substantial miniority of whites up to 1975, when all schools' enrollments were readjusted under a desegregation order, while Male High School, the counterpart of Baltimore City College, had long since become all black. The reason for these differences appears to lie in the fact that technical training facilities and teachers can less easily be duplicated in a comprehensive school than can purely academic training, which requires little in the way of facilities. In fact, it may be argued that the principal ingredient for an academically elite school (especially in nonscience areas) is a high ability student body, while both special facilities and specially trained teachers are necessary in technical schools. These points are useful ones to be kept in mind by persons engaged in designing "magnet" schools intended to attract and hold both black and white students.

5. The transfers allowed in this plan and in similar ones proposed elsewhere are "majority-minority" transfers, to prevent their use by whites to escape from an integrated city school to a white suburban one.

6. Vouchers limited to public schools have been discussed along with full private-public vouchers. I will not consider them here, because they have already been discussed under interdistrict choice, although, like Baltimore's junior high school choice plan, there is no initial school assignment from which a transfer choice may be exercised. From the point of view of the principal, however, some public school voucher proposals are different, in that the principal's resources depend directly on the number of students who choose the school. The principal thus has both the incentive and the resources to make the school distinctive and attractive.

7. In some cases, the possibility for and some of the attractiveness of a voucher system arise from a prior shift to extensive state financing. This, for example, is the case in California.

8. A more extended version of the same argument is that as school costs escalate, parents with higher incomes will vote against increased taxes to increase the voucher value but will instead increase the supplement, making it an ever larger portion of total school costs. However, this argument is probably not valid, because if higher income persons were to vote this way, they would more often vote against increases in school taxes than low income

persons under current school financing arrangements, while in reality they are less likely to vote against these increases. The Coons proposal in California fixes the voucher value at 95 percent of the previous year's public school cost.

9. In the Coons California voucher proposal, supplementation can occur but must be bought from the state as a supplementary voucher. This allows the state to charge different prices for supplementing by family ability to pay, thus combining the virtues of restricted and unrestricted vouchers.

10. In this version, Jews and other religious groups would for the most part attend the "Protestant" schools, just as Jews attend Montreal's English-speaking "Protestant" schools. On the other hand, some picture a more religiously divided education, involving a variety of religiously different schools.

REFERENCES

Coons, John, and Stephen Sugarman. 1978. *Education by Choice.* Berkeley: University of California Press.

Fantini, Mario. 1973. *Public Schools of Choice.* New York: Simon and Schuster.

Index

Ability
  learning and participation and,
    36-37
  See also Intelligence
Achievement, and self-concept,
    reciprocal
  effects analysis of, 194
Achievement scores
  racial composition data on, 107-108
  decline in, 75, 78
    academic course exposure and, 78
    birth cohort size in, 79-80
    demographic characteristics
      and, 105-106
Age disaggregation, in model develop-
    ment, 82
All Information analysis, of longi-
    tudinal data, 166-167
Alternative schools, choice of, 243-
    244
Alum Rock School District, parental
    choice experiment in, 237-238
American College Test (ACT), score
    decline in, 75, 78
American Institute for Research
    (AIR), 94
  Project TALENT of, 109-110
Astin, Alexander, 110-111

Bachman, Jerald, 110
Behavior, and intelligence, reciprocal
    causal effect analysis of, 181-
    184, 183(fig.)

Berkeley Growth data, structural
    regression analysis of, 181-
    184, 183(fig.)
Bernstein, Basil, 99-100
Birth cohort. *See* Cohort size;
    Cohort study(s)
Birth order effects, on test scores, 79

California Assessment Program (CAP),
    school residuals in, 173
CET (capacity, effort and time)
    model of teacher input, 208-
    210, 223
  determinants of, 215-221
  extraction of labor and, 214-215,
    221-222
  organizational structure and, 210-
    215, 222, 223-225
Chief State School Officials (CSSO),
    in school research access, 97
Classroom effects
  between classroom variations in, 23
  of size, 19
  as social system, 22
Cognitive growth
  cross-sectional *vs* longitudinal
    analysis of, 160-161
  reciprocal effects analysis of, 194-
    195
  schooling effects data on, 101-102
  See also Intelligence
Cohort size, education effects of,
    79-80

Cohort study(s)
  alternative modes for, 149
  starting point for, 149-150
  total age in, 134-135
  See also Longitudinal study(s);
      for high school class of 2002,
      National, for high school class
      of 1972
Coleman Report, 101, 108
  cross-sectional design of, 156-157,
      163, 166, 177
Collective bargaining, teacher
      performance and, 223-224
College faculty, labor force partici-
      pation rate of, 82
College preparatory programs, learning
      and participation in, 30
Colleges and universities
  demographic account data for, 87
  enrollment trend model for, 81
  sex disaggregation in, 82-83
Commitment maximization
  frog-pond effect on, 38
  to present *vs* future success, 34
  program inflation for, 34-35,
      43-44, 49-50
  reward and cost functions in, 33-34
  student role relation to, 39-42, 47
Community control of schools,
      parental choice and, 236-237
Community data, in education
      models, 89
Compensatory education effects
  elementary school study of, 135-
      136
  programmatic stigmatization and,
      30, 42, 44
Contextual effects
  individual variables in, 21
  interactive form of, 23
  methodological simplification of,
      19-21
Crime rate analysis
  routine activity approach to, 72-73
  victimization survey in, 88
Cross-lagged correlation method,
      of reciprocal causal effects,
      189-193
  in cognitive growth, 194-195
  in self-concept and achievement,
      194
  and teacher expectancy, 193

Cross-sectional analysis
  equilibrium assumptions in, 177-
      178
  vs longitudinal analysis, 10, 155-
      166
Current Population Surveys (CPS),
      education data of, 104
Curriculum. *See* Educational
      categories and topics

Data banks
  measurement problems of, 96
  of National Longitudinal Study
      (NLS), 119-120
  utilization of, 149
  privacy acts and, 96
Data collection
  on equal opportunity, 102-104
  for longitudinal studies, 109-111,
      137-139. *See also* Longitudinal
      data
  as methodological problem, 100-
      101
  on noncognitive outcomes, 106-
      108
  for period studies, 104-106
  proliferation of, 95-96
  racial identity in, 109-110
  on schooling effects, 101-102
  for social accounts, 66-69
    demographic units in, 70-71,
        86-87
    household and schooling data
        in, 87-89
Demographic accounts
  benefits of, 70-71
  in social indicator models, 71
  of education, 86-89
Demographic change, achievement
      score trends and, 79-80
Desegregation. *See* School desegre-
      gation
Disaggregation by age and sex, in
      education models, 82-83
Durkheim, Emile, 3, 4, 13
Dynamic change models, 174-175
  alternative formulations of, 178
  equilibrium assumptions in, 177-
      178
  of learning process, 175-177
  of reciprocal causal effects, 184-
      186

Econometric models
  of causal effects, 186-188
    educational applications of, 189
  development of, 66
Educational categories and topics
  academic content of, 78
  authoritative *vs* student-directed,
    42-43, 45
  choice among, 238
  institutionalized, 27, 48-49
    student outcomes and, 29-31
  lateral differentiation of, 41-42
  nationally defined, 31, 49
  schooled knowledge and, 41
  social structure and, 2-3
  in specialized schools, 241
  stigmatized programs in, 30, 42, 44
  valued futures related, 28-31, 47
    program inflation and, 49-50
Educational production function
  institutional goals and, 215-216
  learning theory and, 207-208
  statistical equation for, 204-205
  study of, 9-10, 203-204
    conclusions in, 205
    theoretical framework for, 205-
      206
  of teacher inputs, 208
    capacity, effort and time (CET)
      approach to, 6-7, 208-210
    determinants of, 215-221
    extraction of labor and, 214-
      215, 221-222
    school organization and, 210-
      215, 223-225
Educational research
  cross-sectional *vs* longitudinal data
    in, 10, 155-159
  on cognitive growth, 160-161
  methodology of, 166-167
  on school effects, 161-166
  data needs of, 12, 94-95, 98
  expenditure on, 95
  integrated analysis in, 98-100
  school access for, 96-97
  utility of, 97-98
    meta-analysis, 108-109
    Project TALENT, 109-110
  unsponsored, 95-96
  See also Data collection; Longi-
    tudinal analysis; Longitudinal
    data; Longitudinal study(s)

Educational sociology, status of, 95
Education effects
  cognitive data for, 101-102
  cohort size and, 79-80
  cross-sectional *vs* longitudinal data
    in, 161-167, 173-174
  demographic account data for,
    88-89
  learning process models of, 175-
    177
  noncognitive data for, 106-108
  of public policy, 12-13, 14, 85
  of school desegregation, 107-108
  of structural levels, 5-6, 102
    contextual *vs* individual data on,
      19-21
    individual factors in, 21, 35
      ability as, 36-37
      aggregated, 38-39, 85
      family status, 22, 36
      monetary resources, 22
    institutional *vs* organizational,
      7-9, 16-17, 24-25, 31-32,
      58-59
    of institutional structure, 59-61
    interactive, 23
    multi-level complexity of, 19,
      20(fig.)
    organizational structure and, 43-44
    research models of, 18-19
    societal factors in, 44-46, 83-86
    student role properties and, 39-43,
      46
  of teacher expectancy, 193
Education expenditure
  federal priorities in, 100
  model development of, 83
Education models
  demographic accounts in, 86-87
    household and schooling data
      for, 87-89
  future development of, 82-83
  of intellectual growth, 75, 78-80
  longitudinal data in
    dynamic change, 174-178, 184-
      186
  of reciprocal causal effects, 179-
    189
  occupational and labor force
    structure
    in, 81-82
  of organizational change, 80-81

Education models (*continued*)
  of school enrollments and attain-
    ments, 74-75
  social indicators in, 73-74, 76(fig.)-
    77(fig.), 83-86, 84(fig.)
Education system
  commitment maximization in,
    33-34
    program inflation for, 34-35,
      43-44, 49-50
  finance of, 13, 247
    voucher system and, 247-248
  institutional structure of, 5, 26-
    28
    lateral and vertical differentiation
      in, 26, 40-42
    social world and, 59-61
    student role and, 16, 25, 32
    teaching strategy in, 53-55
  organizational structure of, 4, 23
    centralized *vs* decentralized,
      51-53
      internal autonomy and, 7-8
    consolidation of, 80-81
    enrollment effects on, 185-186
    equal opportunity and, 102
    institutional legitimacy of, 48-49
    loosely coupled properties of, 17,
      18, 50-51
    nested concept of, 19, 24
    student role and, 18, 24-25
    teacher performance and, 210,
      222, 224-225
      autonomous model of, 211-
        212
      bureaucratic model of, 212-215
      collective bargaining and, 223-
        224
  parental choice in
    of alternative schools, 242-244
    of magnet schools, 244-245
    within school, 237-239
    of specialized schools, 241
    transfer requests, 242
      within district, 239-240
      interdistrict, 245-246
    voucher system and, 248-
      253
  state expansion of, 56-57
  state regulation *vs* parental control
    in, 233-237
  structural levels of, 15

Elementary schools
  alternative, 243-244
  curriculum choice experiment
    in, 238-239
  longitudinal study of, 135-137
Enrollment rates
  for higher education, 81
    sex disaggregation of, 82-83
  models of, 74-75
Equal opportunity
  college preparedness and, 102-103
  federal policy on, 100
  structural *vs* socialization factors
    in, 102
  voucher system and, 251-252
  See also School desegregation
    plans

Family effects
  demographic account data for,
    88-89
  size and, 79
  status and, 36
Federal government
  educational policy objectives of,
    100
  agencies of
    in child development research,
      148
    in longitudinal study manage-
      ment, 126-130, 147
Follow-up systems
  in longitudinal study(s), 115, 117,
    142-143
  Migrant Student Record Transfer
    System (MSRTS), 148-149
Frog-pond effect, on learning and
    participation, 38

Glass, Gene, 108-109
Growth Study
  augmented sample in, 144
  cross-sectional *vs* longitudinal
    data in, 160-161
  follow-up problems in, 142-143

Higher education. *See* Colleges and
    Universities
High schools
  alternative, 244
  assignment to, 234-235
  demographic account data for, 87

High schools (*continued*)
  education effects in. *See* Longi-
    tudinal study(s); of high school
    class of 2002, National, of
    high school class of 1972
  magnet, 244-245
  specialized, 241
  transfer options in, 242
Household data, in education models,
    87-89

Individual level effects
  methodological simplification
    of, 19-21
  in substantive simplifications,
    21-22
Intelligence
  achievement score decline and,
    75, 78-80
  and behavior
    reciprocal causal effect analysis
      of, 181-184, 183(fig.)
  measurement of, 37, 38
  properties of, 36-37
  See also Cognitive growth
Interactive models, of contextual
    effects, 23

Labor under capitalism, hiring *vs*
    extraction of, 213-214
  educational applications in, 214-
    215, 221-222
Labor force participation, of instruc-
    tional personnel, 81-82
Lateral differentiation
  commitment and learning effects
    in, 41-42
  national uniformity of, 26-27
  programmatic membership and,
    26
Learning
  dynamic change models of, 175-
    177
  theoretical approaches to, 207
    in education production context,
      207-208
  and participation
    ability and, 36-37
    in authoritative *vs* student directed
      curricula, 42-43, 45
    in centralized *vs* decentralized
      systems, 52

expansion of, 56
family status and, 36
institutionalized topics and, 29-31
institutional role changes and,
    55-56
reciprocal relations between, 17
school status and, 22, 38-39
state strategies for, 56-57
teaching strategies for, 53-55
valued futures related, 13, 28-
    29, 30-31, 47
  program inflation and, 49-50
  vs student role expansion, 39-40
See also Cognitive growth
Least-squares regression analysis,
    174
Longitudinal analysis
  vs cross-sectional, 155-159
  of cognitive growth, 160-161
  of school effects, 10, 161-166
  of discrete data, 154
  function of, 154
  of hierarchical data, 173-174
  measurement error in, 195-196
  methodology of, 154-155, 166-
    167, 196
Longitudinal data
  defined, 153-154
  in dynamic change models, 174-
    178
  hierarchical components of, 11,
    168
    analysis approaches to, 170-173
    structure in, 168-170
  matched *vs* unmatched, 160
  of reciprocal causal effects, 178-179
    cross-lagged correlation of, 189-
      195
    dynamic change models in, 184-
      186
    multiple time-series model of,
      186-189
    structural equation models of,
      179-184
Longitudinal study(s)
  on elementary school level, 135-
    137
  of high school class of 2002, 11-
    12, 133-134
  field trials of, 147
  follow-up to, 142-143
  participant observation in, 146

Longitudinal study(s) (*continued*)
   project management of, 147-
     149
   research agenda in, 137-139
   research design in, 139-140
   response rate and, 141-142
   samples in
     add-on, 144-146
     augmented, 143-144
     base year, 140-141
     core, 141
   literature on, 94
   National (NLS), of high school
     class of 1972, 11, 111
   background of, 112-113
   conceptual framework of, 130-
     132
   data archive of, 119-120
   measurement problems in,
     120-122
   equal opportunity data of, 102-
     103
   incomplete returns in, 117-118
   management of, 123
     advisory groups in, 124-125
     federal controls in, 126-130
     planning committee for, 125-
     126
     private contractors in, 123-124
   new cohorts in, 118-119
   response burden of, 128-129
   response rate in, 116-117, 141-
     142
   sample depletion in, 122-123
   survey operations for, 113-116,
     140
   users of, 129-130
   projects for, 94
   sample depletion in, 122
   starting point of, 149-150
   for total age cohorts, 134-135
   utility of, 10-11, 109-111
Loose coupling, 17, 18, 50-51

Magnet schools, choice of, 244-
   245
Mayflower Conference, 112
Meta-analysis, utility of, 108-109
Migrant Student Record Transfer
   System (MSRTS), 148-149
Monetary resources, education effects
   of, 22

Montessori public schools, choice
   of, 243

National Assessment of Educational
   Progress (NAEP), household
   surveys of, 105
National Center for Educational
   Statistics (NCES), 94
   in longitudinal study(s), 148
   National Longitudinal Study
     (NLS), 112, 113, 122, 124-
     125, 126-127, 128, 129-131,
     132
   test development by, 149
National Longitudinal Study (NLS)
   of High School Class of 1972.
   See Longitudinal study(s)

Office of Management and Budget
   (OMB), federally funded
   research clearance by, 126,
   127-128, 148
Open schools, choice of, 242-243
Opinion poll data, in educational
   research, 98

Parental choice in education
   of alternative schools, 242-244
   collective control and, 236-237
   of magnet schools, 244-245
   within school, 237-239
   vs state regulation, 233-236
   transfer options for, 242
     within district, 239-240
     interdistrict, 245-246
   voucher system and, 237, 247-
     250, 253
     pros and cons of, 251-252
Parental teaching role, cognitive
   growth and, 79
Period study(s), data collection
   for, 104-106
Private schools, in voucher system,
   247-250
Project TALENT, 112
   achievement score data in, 105-106
   base year sample in, 140
   utility of, 109-110, 111
Public policy
   education effects of, 12-13, 14,
     85
   on equal opportunity, 100

Race differences
on achievement tests, 37
in college preparedness, 102-103
Reading scores, period change data
on, 105-106
Reciprocal causal effect analysis,
178-179
cross-lagged correlation method in,
189-195
cross-sectional data in, 155, 157
dynamic change models in, 184-
186
multiple time-series model in,
186-189
structural equation models in,
179-184
Reed, John, 98
Regression analysis
methodology of, 166-167
of school residuals, 161-162, 173-
174
Regression models, of longitudinal
data, 181-182
Residual index, of school effects,
161-162
regression analysis for, 173-174
Response rate, in longitudinal
study(s), 116-117, 141-142

Scholastic Aptitude Test (SAT),
score decline in, 78
School(s). *See* Education system,
organizational structure
School assignment
methods of, 234-235
to specialized schools, 241-242
state *vs* parental control in, 235,
236
transfer options and, 239-240,
242, 245-246
School attendance laws
parental control and, 234, 235
relaxation of, 235-236
School desegregation plans
education effects of, 107-108
magnet schools in, 244-245
and student assignment law,
235
transfer options in, 242
within district, 239-240
interdistrict, 245-246
voucher system and, 249

School status, education effects of,
22, 38-39
School studies. *See* Educational
research; Longitudinal study(s)
Self-concept, and achievement,
reciprocal effects analysis of, 194
Sewell, William, 93, 110
Sex disaggregation, in model development, 82
Sexual behavior accounts, units of
measurement for, 68, 70
Social account design
econometric models and, 66-67
units of measurement in, 67-69
demographic, 70-71
for education, 86-88
dollar equivalents, 69-70
Social change study(s), data collection
for, 104-106
Social indicator models
of competitive activities, 71
subject to risk approach in, 71-72
for routine activity, 72-73
Social indicator research, 65-66
for education models, 73-75,
76(fig.)-77(fig.), 83-86, 84(fig.)
achievement tests in, 75, 78-80
organizational trends in, 80-81
social accounts design in, 66-71
Social science models, contextual
vs individual level effects in,
19-21
Social status effects
on educational success, 22, 36,
44-45
family, 36
school, 22, 38-39
Social structure, education system
and, 1-3, 15
Sociolinguistics, and class structure,
99-100
State regulation of education, *vs*
parental control, 233-237
Stigmatization, programmatic,
learning and participation
effects of, 30, 42, 44
Stromsdorfer, Ernst W., 100
Structural equation models, of
reciprocal causal effects, 179-
184
Student assignment. *See* School assignment

Student outcomes. *See* Learning
and participation
Student role
commitment to, 33-35
demographic account data on,
86, 88
expansion of, 39-40, 46
institutionalization of, 40-
42
organizational concept of, 24-
25, 32
research designs on, 42-43
school status and, 38-39
Student-teacher interaction
data collection on, 101-102
expectancy effects study of, 7,
193
Study of Sustaining Effects (SSE),
135-136
Survey research. *See* Longitudinal
study(s)

TALENT data bank. *See* Project
TALENT
Teacher performance
autonomous professional paradigm
of, 211-212, 215-216
in bureaucratic model, 6-7, 212-
213
extraction of labor concept
and, 213-215, 221-222
capacity, effort and time (CET)
approach to, 6, 208-210, 220-
221, 223
capacity in, 216-217
collective bargaining and, 223-
224
effort in, 217-220
time allocation in, 220
institutional goals and, 215-
216
strategies for, 53-54
research design of, 54-55

Teachers
labor force participation rate of,
81-82
parental choice of, 239
and student interaction
data collection on, 101-102
expectancy effects study of,
7, 193
Time allocation, teacher
determinants of, 220, 222
institutional rules and, 211-212
learning effects and, 209
Time-series model, multiple, of
reciprocal causal effects,
186-189
Transfer options
within district, 239, 242
interdistrict, 245-246

Universities. *See* Colleges and
universities

Vertical differentiation
national uniformity of, 26-27
schooled knowledge and, 41
structural form of, 26
student commitment and, 40-41
Victimization surveys, 88
Vocational programs, learning and
participation in, 30, 43
Voucher system
future role of, 253
objections to, 250-251, 252
parental control in, 248
practical applications of, 237,
249-250
proponents of, 251, 252
school finance and, 247-248
variations in, 248-249

Weber, Max, 2, 4, 12
Women in labor force, educational
expansion and, 82

About the Editors

Charles Bidwell is Professor of Education and Sociology at the University of Chicago, where he is also Director of the Educational Finance and Productivity Center and Chairman of the Department of Education. His interests include organizational theory, its applications to educational organizations, and the productivity of educational organizations. He is the author of a monograph and 31 articles in these areas of interest.

Douglas M. Windham, an economist, is Professor of Education at the State University of New York at Albany. Until 1979, he was Associate Professor of Education, Director of the Comparative Education Center, and Codirector of the Educational Finance and Productivity Center, all at the University of Chicago. He is a specialist in the finance of educational systems and the economic analysis of education and national development. Professor Windham is the author of numerous monographs and articles.